Also by Peter Dorney

Chip Butties

Second Printing January 2004

Pennine
12 Lorong 19, Geylang,
#04-01 Bougainvilla Apartments
Singapore 388493
Tel: (65) 6842-4413 Fax: (65) 6842-3756
e-mail: sammylah@pacific.net.sg

ISBN: 981-04-5495-3

Cover Photo & Layout Design: Robert Stedman Pte Ltd., Singapore
featuring Angie Chua & Elliot Lewis

Printed in Singapore

For Sammy, Alan and Rudy

taking care of the beloved 'Heaven On A Stick'

with special thanks to Robert Stedman
and Sue Seys-Phillips for their
continued help and encouragement

Chinese Takeaway

Peter Dorney

Chinese Takeaway is the second novel by Singapore-based writer Peter Dorney.

His first book – *Chip Butties* – was described as an hilarious "lookback through laughter" at growing up in his native Manchester after the war.

His new novel *Chinese Takeaway* illustrates many of the cultural surprises and experiences of living in Southeast Asia for almost two decades .

Traditional customs, attitudes and images are gently turned upside down, inside out and back to front — with side-splitting results. No one is spared as Australian and English characters come under a spotlight of fun and invariably misunderstood communication.

CONTENTS

Chapter 1

The Dingo Has Landed

'Welcome to Singapore's Changi International Airport.' the mechanical sounding voice announced over the aircraft intercom 'Please remain in your seats until the aircraft has come to a complete stop and the seat-belt sign has been switched off.'

This was it then, a new experience awaited outside the window as for the next two years a certain Simon Skeer would be a Teacher in Residence, at the Antipodean Academy of Learning in Singapore. Looking back, it hadn't taken all that long to arrange.

Having spent the previous two years teaching English in the town of Tom Price, in the far north of his native Western Australia, an advertisement on the Internet for school teachers in South-East Asia triggered his growing desire to strike out from the Outback and see more of the world. It would be quite a change from the dust and barren emptiness of the Pilbara region and the thought of spending time in *exotic Asia* was rather appealing. Three months later and the deed was done, signed and sealed, and Simon was preparing to be delivered to tropical climes come the approaching New Year.

The family had been at the airport to see him off. Complete with farewell gifts which included a furry dingo and a cork-dangling Aussie bushman's hat. Why do Australians abroad always have to advertise where they come from so emphatically, he wondered.

He said his farewells to a tearful mother, deep-breathing

father, a grinning fifteen year old brother relishing the thought of a bigger bedroom at long last, and sniffing seventeen year old twin sisters who had adored him since birth. Why do people insist on seeing you off at airports he wondered. It's always the same, tears and terror as the Final Call time draws closer. It never gets easier and he'd much rather have said his farewells at home, hopped in a taxi and had a tranquil departure. But it doesn't happen, ever. Such is life.

'Weez gonna come an' see yewz soon, 'his father threatened as he walked away from the group and into the Security area, waving the grinning dingo and hat. He nodded, smiled, and fed the animal into the security scanner.

The dingo bleeped. 'What's this?' the bored checker asked picking up the offending mutt.

'It's a dog,' he answered… wanting to add 'What do you think it is!' but didn't.

'Gotta name?'

'Arthur,' he responded, giving the first name he thought of.

'That's my name.'

'Well there you are then, you are famous in the Outback world,' he responded with a smile as Arthur Two passed the furry animal back to him, growled quietly, and sent him on his way.

As he turned into the aircraft cabin he saw with certain alarm that half the passengers were wearing bushman's corked hats. The scene before him resembled a hat-makers convention of which Simon was now a recent, and rather reluctant, member. How embarrassing, he thought, and uttered a silent prayer to the God of Hat Travellers *please don't sit me amongst the hat-band*. He was thankful to end up quite a few rows forward of the main party of milliners and stuffed the hat deep into his hand baggage as quickly as possible.

The rather robotic crew offered him a choice of juice, beer or wine with smiles that had no doubt supported their bubbling options a few hundred times. He sat back with a glass of orange juice and started to fiddle with the in-flight entertainment gadgets which would help pass the next few hours. After the last minute rush before leaving he was quite tired and slept most of the way, missing the film he rather fancied seeing. Another time.

It was dark as they taxied towards Singapore airport terminals, though the blinking lights of aircraft making their way into and out of parking bays together with the bright lights of the building, presented an almost Christmas tree effect. Seeing that it was just into a new year the display seemed rather appropriate.

Immigration procedures were swift and a few moments later he loaded his suitcase onto a trolley and made his way out of the Customs area.

A tall man stood outside the glass doors holding a sign reading 'Antipodean Academy Teachers' and Simon duly reported his presence to the 'Meeter & Greeter' as his badge read.

'Wait over there, please,' he was directed towards a clutch of three girls in their mid-twenties. Each of them wore her Aussie identity rather loudly, one had a furry koala on her left shoulder, another a kangaroo painted on her sleeve and the third a duck-billed platypus across her t-shirt front. He groaned on the inside thinking *It's The Animal Kingdom Goes Walkabout* but grinned on the outside as he walked over.

'G'day Bruce,' said koala shoulder 'I'm Sheila.' You would be, he thought.

'And I'm Sheila too,' added kangaroo lady.

'And so am I,' concluded the last of the patriotic Sheilas.

All three shook hands enthusiastically, two were brunette one a red head.

'Is that t-w-o or t-o-o?' he asked of the second Sheila who showed more teeth than a Melbourne Cup winner as she giggled 'Could be.'

'And my name is Simon, not Bruce,' he clarified to all three.

'Good for yew, Blue,' said Sheila Two 'where have you arrived from?'

'Perth,' he answered as two more male newcomers joined the group.

'G'day. I'm Bruce from Brizzie – Geography. And this here is Tyrone from Tasmania – Phiz-Ed and Athletics,' the former was in jeans and t-shirt, the latter in a tracksuit of green and gold, his country's national colours. With 'G'days,' all round plus smiles and handshakes of great emphasis the merry band of academic arrivals came together.

'Is that it then?' someone asked their Meeter as he ticked them off his list having steered his way through the dense waiting crowd in the wake of Bruce and Tyrone.

'One more,' he advised as a loud 'Cooooeeeee…' announced the arrival of the final member of the party.

Mouths dropped, eyes opened wide as a wobbling kaleidoscope on stilts came towards them pushing a luggage trolley as well-stacked as she was.

'Sorry to keep yewz. I was just getting some duty-free things to keep me going,' the young lady smiled at each of them.

Stick thin and wearing dark red tights above high cork-heeled shoes, her multi-coloured top was both sleeveless and skimpy to say the least. The tanned surfer's face was topped by a thatch of shiny blonde hair which stood upright on the top of the head before it cascaded down her slim back.

Looking at her bulging bags of cocktails and wine, giggling and tottering somewhat on rather perilous heels, she smiled at them demurely.

'And they didn't charge you any duty on that lot?' Bruce asked taking in the mini bottle shop displayed before them.

'Oh no, his eyes were on other things I was carrying,' she giggled as she shook her upper body and rather ample assets, one pineapple the other orange from the way the colours slashed across her tight tropical top.

'Anyway, I'm Cazza from Cairns. I'm the Librarian,' she announced, bending her knees slightly in a body-shaking giggle. The dip was much appreciated by the three male members of the party as it afforded a top-down view of Cazza's major attributes.

'And you're the Librarian?' the Tasmanian checked her academic position 'Bet you'll have no trouble getting the kids to return the books early just to have a look at what's on the top shelf.'

'Oooohhhhh, cheeky,' came the giggling response 'and I'll soon be stamping your library card Expired if you're not careful.' The youngest member of the party admonished him with a smile.

'Seven,' announced the still-ticking Meeter 'correct. Follow me please,' the party wheeled their luggage trolleys after him along the brightly lit concourse towards the distant Exit signs.

The three Sheilas led the way followed by Bruce who was soon chatting up Number Three rather emphatically. Tyrone in his track-suit of Australian colours jogged along next to Cazza while Simon made up the rear.

Looking at them from the back it occurred to him that they could only be from Oz and was thankful that he'd hidden his own Outback farm stock deep in his hand baggage. Not that he didn't love being a genuine 'dinky di' Aussie but banner broadcasts of the fact were not his style.

The automatic Exit doors opened as they approached and the outside heat smacked each of them full in the face, providing the usual extremely warm welcome to Singapore.

'Wow,' they exclaimed as each stepped outside the building.

'Like is this hotter than the plate on me uncle Ernie's barbie or what!' announced Bruce. The others agreed, starting to perspire and slowly drip onto the pavement in a rather quaint combined mini-waterfall effect.

Before leaving Australia they had each received a Newcomers Orientation Pack from the Academy. Amongst many points of interest the prevailing weather was described as either *hot and dry with occasional showers* or *hot and wet with occasional sun*. All bases had been nicely covered it seemed. No snow though.

Their own humid welcome consisted of the evening leftovers of one of the forecasts between which there was little difference anyway, just the order of delivery.

Their Meeter whistled, waved to a minibus parked across the road and within seconds it had pulled up in front of them. Suitcases were loaded in the back, hand-baggage on and around seats and they were soon underway.

The air-conditioned vehicle was comfortable and cool as they headed towards the city along a fast moving highway with the sea on the left. All seven were captivated by the endless rows of ships lights that looked rather like bright necklaces on a rich black base which was in fact water. The realisation that they were now in Asia began to sink in.

The school had arranged for them to be accommodated in a small downtown hotel for a few days, after which they were on their own. During this time they were to attend a Welcoming Staff Meeting in the school hall, familiarise themselves with the city and arrange their own accommodation. The new term would start almost one week hence, time then was of the essence.

The 'Double Happiness Inn' was set on a narrow street not far from the centre of the city. It offered a small gravel-covered curved drive between sheltering frangipani trees to welcome its guests. The archway of the Inn was a faded lime green, the entrance door the same rather tired colour. The once white, now grey, outside walls kept up the flaky-pastry effect as did the peeling brown wooden shutters protecting aged windows. The minibus stopped in the beam of the dim porch-light and the band of travelling teachers collected their suitcases and hand baggage and trooped into the Reception area.

A somewhat sleepy fellow with half a dozen long whiskers

dangling out of a mole on his chin sat behind the desk. He was wearing a rather limp vest and black baggy pants, no shoes, and a rather tired look of disinterest. A television set on the corner of the counter blared out its message in Chinese.

'Passport,' he requested and seven Kangaroo & Emu covered booklets were handed over. Nothing was said as fourteen eyes were drawn to the screaming television, each trying to make out what was happening on the small screen as robed figures flew threw the air chased by pursuing explosions.

'You stay five night. Breakfast at seven morning time. And no smoking in rooms.'

The instructions were passed on by those at the front to they in the rear who couldn't quite hear what was being said due to the Battles of Old Beijing Show currently blasting their way via the telly.

'Ridgie didge,' declared Sheila One to the fellow 'she'll be apples. And the party's in my room kids, bring your own nuts,' she announced, turning to the remaining travellers. 'Shower, shave, shampoo and whatever …and I'll be entertaining in half an hour. It's called a *Getting To Know Yewz Session'*.

All agreed on the rendezvous and shuffled off up the staircase of the four-storey hotel. Each avidly sought out their temporary home leaving the fellow on Reception wondering exactly where the apples were that Sheila One had just mentioned.

Simon's room was cramped but clean. You couldn't swing the proverbial dingo around in it though so he left Arthur in his hand baggage, not wishing to test the adage fully.

He switched the air-con on and opened the door to the rather functional bathroom which had just a loo, shower and sink, no bath, which was fine. The humid musty smell of Asia was now with him and would remain so for the rest of the year.

Twenty minutes later he was showered and refreshed. Pulling on a pair of shorts and t-shirt he tugged a few cans of West Aussie beer out of his hand baggage and made his way down two floors to Room 12 – Sheila One's temporary abode. The door was open and pop music was coming out of a radio providing a sound target for arrivals. Songs they knew played and as Simon arrived the compere gave out the weather forecast – hot and humid with showers in the afternoon, temperature range between twenty six and thirty two. What his new listeners didn't realise was that the weather forecast was basically the same every day.

All the girls were there, including Cazza in a clinging white t-shirt top two sizes too small that read *I did it on the Barrier Reef* in shell-like lettering across the front. I bet you did, Simon thought to himself as he squeezed into the room. Bruce and Tyrone arrived just after him, both with wet hair, wearing just shorts, no shirts.

Cazza was sipping on a long pink drink and proclaiming 'Ooooh, it's gorgeous.'

'What is?' asked Tyrone in patriotic green and gold satin shorts. 'This is a Singapore Sling…very exotic. Nice and pink just like your muscles,' she added for good measure, reaching out and squeezing his upper right arm.

Simon wondered what effort she put into making the request 'Shhhhhh…' come to life in a library, an experience they would all be exposed to very soon no doubt. The place could easily become more popular than the tuck-shop this coming school year, he reckoned.

The three Sheilas all came from New South Wales, though from different towns. They had never met before the flight but had all sat together, shared a few 'tinnies' of beer, as good old Aussie *sheilas* do, and were now as inseparable as a bunch of grapes ripening on the vine under the hot Australian sun.

Somehow or other Cazza had managed to get supplies of the most appropriate drink for the occasion – the Singapore Sling – which she willingly shared amongst her new colleagues, pouting and posing as she did the pouring. The three Sheilas tried it and thought it delicious, the boys each had one sip, declared it rather sweet and went back to the more familiar, and preferable, taste of beer.

Half an hour later and one would have thought they had known each other for years, had trekked waterless across the Nullabor Plain together and would die for a just cause as one. Camaraderie, with a background of instant noodles and laughter, had set in.

The noise in Room 12 soon matched that of the downstairs telly. One by one they bonded in the best Aussie style - over a drink - as they realised they could each trace their own family lineage back to Ned Kelly. Well almost, sort of, kinda. They'd all read the Booker prizewinning 'True History of the Kelly Gang' anyway so that was OK.

Come midnight and a close to the festivities was called by Sheila One as the next morning they were to be collected just after nine and taken to the Academy for a Welcoming Assembly of Staff. Simon had enjoyed both the company and the laughs shared with new-found friends but, like all of them, was ready for bed after a long day.

Sleep came easily and the next morning the troop gradually appeared in the sunny dining room with its high ceiling and fans lazily moving the warm air about. The room was painted the same faded green as the entrance.

They probably got a bulk discount on paint at the time thought Simon as their Singapore adventure began in earnest, as well as daylight.

The same minibus they had travelled in the previous evening appeared just after nine and they climbed aboard. Tyrone was in yet another version of his Australian tracksuit wardrobe, this one involving a green and black top with gold 'trackie' bottoms – in recognition of his position. One didn't need to guess what subject he taught, Simon thought, the others though were somewhat less obvious.

The three Sheilas were classed under maths, chemistry and history – in ascending order. Bruce carried a small geography book on Asia which gave his area of activity away and Simon had some English publications under his arm – another dead giveaway.

As for Cazza well she carried nothing but her two main points of interest and a purse before her. She wore another skimpy white top above a wraparound navy blue and red batik skirt which opened at one side to show a great deal of left leg. This girl is going to be amazing in this place, Simon thought, for just twenty-two she had a certain style he had soon decided.

The journey to the school was short and they were passing through the portals of learning of their new workplace by half past nine. A Registration Desk was positioned just inside the entrance at which two Singaporean ladies were obviously very busy.

Each reported their arrival to the duo, were swiftly and most efficiently ticked off a list, then directed to the inner courtyard of the square shaped four-storey building.

They were told to gather in The Hall on the fourth floor at ten, in the meantime there was a chance to wander around the Academy, take in the atmosphere and get the feel of the place.

Coffee, tea and iced-water were available from a canteen to the right of the entrance and the little group slowly made their way across the quadrangle lawn to sample the delights on offer. The place was buzzing with people as old and new teaching staff came together, many with excited cries at catching up with old friends.

'And how are ya then?'

'G'day Blue.'

'G'day mate.'

'Well I'll tickle my tits till Friday – look who it is!'

'Great to see yewz.'

'So ya did come back after all, ya old bastard. Can't bear to leave us, can ya?'

Down Under friendship in advanced format.

The Hall was large with a dark wooden ceiling, window frames and floor. There was a stage at one end towards which the rows of chairs in the centre faced. The area was filling rapidly as the seven newcomers entered and took their seats amongst present strangers, future friends.

At ten exactly a tall, thin lady of some fifty or so years, wearing a cool-looking pale blue suit, climbed four steps at the side of the stage and made her way to the singular microphone at the front. Her audience hushed.

She was followed by a slightly younger lady in a black dress who kept a respectful distance behind her leader and took a chair to the right of centre a few yards back from the mike.

'My name is Matilda Wilson and I am the Headmistress of the Antipodean Academy of Learning in Singapore,' the speaker announced. 'Before we go any further let me say that though my name is Matilda, and I am Australian, I do not dance and if I did it would certainly not be the waltz,' she paused before adding 'I am much too modern,' at the same time keeping a straight face.

Her audience laughed readily. Nice opening, thought Simon. Bring in a little levity straight away and relax the gathering.

'Let me welcome the twenty or so new teachers who join our ranks today and at the same time welcome back a similar number of old hands who return for a new year with us,' she added a 'well done all of you,' presumably in a message of general encouragement in taking on what the year ahead would bring.

'The lady who has joined me on the stage is the Deputy Head, Ms. Dorothy Comardy – or as she is known in this Internet age, Dot Com.'

Her audience again reacted with the anticipated laughter and Simon once more gave the speaker ten out of ten for preparation, originality and overall content.

'One, or both, of us is always on site and is available at any time for school or personal matters of any nature.' She paused before continuing 'I address my opening remarks to the newly arrived teachers, those who are returning have heard it before but at the risk of repeating myself every twelve months, let me mention a few basic facts.

We are all guests in this country. It is not Australia or, for that matter, New Zealand or even England…yes we do have a few Poms amongst us,' she smiled knowingly.

'We are now living in a part of Asia and the culture is in many ways quite different to what we have been used to back home. What goes there may be a no-go here.'

Matilda looked directly at Cazza, who had taken a front row seat to best show off her batik, boobs and legs, and continued

'There are certain behavioural standards we should recognise. Do what you wish behind closed doors but when out in public please remember that displays of bosoms and buttocks are mainly seen as a No-No here, especially in a working environment.'

Cazza quietly marked her library card and made out to listen intently, slowly smoothing the batik skirt to cover her left leg. The movement was seen as being semi-erotic by those sitting along the front row on her left.

Madam Speaker continued 'The Academy has been in business – and education is a business these days – for five years. The first year saw around 75 students from 9 countries here. This year we will have over ten times that figure with students from over 20 countries amongst us, and what started with half a dozen or so teachers is now close to fifty.

Your tasks though are not easy. You are reminded that while many of our students are Australian or New Zealanders, the majority are not. Each of them needs careful handling appropriate to their own background and way of life. You are now teachers, counsellors and academic psychologists rolled into one.

The experiences you have during your time at the Academy will prove invaluable in your future work, and life, and let me say that you will get out of this exactly what you put into it.'

The speech then moved on to more pedestrian matters such as school rules, class times, facilities, layout of the school and term dates. Details came forth regarding the city-state of Singapore, language - officially English but often not quite what you'd expect – population, 4 million plus: ethnic split - 77% Chinese, 13% Malay, 7% Indian…

'And we are found amongst the remaining 3% under the 'Others' category,' she paused.

'So you can tell your friends and relatives that you are now officially categorized as an 'Other' and that you will soon know how the 'other people' think.'

In reference to communication mention was made of the local word *Lah* 'In Singapore you will find that many people use the word 'Lah' when speaking to each other. The nearest equivalent to which would be the term 'Mate' as used 'down under'. The 'Lahs' that you get can be taken as a friendly additive or emphasis to whatever has been said to you. Let me say though that in the Music Department Miss Finn has not added an additional 'Lah' to her basic Do : Ray : Me : Fa : So…so far as I know. She still maintains the one La I believe.'

The audience loved it. Head of School then ended her speech and called upon Dot Com to detail the more specific areas to be covered.

The Deputy Head spoke briefly about her work and role in school events and activities. She provided information on the local environment such as the whereabouts of various High Commissions, Clubs, Entertainment Centres, buses, underground MRT trains and other social facilities in and around the city.

In summary the audience was told that various types of literature on living in Singapore could be found in the Staff Room and if anyone had any specific questions then they should just ask – and they would be given the answers, if known.

After the speeches everyone stayed in the hall until the two leading ladies had positioned themselves at the Exit. As the gathering then slowly left the area personal words of welcome were passed between speakers and their staff. No one was missed.

By eleven the basics were over and done with. Teachers had been asked to gather under their own particular discipline in various parts of the building and Simon made his way to the English Group which was meeting on the first floor. There were just five teachers in total, plus Cazza who had been attached to them as she was the only Librarian and as such could not hold meetings with herself very easily. And as the books on site were mostly in English she thus qualified as a de-facto member of the English squad.

'Hi,' the last member of the unit walked into the room, warmly greeting all as he did so 'my name is Rupert Nelson and I am in charge of all English activity here.'

The man was in his late forties and obviously an old hand in terms of the Academy and what went on. He sat on the edge of a desk at the front of the classroom and spoke to the seated sextet.

'What we need to do today is go over who is taking which classes, where and when – and the students you have in your care. The appropriate syllabus for each particular class has already been detailed in the papers which will be passed to you in a moment.'

Rupert was from Napier in New Zealand's North Island and had been with the school since the opening. He seemingly 'loved' Singapore he told them, adding as part of his preamble 'Oh the food! You have many delights in store, including expanding waist-lines if you're not careful. I don't recognize any faces so take it you are all new this year?' He posed the question and received six nodding heads in response. They must have looked like a row of twitching dogs on the back shelf of a Holden saloon car Simon mused.

'Let me tell you, before anyone else does, that I am known as 'Lord Nelson' around here which neither pleases or displeases me. It

26

is though a fact and if it helps people remember my name then I accept it.'

What he was doing was letting them know that he knew what everyone called him and that it didn't bother him. Supposedly. He passed each of the teachers a folder containing class details, an already planned timetable, subject list, books to be studied as well as names of students under their care. Whilst the recipients of the documents examined them he turned to Cazza and explained how the library system worked in simple terms before passing her a detailed directory of books in-house for familiarisation in her own time.

Rupert was finding it difficult to keep his eyes from straying south of the directory which Cazza had carefully positioned on the left knee of her crossed legs. A nearby fan was blowing her way the result of which was that much of her left thigh was on general display, the exact amount of which varied at any given time according to the movements of the oscillating metal.

'I shall personally show you the library after we finish here,' he whispered quietly to the lady from Cairns who responded with a breathless 'That will be beaut.'

'I'm sure,' he mumbled to himself, voice floundering on the jagged barrier reef within his excited mind. He could already see Cazza climbing the library ladder in search of a specific book he'd requested and which was filed at the very top of the shelves.

Half an hour plus a few questions and queries later and everyone seemed satisfied. The English team was then taken to the various classrooms they would be using after which Miss Exotica Queensland was escorted to her book domain by her personalised Kiwi mountain guide.

Rupert introduced Cazza to her assistant, Madam Tan, who was busy checking on new book arrivals. The lady obviously approved of the batik skirt but marks for the minimalist white top which Cazza wore were perhaps somewhat limited. She hadn't spotted the gap in the skirt so did not realise the many provocative possibilities of her younger colleague – as yet.

The pair seemed to be instantly comfortable with each other and after twenty minutes or so on the computer checking out the various systems used Cazza declared herself 'Ready for anything,' I bet you are, thought Rupert before banishing such ideas to dry Outback sand and concentrating on herding his charges towards the canteen where lunch was to be served at one o'clock.

On arriving the small groups split up, some went in search of Western and others of Asian fare. At least they haven't arranged an Aussie bar-b-q, thought Simon, which would be been rather obvious and inappropriate he felt. Having gathered together a plate of various meat dishes plus a couple of veggies well endowed with chilli, all on a bed of steamed rice, he threaded his way amongst the tables until he found one less occupied than others. Quite comfortable with chopsticks he sat down, popped open his can of low-calorie soft drink and set about his first meal on Singapore soil.

'Hiiiiiiiiiiiiiii….' the voice reverberated into his right ear. Simon paused in mid chopstick movement and looked up, mouth still open.

'I'm Chauncy,' his visitor announced before adding 'Art,' and asking 'Look may I join you?' He sat without waiting for an answer parking himself opposite, grinning excessively.

The newcomer was in his mid forties, wore pink walking shorts, which matched his footwear, and a droopy collarless white shirt covered in green and gold blotches. His hair blended with the shorts though was actually more red than pink, perhaps the lighter tone will appear when the dye starts to fade Simon considered.

Chauncy noticed Simon taking in his shirt colours and responded 'I know, isn't it DIvine. So appropriate don't you think…Aussie colours on the first day of school. Well, not the first day for the kids but it is for us teachers, you know what I mean…' he trailed off, finishing with a rising 'Mmmmmmmm……' which gained rapidly in pitch much like a whistle on a kettle.

Simon gulped down his first mouthful and asked 'Sorry, did you say your name was Arthur?'

'No, dear bois,' came the smiling reply 'now pay attention, there will be questions later. It's Chauncy. I am the art master – hence the Art, as in position, not name. Why, do you know many people with the name Arthur?'

'My dingo's called Arthur,' Simon responded with a straight face and scooped up another delicious mouthful. Chauncy's eyes opened wide. Simon clarified 'He's a toy one actually. Airport farewell present from the family, all that sort of stuff.'

'Is he? That's nice, maybe I can paint him one day against a backdrop of dry, arid desert…not that you can find many such places around here,' he proclaimed, laughing happily away to himself before digging into his own food.

'Oh, oh, oh, oh, oh…' he suddenly proclaimed, twitching on each rising and falling 'oh' as he did so. Simon thought he had a case of wobbling lockjaw sitting opposite and wondered where the Medical Centre was.

'Are you ok?'

'Oh yeeeeessss,' came the response in deepening tones 'it's just that this food is just so, so, so, so, well you know...so…so…yes…that's it…so wonderful.' His left arm shot into the air in emphasis and another rising kettle exclamation of 'Mmmmmmmmm…' followed, with an added 'Wow!' coming in fast behind as Chauncy's head quivered for final emphasis.

Well he's a bit of life thought Simon before asking 'Are you Australian?'

His companion spluttered on a slippery piece of fish and proclaimed with certain vigour 'No, no, no, no, no, of course not. I'm a Pom. Or should I say *bloody Pom* to you? But I've been to

Australia and want to go back sooooooon. Oh yes... Love it. Just LOVE it! Oh those bronzed ANzacs, show me the beach and a slippery surfboard and I'll get into deep water difficulties for anyone.'

I like the emphasis on certain syllables Simon thought to himself as another 'Oh yes...' was added to the last comment.

'Do you do nude paintings?' he passed a tricky one across the wooden table.

'Certainly. In this climate, who needs clothes? I just love standing before a canvas au natural. In fact I'm at my best when there's nothing between I and my current masterpiece except air,' the straight-faced response came from the chewing artist-in-residence who couldn't keep still.

'Live and let live, I say,' Chauncy continued after clearing some spicy spinach 'and let your cobalts run into your aquamarines any time the fancy takes you. That's my motto anyway.

So let the world come and ogle ... I am a free palate for all to see. That's me,' another 'Mmmmmmmm...' came in behind the declaration of poster paint independence.

Well he's quick, thought Simon, and quite funny too, as he warmed to his lunch companion.

'And what do you teach?' he was asked as a piece of bright red chilli lodged between two front teeth of his artistic colleague took his eye. It rather matched his hair colour Simon thought before answering.

'Boring old English, I'm afraid.'

'Don't! Don't! Oh don't, puhleesseeee...' came the cry, accompanied by more twitching.

'Don't you DARE say that the English language is BORING!' the volley was fired back at him fast and low 'It is the most BEAUtiful (heavy accent on the first syllable again) language in the world. Oh how I give thanks every day for being born an Englishman and growing up with this most expressive of languages flowing through my veins.'

Right oh okker, Simon thought, point made 'I was meaning that it is probably not half as varied or spontaneous as Art, especially with someone like you in front of the canvas.'

'Quite correct,' the somewhat huffy answer came back to him across the chilli sauce 'I live for Originality and Imagination – who are also my two Persian cats, by the way – as well as creativity and spontaneity in the art-room.'

Now it was Simon's turn to think 'Wow,' though he tried not to twitch.

Cazza sashayed into view and headed their way, presented a melting smile and two wobbling upper-level jellies to each of them and asked if she could join their table.

'My dear,' exclaimed Chauncy, standing and bowing extravagantly 'you are a vision of well-balanced colour,' he paused to take in the batik skirt 'the likes of which I have not seen since my tubes were tied and squeezed as one across the canvas of life. Sit – do,' he insisted, guiding her to a seat as he cleared a place.

She did as bid, glancing rather apprehensively at Simon who raised his eyebrows in silent acceptance of the artistic exhibition they were witnessing. 'I'm the new Librarian,' she advised the Shirt of Many Aussie Colours.

'Oh shush,' he responded immediately in mock disbelief before collapsing laughing across the table, slapping his bare knees as he did so 'and what will you fine me if I'm a day late in returning my book 'Painting by Numbers – Parts 1 to 10'? Mmmmmmmm…?????' the kettle was again steaming.

'It depends which of the numbers are late, as I've already got your number,' she looked up from her gastronomic delight.

'Ooohhhhh…cheeky monkey. I love it!' Chauncy proclaimed, adding 'Don't worry, I'll never be late for you.'

'How long have you taught here?' Simon asked the Art master, giving Cazza a chance to start her meal.

'Three years dear bois, and if you're wondering how come a Pom like I is here I shall reveal all. Pay attention,' Simon wasn't really wondering at all, but waited for the story to unfold anyway.

'I just happened to turn up one day with my palate of persimmon tones and Madam White Snake up there – the Head of School to you, Matilda to others – simply could not resist my work and offered me a job immediatement. And as I was *between exhibitions* at the time I took it. And here I have been ever since.'

'Who's Madam White Snake?' asked Cazza taking up on the title.

'Originally she is a famous character in an ancient Chinese opera who worked for the good of the enclave against the surrounding forces of evil, much like Matilda upstairs does. Our very own Madam White Snake spends much of her time keeping rival schools at bay when they try to nick our kids.'

'Other schools nicking the kids - isn't that a little queer?'

'Oh, where?' Chauncy sat bolt upright quickly scanning the horizon 'Can't see anyone of note my dear,' he announced the result of the survey as he sat back 'but we live in hope. Keep up the surveillance.' A quick 'Mmmmmmmmm….' followed, as each got on with their meal.

They ate between a repartee that became increasingly potent as the contents of their plates diminished and exchanges grew in both double meaning and definition.

'We're off after this, aren't we?' Ms. Iggle-Oggle-Wiggle-Woggle-Jelly-On-A-Plate asked neither of them in particular.

'I've been off for years, dear. As anyone can see!' Chauncy shot back before bursting out loud yet again in rolling laughter.

'I'm sure,' added Simon.

'Cheeky,' came the artistic response followed by another knee slap and a slow swaying movement. It almost ended up with him falling amongst the student - this was a school after all - ants below the table who sat in neat lines awaiting any scattered rice from above.

'Yes we are,' confirmed Simon to Cazza 'and we are supposed

to all meet back at the hotel to discuss options on permanent premises for our own little group.'

'Oh yes, I remember all that,' Chauncy offered 'it's so GHASTly all this looking for digs isn't it? Never mind, I'm sure you will find somewhere nice but remember to ask about the Hungry Ghosts.'

They looked at each other and then at Chauncy.

'The Hungry Ghosts?' Cazza sought clarification.

'Oh yes…come the seventh moon of the Lunar Calendar they are all out and about. People hold noisy rituals, gatherings and songs for a month or so just to keep them settled and under control. All of which can be extremely loud if you happen to live near a place where performances, auctions or dinners are taking place.'

They again looked at him questioningly, unsure if he was serious or joking.

'And when will all this happen? asked Cazza.

'In the seventh month, around August or September.'

'But it's only January now so why worry?' continued the puzzled librarian.

'Because rehearsals start very early my dear, that's why,' he advised, adding a finishing 'Mmmmmmm' and laughing happily as they finished the meal. 'So don't forget,' he reminded them as they stood to take their leave 'ask about the Ghosts.'

'Oh we will,' confirmed Simon as he and Cazza made their way out of the canteen.

'See you next week.'

'Oh YES….' came the returned promise, followed by a threatening 'And don't be late on Monday, otherwise I'll keep you in after school.'

The pursuing laughter faded as they cleared the building and took a taxi back to the Double Happiness Inn. They sat in the lobby reading the Real Estate pages of The Straits Times while awaiting the five other members of the team to arrive.

The three Sheilas took gold, silver and bronze in crossing the

Inn entrance closely followed by Bruce after which came Tyrone tailed off a rather bad last. So much for the fitness of the Physical Education master, they thought.

'How'd'ya go?' asked Sheila Three of her two companions.

'Great,' they chorused.

'Wha'd'ya reckon to old Waltzing Matilda then?' asked Tyrone now back in the leading pack.

'OK,' they both agreed 'Seemed nice enough, though obviously allergic to a bit of thigh,' added Simon as Cazza punched his arm in response.

'And what about Dot Com eh?' Bruce tabled the question 'Bet her website would be worth looking at on a dark night in Dandenong.'

'That's for sure. Quite a few cobwebs must have appeared in the chalk cupboard over the years and would probably make interesting reading,' agreed Sheila Three, giggling at the thought.

Simon called the meeting to order and they all sat around a low cane table with a stained glass top, the stains probably originating from beer bottles.

'OK then folks, we need to contact a few Estate Agents and see what's going in the way of a likely home. Are we agreed that we all move into the same location if we can find one big enough, as that way we should be able to bargain for better prices because of the numbers in the group?'

The remaining six nodded 'Better the bastards you know that the ones you don't,' Bruce summed things up.

'Right then, so here are some adverts we've cut out of this morning's paper while we've been sitting here. I'll pass them around and we can start calling and see what's what. Is that OK?' all nodded in silent agreement.

The unit was unanimous in its goal and each collected half a dozen or so ads. before making their way to various telephones to start the calling.

Cazza went upstairs to her room as there were not enough 'phones downstairs. She settled on the edge of her bed, arranged pen and paper and dialled her first number.

'Granmetrohuldingandrealestate may I helpt chew?' the other party asked.

'G'day, is this the estate agents?' she was trying to work out what had been said.

'Yest sir may I helpt chew?'

'I'm calling about the ad. in this mornings paper for the 'Large old house with character' in District 14,' she advised, raising the pitch of her voice to emphasise her gender to the listener.

'Sorry not in,' came the response 'please call back at four o'clock, can.' Click. End of story. End of call. She sat back looking at the receiver. Rather stunned she told herself that it was a start anyway and dialled the next number on her paper.

'Ah,' the grunt came down the line like a popgun going off.

'Hello?'

'Ah?' the echo bounced back, short and sharp.

Ploughing on Cazza asked 'Is this Dolly Tan Real Estate?'

'Ah. Yest but no in ah. Out for luncht.'

I got that, she thought and moved on, rather flushed with opening success.

'When will she be back?'

'No idea. Please to call back free later can.' Click.

Free what? What's with all these cans? Two down, four to go. Third time lucky…perhaps…and dialled once more.

'Hellloooo?'

'Can I speak to the person handling property in Siglap?'

'Who is dis?' came the questioning response. Ooh, a conversation. We're on our way here, she felt quite triumphant.

'My name is Carol Latham,' she informed her new phone-mate thinking it best to use the name she'd been given at birth, rather then her nickname, and thus keep things simple.

35

'How to spell?'

'C….'

'D…'

'No…C as in Cairns.'

'What?'

'C as in Cairns.'

'Ah why? We don't sell cans.' Here came the cans again!

'Why what?' the Queenslander was puzzled.

'Can what?'

'C as in China,' Cazza tried again, going regional this time

'You speak Chinese ah?'

'No. Never mind, can I speak to the boss?' she sought high office this time.

'Smee lah,' Oh, she thought, getting rather excited about hearing her first Lah and remembering Matilda's earlier words about same. Feeling they were perhaps now on the same wavelength she asked if she could make an appointment to see the house in question.

'He no come yet. Please to call back later, can?' More cans.Click.

She gave up after that, wondering what all these cans were about, must be something to do with the heat. She actually felt the urgent need to open a bottle, more so than a can, of her Singapore Slings and reached into the fridge to release one from its chilly abode.

The contents were knocked back rather urgently and feeling somewhat calmer Ms. Cairns rejoined her team downstairs, as previously agreed, at three thirty.

'Any luck?' asked Simon of the gathered assembly. They all shook their heads.

'I'm actually expecting, hoping, wishing, praying that someone will call me back. But I can't be sure because I don't know if they really understood what I wanted,' reported Bruce.

'We neither,' the three Sheilas added looking rather drained and badly in need of a quick pick-me-up. Tyrone shook his head as his right hand indicated a Big Zero and six pairs of eyes moved on to Cazza.

'Bloody hopeless mate,' she announced 'enough to turn a girl to drink,' thinking back to the cool Sling she had just savoured. Despondency and failure were fast setting over the party.

Simon had also had no luck so they agreed to adjourn to the nearest pub and discuss the project further. They asked the same whiskered fellow on the Reception Desk as the night before, his telly still blasting away, where the closest pub was.

The secret of happiness, tranquillity and cold beer could be found by following his directions…Right out of the gate, three streets down the road, turn left and twenty yards past the '*mamastall*' they would then find the 'Ever Famous Golden Sunset Palm-Reader and Karaoke Bar.'

'What's a '*mamastall*'?' Sheila Two asked between television explosions.

'Can lah,' came the smiling answer.

'It's where you buy cans, obviously.' Sheila Two felt.

The unanimous vote was that they adjourn to said Bar, if they could find it, for regrouping purposes and discussions in how best to fight another day. Well, summon up enough bravado to call another real estate agent actually, but only after much-needed fortification and encouragement by bottled sustenance. In other words, get pickled rather quickly.

Some four hours and numerous jugs of Tiger beer later they staggered back into the Inn. Feeling much the better for their liquid intake each now loved the world totally, loved Singapore – not that they'd seen much of it yet – and loved everyone they'd ever met during their short time on this earth.

A message awaited Bruce. It was stuck on side of the screaming telly at the Reception Desk which they agreed was a great place to leave messages as everyone arriving was automatically drawn to the noisy set and would look that way anyway.

It read '*Will collect you and your party at 0900 tomorrow, Fri-*

day, to take you to see 8 bedroom house in East Coast.' It was from a Desmond Tan of Tan, Tan, Tan & Tan Real Estate. The overall mood of the group lifted even higher.

'Wow, well done mate, a bloody Bulls Eye. Must be a family business with all those names being the same dontcha think?' asked Tyrone. All agreed.

'That's really bloody beauty Brucie. You've done well, we gave up after the fifth *'Ah,'* announced Sheila Two before tripping over the resident tabby cat lying at the bottom of the stairway who never moved for anyone, not even the owner. There were no eating arrangements and most of them simply crashed out in their rooms, well oiled from the late-afternoon early-evening sundowners.

The next morning quite a few sore heads sat around the 'brekki table' trying to take in enough toast to soak up the lingering overnight residue. As promised, a minivan arrived just after nine and a fellow in smart black pants and open necked light blue shirt hopped out.

'I'm Desmond Tan,' he announced to the party. They introduced themselves around the circle which surrounded him and he promptly forgot every name except Bruce who was the one who had called.

'OK then shall we go? I have a nice old house out in the east coast which could well suit your needs.'

'Great,' the collective reply came back to him.

As they drove along they filled Desmond in with answers to various questions such as to when they needed a place, how many people exactly, garden preferred or not and such like.

Half an hour later they pulled up outside an old three-storey house painted in the same pale green as the Inn they'd just left and agreed that there really must have been an over supply of this paint some twenty years or so ago. Desmond took them through the property, pointing out the best features, ignoring the worst.

'It has 8 bedrooms and has been used for student accommodation until recently. The students came from Indonesia but have now gone back, just a few weeks ago in fact, so your timing could be right.'

There was a sizeable garden at both front and back as well as a wide wooden verandah at the front. An old kitchen and well-worn living room of ample size for their numbers made up the downstairs delight. The upstairs bedrooms and bathrooms were rather weary but acceptable.

Although the rent was somewhat higher than they had budgeted and some fast finger work on seven flashing calculators ensued, followed by serious negotiation on lowering the price, the deal was finally done. Number 8 - an auspicious number, they were told – Trent Way, Katong was signed up by the Super Seven for one year with an option for an additional year thereafter, subject to all parties wishing it so.

'The address doesn't sound very Chinese,' Sheila Three commented as they drove back into town.

'I thought that,' added Sheila One 'my mum will think I'm in bloody Wollongong, never mind Singapore, when she writes to me at Trent Way.'

'That's OK,' decided Simon 'better have a European name at this price than a lucky Chinese one twenty percent dearer.' The point was well made.

The required paperwork was completed in the office of The Allover Tans, as they had dubbed the Real Estate agency due to the fact that much like a nudist beach there seemed to be full frontal rows of Tans everywhere they turned. A deposit was paid and they duly collected 8 keys – one each plus a spare – before heading back to the Inn.

Sunday morning was set for the day of the move and seven excited Aussies duly celebrated Phase Two of their teaching experience in the tropics with a tinnie or two in the hotel lounge.

Chapter 2

Cymbals Of Success

The move from the Inn to the house went off without any real hitches. It wasn't as though they were moving from one established home to another and had to pack tons of belongings, carry and position settees, fix washing machines, arrange beds and the like. In this case, as the new place was semi furnished, it was a matter of simply packing their bags into the minibus and heading east.

With three bedrooms on both the first and second floors and two on the ground floor a certain amount of jockeying for prime positions went on. Finally it was agreed that Simon, Bruce and Tyrone would be 'banished' to the top of the house and therefore have the greatest number of stairs to negotiate, a situation seen as right and fitting for three fit young men. The Three Sheilas would take the first floor and Cazza would have one of the ground floor rooms, the one furthest away from the kitchen and lounge as it turned out.

The furniture which greeted them was functional if not fantastic and would do until one, or all, of them won the lottery. Being typical Aussies with an eye for a flutter they had already sussed out the weekend and midweek lottery systems in Singapore. There was unanimous agreement in putting a small amount of money on combinations of numbers which offered thousands of dollars in reward if the numbers came up. The draw was on both Saturday and Sunday nights so hope and anticipation filled the weekend.

Most had picked the number of the house, especially as they'd been told it was 'lucky', and combined it with things like the number of kids in their classes, population of Australia, number of koalas in the backyard (zero) and the estimated size of Cazza's upper jellies – though there was no area on the entry forms for letters such as 'D' or 'E'.

After lunch the Three Sheilas and Cazza announced they were going to the beach. Dining arrangements had consisted of fast food delivered by a not-so-fast fellow who got lost on his motorbike and took ages to turn up. When he finally did so the supposedly 'hot pizza' was colder than when it had started life on its foil tray. The weather though was hot, as usual, so a 'cold collation' was dished out to all helping hands on site, with some cheap dry white Aussie wine in support.

The three lads elected to also head for the beach. Their choice though was to one of the beach-side bars more so than a quiet four-seater sand-dune which the ladies were seeking by the waters edge. Two taxis finally headed off in tandem in basically the same direction. The first, with the girls aboard, turned off at the East Coast Flyover while the other carried on down East Coast Parkway heading towards the airport.

Tyrone sat in the front seat next to the driver. His green and gold Aussie beachwear looked very smart though his manner was one of growing concern.

'Weez going back home by the look of it fellers,' he announced, pointing at a descending red and white aircraft on which they could clearly see a white kangaroo on the tail.

All three waved and shouted at the 'plane which caused the taxi driver to ask 'Your friends ah?'

'Sure, weez Auzzies and all our mates are on that,' Bruce told him. Patriotism to the fore again, thought Simon. A little further down the road the driver swung onto an off-ramp and moments later deposited them at a busy fast-food and shopping complex by the beach. A quick walk through a packed car park, carefully avoiding suicidal skateboarders, and there it stood before them — The Famous Ever Beach-Bar & Karaoke Korner - awaiting their pleasure.

'Let's hope they have some 'Famous and readily available cold beer' and we'll be apples,' Bruce itemised their immediate needs. There came those apples again, thought Simon, though there was no obvious indication of the bar selling cider from where they stood.

A row of cane tables and chairs was set against a slate wall next to a cycle path which itself was separated by sand and palm trees to the waters edge. A few yards back from the tables stood the focal point of the establishment, a dark bamboo bar with tall cane stools standing guard in front of much sought-after contents. Soft guitar music coming from a couple of speakers in the thatched roof added to the ambiance.

Happy Hour 12pm to 8pm. The chalk sign above the giant glass fridge read.

'What do you make of that?' Bruce asked 'Do you think they mean midnight until eight the next night or noon till eight at night the same day?'

'Dunno,' offered Tyrone who was showing more interest in the busy bikini parade passing along the cycle track than the bottled options to his left. All three settled at a wobbly wicker table and soaked up the sunny setting in absolute delight.

'Well it sure is different to Brizzie,' announced Bruce.

'And Tassie,' added the Australian flag carrier.

'And Tom Price,' imparted Simon who was also taking in the situation with certain relish.

'Can I helpt chew?' a friendly voice brought them back down to earth. It belonged to a Chinese waiter dressed in bright floral shirt, khaki shorts, no socks and white jogging shoes.

'Owmuchizzajugabeer?' asked Bruce in his best Brisbane surfie accent.

'Ah why?'

'Because weez thirsty,' Bruce announced 'and we'd like some of yer *Famous Ever* beer, mate. Please.'

The other party seized on the mention of beer and advised his trio of thirsty travellers 'Special half price until eight. No worries mate,' he finished off, grinning.

'Had a few okker Aussies through here have you?' asked Tyrone

'Then yer'll know what weez like, won't yer?' Bruce finished the question.

'Two jugs?' the smart salesman asked 'With ice?'

'Who said two!' Simon asked 'One to start with. And why would we want ice?'

'Because it warms up quickly and ice will keep it cold longer.' The explanation from the smiling Mr. Flower Power seemed sensible though it was something they'd never thought of.

'OK but let's have the ice in a separate bucket.'

'Good thinking my man,' Bruce praised his colleague with a thumbs-up sign.

'Now how about a lump of ice on top of that?' he asked as his gaze swept over a passing beauty in black bikini top and tight white mini-pants. Miss Singapore Beach went gliding past on roller-blades, hair flowing behind in the light breeze. All three gasped.

'I think it'd be me needing the ice, not her,' Simon gaped at a vision sailing by. The others agreed. Their beer and the ice came and went. As did the next order and the next and so on until they lost count.

By sunset they were feeling no pain, were in love with the world – including every skating Miss Singapore Beach entrant gliding by – and felt there could be no finer place on earth, other than Australia of course, to be in at that very moment. The long running Happy Hour ended at eight, as did the visit.

Collecting fast-food dinners as they meandered back through the shopping area they hailed a taxi and each sang a verse of Waltzing Matilda to the driver on the way home. Why do we always do this as soon as we leave Oz? Simon asked himself but was too pickled to provide a sensible answer.

Four faces bright red from the sun welcomed the three faces bright red from the booze when they tumbled out of their home-delivery taxi. Cazza was sitting on the verandah reading a magazine, her jellies had a luminous strawberry sheen to them which gave her a rather fetching glow in the semidarkness.

'Had a nice time boys?' Sheila Three was perched on the verandah railing taking in the light evening breeze. There was no response as all three rushed urgently past heading for the nearest loo, each hoping their target wouldn't be occupied.

'Bloody beaut Sheil,' finally advised a returning and greatly relieved Bruce a couple of minutes later. 'Ask the two other plonkers about it when they get back from *pointing Percy at the porcelain*,' referring to Simon and Tyrone.

'Weez had a bloody great time, doncha just love it here?' he turned back into the house and fell over an arm of the settee. The place was new to him so he had the excuse of not knowing the geographical layout of the furniture all that well.

'And yews, how was it all?' the rather muffled follow-up question came their way from the faded carpet runner behind the cratered three-seater settee. Cazza had moved inside and was now glowing on a battered beanbag, hair filled with what looked like half a pound of jellybeans. Her shorts seemed to start around her waist and end just below the same area. This girl brought new meaning to the word *relaxing*.

'Terrific. We had a great time and did you know you can hire bikes down there for just a few dollars an hour and ride for miles and miles?' Sheila Two asked, red hair and red face almost the same tone.

'And we're all going skating next Sunday,' announced Sheila One,the new Social Secretary of the Residents Fitness Group.

'S'roight' added Sheila Three as she reached out to pick at one of the quartet of hamburgers they had obviously brought for their own dinner and which Sheila Two had just opened. The food lay on paper in the middle of a threadbare carpet which covered the centre area of the once highly polished wooden floor. The greatly relieved Tyrone and Simon finally returned.

Collecting their own fried chicken packs from the table they joined the team lying on the floor, grinning and happy with life thanks to the copious amounts of amber liquid consumed earlier beneath swaying palms. During the next hour or so they set the world to rights. Opinions on Didgeridoo Night-school courses, Germaine Greer doing a duet on the next Kylie Minogue album and *Wombat Breeding for Beginners* handbooks were passed around faster than the cans of beer and bottles of cold Aussie wine. Which took some doing. After much heated debate Sheila One made the comment that if they planned to be on the 8.02 am Number 14 bus to town the next morning they'd perhaps better get their material ready for the first day of the new term.

Sheila Three announced that none of them had won the lucky Numbers Draw that evening so would indeed all have to go to work for another week, or in this case for the opening week.

'What a bummer!' proclaimed Tyrone in the usual patriotic green and gold striped shorts as Bruce began to snore in agreement from his obviously comfortable position behind the settee.

'OK let's go gang,' Sheila Three called it a night. Tomorrow was a new day, a new beginning, a new experience for them all and undoubtedly a new hangover for three of the party.

The 'two minutes' walk from the house to the Number 14 bus stop, as advised by Desmond Tan of the Allover Tans, was exactly that and the 8.02 duly arrived on time. They had all bought stored travel passes and knew how to use them, having been coached by their helper from the nudist real estate company who they had declared to be a 'Really Bonzer Bloke.' The title had been conferred in view of his great assistance and help in their time of need, which in this case was the need for somewhere to live.

'Good on yer Dezzo,' they had toasted his talents in unison, and in Tiger beer, at an appropriate moment the previous evening during a '*Cheers to Great Mates*' session.

All of them sat upstairs on the air-conditioned double-decker bus and took in the sights of the morning as it slowly made its way into the city. Overall visual reception for three of the seven travellers was not as clear as for the remaining four but things on the outside of the windows still managed to look pretty good. At twenty-past eight they hopped off their red, purple and white chariot close to Orchard Road and three minutes later entered the Antipodean Academy portals.

Wishing each other well they split up and made their way to their own classrooms – and library – to set things in place before Assembly at 9am.

Simon's room was 106 on the ground floor, and his documents told him to expect twenty three kids around thirteen years of age from some seven countries. The classroom door was open when he arrived and four boys were already sitting at single desks at the back of the room.

'Good morning,' he smiled at them making his way to the desk in front of a large blackboard. None of them answered but they did smile which was a fairly encouraging start he thought.

'Where are you all from?' he looked up as he laid his books and bag on the desk.

'Australia,' three of them answered.

'Japan,' came the final entry.

'Great, and Hello to you all. My name is Simon Skeer and I'm also from Australia so I'm afraid you, Mr. Japan, are already down 4 –1 and we haven't even kicked off yet.'

He smiled at the Japanese boy who looked at him blankly 'Don't worry, there's always the second half,' he was trying to give some hope to the somewhat puzzled pupil.

He enjoyed teaching kids around this age as they were starting to form their own opinions about life and had views they would often share with you, if you could get them interested in a subject in the first place of course.

Two girls walked in, smiled at him and sat next to each other on the second row. Simon gave them a welcoming 'Hello,' and set about sorting out his books for the first day of the first term. By ten minutes to nine all twenty three students were in-situ and he realised that the first foray of his new Asian academic voyage was about to set sail.

'OK folks,' he killed the chatter and gained their attention 'at the risk of repeating myself, my name is Simon Skeer – as on the blackboard, here,' he pointed to where he'd written his name in the top right-hand corner.

'I am from Australia and I will be your class teacher for the coming year. Right now though we all have to make our way to the 9 o'clock Assembly in The Hall which is on the fourth floor. I would ask that you make your way directly there, out of the door, turn left and up the first set of stairs all the way to the top, and I'll see you back here afterwards.' They all left. Simon made up the rear to rein in any possible strays, of which there turned out to be none. The group duly followed instructions to The Hall which was filling fast when he and his charges arrived.

The boys wore black shorts, white shirts, green and gold striped ties, belts and socks – an overall combination of the Australian and New Zealand colours he realised. The girls were in white dresses with black polka-dots and waistband sashes of green and gold which tied at the side. Their white ankle socks had green, black and gold edging.

Some fifty or so teachers and staff were seated along the side-walls discretely watching over their pupils on the forward-facing centre rows of chairs. At nine exactly by The Hall clock Matilda Wilson, looking thin and angular, with obviously more bones than beef about her, made her way on to the stage. Ms. Dot Com followed at the usual respectful distance. Their audience hushed and stood as one.

'Good morning,' the school head greeted them 'please sit down.'

Almost eight hundred souls did as bid and the speech began. The welcoming words went on for some fifteen minutes and as they did so Simon surveyed the gathering, slowly taking in all that sat before him. Across the room sitting midway along the far wall amongst twenty five or so other teachers he spotted Chauncy at the same time Chauncy spotted him.

The artist was wearing a pale blue smock that clashed terribly with his now heavily gelled and spiky red hair, advanced modern art thought Simon as their eyes met.

Chauncy had his hands clasped in front of him and as their eyes locked across the crowded space three fingers of his upper hand wiggled in welcoming salute. Simon smiled and nodded imperceptibly before continuing his radar sweep of the rows thinking to himself that things were probably not going to be dull over the next few months with someone like this colourful fellow around.

Words from Dot Com followed Matilda's speech, filling in the administration blanks left by her leader and by a quarter to ten they were all back in their allotted classrooms.

The day went well, Simon felt that his charges were all quite smart and that a common thread of creativity ran through them, even if their nationalities were quite diverse. Like all teachers he moved between classrooms to take other lessons before returning to home base and his own particular flock at the end of the day.

Life gradually settled into a routine in that all seven occupants from the House at Number Eight travelled to work on the same bus most mornings, cars quickly being filed under 'Impossible' due to the high costs involved in buying or leasing and running same.

Each returned home according to their own timetable and most weekday evenings were spent preparing lessons for the next day, watching television and going to a fast food outlet for dinner.

On the Friday afternoon of the third week the final school bell rang at 3.40pm as usual. Simon gathered up his goods and chattels and made his way slowly towards the gates. As he rounded the final corner the school's *Resident Rembrandt* came rushing down the stairs on his right.

'Simon!' Chauncy exclaimed, grinning happily 'Look, how are you? I've been meaning to catch up with you but you know how it is during the first few weeks of term. Oodles to do. I have endless jars of paint to sort out as well as stiff brushes to soak,' he raised knowing eyebrows at the thought and continued 'Umpteen canvases to prepare, easels and other things to erect,' another knowing pause before 'God, it never ends! Same for you, I'm sure.'

'Oh I'm fine, the kids are great and I'm getting used to things here though it's very different to The Outback of course.'

'Of course it is dear bois,' the artist agreed as they walked out of the gates, fending off pushing kids with a handy extra-length paintbrush 'there's people here for one thing as well as roads, cars and buses. Where you've come from I suppose there were just a couple of cows and the Flying Doctor. Mind you I could find you the cows with ease if you felt the need. Not so sure about a doctor with wings though.'

'Exactly,' back came the agreement from Simon 'and no dingoes.'

Chauncy looked at him.

'Except for Arthur.'

His artistic companion got the message, smiled knowingly and nodded 'Quite right, quite right. Look let's go for coffee and have a nice chat. I might have a 'still life' assignment later but that's OK, no rush.'

The idea was accepted and they wandered slowly down side roads heading towards Singapore's main thoroughfare of Orchard Road. As they finally turned into the busy road a young Asian fellow popped up in front of Chauncy, grinning at him face to face, nose to nose almost.

'Ohhh, hellloooo,' the art master gasped and greeted the new arrival with fluttering delight. Turning to Simon he informed him 'This is Jacob — as in biscuits,' they shook hands.

'And 'Creek'?' asked Simon in reference to the brand of Australian wine. Chauncy smiled in acknowledgment 'I take it this is your 'still life' assignment then?'

'Well, yes and no. The truth is I'm not really sure. He's actually Thai and his real name is Jakubaprorn, or similar, so from that one gets Jacob. Well I do. Perfectly reasonable name process if you ask me. Annnnnnnnnd…' he was starting to flow 'he works on one of the building sites around here, of which there are zillions of course so I can't tell you which one exactly,' he smiled happily.

'Annnnnnnnnd… you see, we met whilst I was watching a cement mixer rotate from one of those wooden viewing platforms they kindly construct so one can take a squizzy and have a good gander at what they all do.' Simon was enthralled.

'Annnnnnnnnd… he, Jacob, was controlling an outpour which was taking place right in front of the platform I was standing on. Annnnnnnnnd… it was all very interesting you see. And he looked at me and I looked at him as it all poured out, so I asked him how long it took to get hard and he said it was almost instantaneous – or at least I think he did – and we sort of moved on from there.' He paused to let Simon take in the story so far. Deep breath.

'Annnnnnnnnd… before I knew it we were chatting away quite happily. Then he came round to my place as I felt I wanted to capture his quite exquisite and exotic features on canvas in a rather creative still life. Are you still with me?' Simon nodded.

'Annnnnnnnnd… so …before long I had him beautifully positioned on my old whatnot by the window just as the light faded and brought out the best in his attributes – all of them,' a glazed look flashed across his face and his head twitched from the recollection.

'However, every time I gave him a bunch of grapes to hold in a certain way he kept eating them before I could get the colours fully committed to the canvas. Annnnnnnnnnd… in the end they'd all gone before I could complete the work properly and by which time it was dark anyway.'

He sighed in exasperation 'So I told him he could come at the end of this week, preferably after he'd eaten, and we'd try again. Annnnnnnnnnd… what do you know, here he is, ready to display all his delights once again. I suppose. Who knows!'

He gasped and smiled at the boy who was walking along with them quite happily as well as silently 'Complete surprise actually as you can never tell if they will or won't turn up.'

Chauncy turned to the subject of the discussion 'Anyway, now where have you been, you NAUGHty bois? I've been looking for you for days,' he admonished the young man, laughing slightly hysterically to himself as he did so 'I just hope you're not very hungry today.'

Turning to Simon he added 'Unlike your wine I'm not sure if he's sweet or dry … maybe I'll find out later.' Turning back to his model he informed him 'Anyway Jacob, Simon here is my friend from school and we're going for coffee so would you like to join us?' The new arrival was formerly invited. Jacob nodded and the duo became a trio as they made their way into a welcoming Bun In The Oven Cakes & Koffee Korner, one of many coffee outlets along the wide boulevard.

Having decided on two cappuccinos and an ice water as their immediate needs Chauncy made his way to the counter to advise their order to a fast-talking attendant.

'Where are you from?' Simon asked his new Thai friend at the table.

Jacob smiled at him before answering 'Yes.'

Try again, he thought 'Are you from Bangkok?'

'Nineteen,' came the reply Well, he thought, now I probably know either his age or number of the flat he lives in. It was all very interesting so he continued 'And how did you meet Chauncy?' although he'd been told by the artist he felt it was a question which should get the lad talking

'She is my mother,' came the family-based response.

Puzzled somewhat he checked the statement 'Chauncy is your mother?'

'Last time,' was the clarification before a puffing Chauncy returned with a tray on which were two coffees and an iced-water. Grins and mugs were passed around before the painter sat down and asked Simon 'Getting on OK are we?'

'Well I think so,' he took the next bit slowly 'though I think that he thinks you were his mother in a former life.' Simon presented his summary of the collection of answers so far received.

'Oh I know,' Chauncy responded, totally unconcerned 'quite correct actually. He was once a budgerigar that my aunty Madge kept at her home in Reading when I was a kid which I used to care for like a mother hen. And every Saturday morning I'd go round and paint its feathers. Blue one week, Green the next week, Red the next, then Gold, Purple, Orange and so on all around the paint box as the months went by. Then one day it fell off its perch and passed on to the great birdcage in the sky – lead poisoning they said it was.' He paused in fluttering sadness.

'But now, you see, he's flown back into my life this time around,' the eyelashes flicked up and down for emphasis as he looked over at Jacob and patted his nearest knee 'So I can now have another few attempts at painting him – though on canvas and using lead-free paints this time.'

Simon was somewhat stunned by the calm, concise and *perfectly-reasonable-to-some* explanation which had just been tabled alongside the coffees.

'Well if that's what you say then it's fine by me,' he declared before sipping his cappo. in contemplation of his own previous lives, though nothing sprang to mind.

A loud 'Hello', which reverberated off the wall in triplicate, interrupted his thoughts just as his nose dipped into the frothy coffee. He looked up to see the three Sheilas standing before them, each grinning happily at those sitting down.

'Oh hi,' he responded, standing up as he did so 'have you met Chauncy?' he directed their focus to the artist. The creator of canvasses stood also and bowed extravagantly before the ladies.

They screamed in delight and answered 'No….No….No…' with a following 'Hello…Hello….Hello...' to the table's unknown occupants, shaking hands with Chauncy and Jacob, who also stood. Going anywhere with these girls was like being in a three-sided echo-chamber, Simon thought.

'Chauncy. Art,' the artist gave them his standard introductory line, before adding 'not to be confused with dingoes.'

They looked puzzled.

'Don't worry, it's an in joke…' he laughed. Turning to his Thai companion he added 'and this is my handsome still life model Jacob,' instructing 'Don't move!' to the boy.

'As in Creek?' Sheila One asked, another on the wine trail tour.

'No, crackers.'

'Those that break up into little puffy bits that fly all over the place as you try to get them into your mouth?' asked Sheila Three.

'Could be. Just imagine…' Chauncy muttered, half to the girls and half to himself 'I'll let you know next week,' the eyes misted somewhat at the thought. 'Look come and join us do, please sit down and have a drink,' he bid them with another flourish.

They did as asked, gathering three more chairs from a table nearby and settled on medium-lattes all round. Soon they were all nattering away like long lost friends, even Jacob was joining in things quite merrily which they were happy to see.

Chauncy was wearing a striped kaftan that looked as if it had come from a discarded deck chair 'Love your top,' commented Sheila Three.

'I know, isn't it just …just…WONderful. Give me fifty cents and you can sit on it for half an hour. But don't drop your frothy coffee over it otherwise you'll get a dry-cleaning bill!'

'Oooooohhhhh, fancy that,' said Sheila Three, lost in thought at the prospect for a moment.

'Which beach did you find it on?' Sheila Two asked with a straight face.

'Not sure if it was Blackpool or Bondi,' the seaside scenery painter answered.

'Nice. Very nice,' the remaining two Sheilas echoed agreement.

'Thanks darlings, I shall sketch you in burnt tones any time you wish. I get much of my charcoal from the remains of good old Aussie barbecues around town, so don't forget to save me some embers when you next throw a shrimp on the barbie. If I'm not invited, that is…' he added in shocked horror at the thought, clasped his right hand to the centre of the deck chair stripes and gasped. They loved it.

Turning to Jacob he asked if he was OK and was given a warm smile in response.

'Oh gooooood,' the painter smiled happily as he informed the others at the table.

'My still life is still alive.....and kicking. I hope!'

The animated chat continued for half an hour or so as the week's events, thoughts and opinions were laid on the coffee table for scholarly consumption. Finally Chauncy announced that he and Jacob had to leave as he wanted to catch the dying rays of the sun on the young man before it was too late to bring out the best of his talents.

'Have you got the forbidden fruit ready?' Simon wondered.

The girls looked puzzled again 'I'll explain on the way home,' he told them.

'Certainly, my dear bois,' Chauncy informed the table and continued 'today, melons and grapes await our arrival, and any pips will be spat out one by one. It will though all be done slowly and only after the fruit has been captured fully for artistic posterity.'

The terms and conditions related to his canvas activity were spelt out clearly for all to understand, though not in Thai. And so saying their farewells Mr. Deckchair Cover and companion swept out of the coffee shop in a flurry of wafting bags and clothing, waving and grinning excessively to all as they went.

'I love him,' declared Sheila One. Her namesakes nodded in frothy agreement 'and for a Pom he's very funny.'

'Yes, this one is,' agreed Simon 'and I think he must be very talented as he tells me he has numerous works in quite a few galleries and posh homes around town.' The three remaining members of the coffee set looked suitably impressed.

The weekend was pleasant with each member of the household establishing their own pattern of activity. The girls went to see a film on Saturday evening, the lads went down trendy Boat Quay to 'check out the bars'. Their verdict was that it was a nice view and a nice setting but the drinks cost much more than they expected. Their tour was thus cut short somewhat as their budgetary limits were reached rather earlier than anticipated.

'Never mind,' said Bruce 'we'll put it all down to experience, and find a cheaper area next weekend.' His two boozing buddies agreed with the comment and they spent a quiet Sunday lolling about the house and garden before heading off for the usual sundowners at the beach.

Early the following week Chinese New Year notices appeared on the school Notice Boards.

The described event was the first 'big thing' of the new school year and both Matilda and Dot Com wanted it to be a success. Their view was that if the year started with a bang — of a Chinese drum— then what followed would also be a success.

Chinese New Year *this year falls on February 15th and 16th. The school will be closed on both days, which are Public Holidays. General school activities will end at lunchtime on February 14th.*

The arrival of the Year of The Sheep will be celebrated by the school in various ways...

Head of Art (Mr. Chauncy) will run a Chinese New Year painting competition. Prizes will be given by age groups – all entries must have the theme 'The Year of the Sheep' and should be submitted by February 4th. Entries will be displayed around the school the following week.

There will be a prize-giving ceremony in The Hall on the morning of February 14th.

The Head of Domestic Studies (Miss Winterbottom) will run a cookery competition. Rules, requirements and results are the same as for Art.

Students are also invited to participate in a Lion-dance Extravaganza. Those interested should report to Miss Finn in Music who will explain the requirements. Miss Finn will coordinate all dance, music and related activity with Mr. Chauncy and the chosen dancers and musicians.

The school recognizes this auspicious occasion and asks that as many students as possible become involved in the activities.

The notice was signed by Matilda.

Simon had seen Chinese New Year celebrations in brief television clips over the years but had never been very interested or closely involved in them. He had never really known much about it but the time for both education and initiation was obviously fast approaching.

Everyone was back in the house early on the Wednesday evening the notices appeared. Cazza pointed out that as the two-day Chinese New Year holiday fell on a Thursday and Friday, and as they would finish at lunchtime on the Wednesday they would in fact be getting a four and a half day break in total.

'Anyone fancy a holiday somewhere then?' asked a green and gold t-shirted Tyrone.

All seven members of the household agreed that it was a 'Beaut.' idea. The difficult part was deciding where to go. Not too far, but far enough for a nice change was the agreed criteria. Bangkok was out as it wasn't quite what a mixed party wanted – nudge nudge wink wink, some other time boys - so Malaysia or a Thai resort was settled on as the ideal options.

As Tyrone had a couple of free periods the next day he was nominated as Coordinator of Travel Operations for the task in hand. In other words, he would call a travel agent and check out what was available. They agreed that there would be a second Chinese New Year Holiday Meeting in the house that coming Friday evening at eight during which a detailed Update from Tyrone would be presented to the floor – and all those sitting on it.

It was also agreed that each attendee was responsible for providing some appropriate 'tucker' (food) and drink for this most important of occasions. Emphasis was laid on the latter item as it would be the end of the week after all.

Chapter 3

Celebration Time

'Have you ever noticed how the clothes on most Singapore girls cling to their bodies like a second skin?' Bruce asked Simon as they made their way to the Number 14 bus stop on the Friday morning.

'I know. Not a bit like the more filled-out Aussie girls who need a bit of space between body and cover to look their best,' he agreed adding 'with certain exceptions' as images of Cazza sprang to mind.

There had been heavy rain for most of the night and the morning was cooler than usual with tall, overhead trees still shaking off the remains of the night's deluge. The three Sheilas caught them up at the bus-stop, just before the 8.02 arrived, their two other housemates were still in the land of nod as they had a late start that morning. Simon himself had a blank period just before lunch and decided it was time to do some bookshop exploring. Being right in the city centre encouraged such thoughts and after his third morning lesson finished just after eleven he duly headed off down Orchard Road in the direction of previously-selected bookshop targets.

The first one was upstairs in a large and very smart shopping centre. Though nice and welcoming with dark wood in most areas it was, as expected, a commercial more than an academic outlet and not really what he sought. *'Will return,'* he made a mental note, and left.

The next shop was in a small off-street setting and gave indication of a more serious tone than the first. The atmosphere was comfortable as he entered and the always-intoxicating smell of new books wafted over him as he meandered between shelves and display stands.

'May I help you?' a friendly voice from behind his right shoulder asked as he gazed somewhat ponderously at the line-up below the heading 'English Classics'. Starting the usual 'No, I'm fine… thanks…' line as he turned around the utterance was stifled on 'fi….' as he took in the stunning beauty before him.

The speaker was about five foot four, slim with long black straight hair. The clear, open face belonged under the category 'Perfect' were she by any chance labelled along with the other items in the shop. She wore a pale blue fitted dress which complemented the shiny hair. Her head tilted slightly to one side as she looked at him expectantly, waiting for his stifled answer to be completed.

Coughing and regrouping his thoughts he swallowed and finally managed an 'I'm just looking at what you have under the *'English Classics'* heading as I may find something I can possibly use in school.'

She smiled at him – causing his knees to tremble – and concluded 'Fine, help yourself. If you need anything I will be at the far end of the store.' He wondered if she had any oxygen down there.

And with that she was gone, leaving a cloud of light perfume that lingered headily around him for a heart-stopping moment. Simon stood perfectly still in some form of shock, having never experienced such a reaction to meeting anyone. He wondered if he was ill or perhaps coming up with some tropical fever. Slowly gathering his thoughts together as he stood before the bookshelf he felt he'd better head back in case he was ill. He quietly took his leave of the shop empty handed and still quite dazed.

He joined the school lunch crowd in the canteen and settled on some steamed fish and vegetables plus a cold drink with lots of ice to help cool things down. He sat at a table, alone. Bruce shortly joined him, looked at him questioningly and asked 'Are you ok?

You look as if you've just seen a ghost.'

'Actually, I think it was an angel,' he corrected his academic mate as the colour gradually returned to his cheeks.

'Oh, really,' came the interested reaction 'well done. Where exactly, which classroom?' the questioning had started.

'No classroom, a small bookshop off Orchard Road.'

'Where abouts off Orchard Road?' his interrogator dug deeper.

'I don't know. I really can't remember,' the honest answer came.

'Oh God! You can't remember! What kind of memory have you got these days, the sun getting to the grey matter is it?' Bruce was getting frustrated.

'I honestly can't remember, that's all. We'll just have to wait and see what happens next,' Simon closed the subject and took in more steaming veggies.

Chauncy trolled into earshot 'Hiiiiiiiiiiii…Hiiiiiiiiii…' he gave his double-edged greeting 'and who's your friend today Simon?' and sat down without waiting to be invited.

'Oh you haven't met Bruce? Sorry, I thought you would have,' he was rather surprised 'this is Bruce from Brizzie and he lives in our house.' Two previous strangers shook hands.

'And this,' he said, turning to Bruce 'is Chauncy – Art – as in dingo.' Bruce looked at him as if he were still in some sort of trance and continued eating his fried rice.

'So you're gonna be very busy then for Chinese New Year by the sound of the details on the Notice Board,' Simon commented to the white sailcloth cape and black flared trousers on display before him.

'Oh don't! It's the same every year. We just get back from the Christmas and New Year break and before you know it Madam White Snake throws the Chinese New Year event smack onto my palate,' he groaned in agony, clutching his chest as he did so and rocking from side to side to add emphasis to the unjust treatment coming his way.

'Never mind, it'll keep you out of mischief. How was your still-life by the way?'

'Still there,' Chauncy advised with a laugh 'stayed the night as we couldn't get the light right.'

'So you took the bulb out and tried candles instead?' asked Bruce, brightening proceedings somewhat.

'Oh, he's a quick one, isn't he?' came the reposte to Simon with a chuckle, a punch in Bruce's shoulder and a slap on the knee; his own.

'Just wait till I get you on my canvas chucko and you won't know if you're Arthur or Martha…or a dingo playing a didgeridoo,' Chauncy added in deference to the mention of the name of Simon's pet.

All three laughed, Bruce somewhat hesitantly feeling he'd perhaps missed something somewhere. In conspiratorial tones Chauncy shared an inner secret after looking round and checking that no one else could hear.

'Do you know what SHE's got me lined up to do?' he asked of them, eyes looking skyward towards the Head's study. Without waiting for an answer he continued 'I have to organise a painting competition for all the little darlings in the school – all 747 of them. Sounds like a 'plane doesn't it! I think I'd better be on one soon, then I can get away from all this,' he trilled before continuing 'and as if that isn't enough I also have to find not one but six fleece from sheep for a special wool dance they want featured at the Chinese New Year Show. And…wait…there's more… just for good luck…I have to have 120 Chinese lanterns made and painted by the first of February so they can be hung all round the school.'

He gasped extravagantly before collapsing across the table, carefully missing his bowl of laksa by a whisker. He groaned for the usual added effect.

'Now how can a mere mortal such as I do all this? Tell me …will someone tell me please. And then tell Madam White Snake' eyes heavenwards again 'up yonder, and maybe I'll be knighted in the next Mao Zedong Honours List,' deep despair set in 'It's all too much.'

'She'll be apples mate,' encouraged Bruce.

'Do you think so? Oh thanks Brian, thanks,' Chauncy bucked up immediately at the thought.

'Bruce.'

'Whatever.'

'You'll be OK,' agreed Simon 'piece of cake.'

'I know…rock cake and I can't get my crampons around it,' the ever-witty wonder painter was hanging free.

'You'd be OK around sheep though wouldn't yew?' asked Bruce with a straight face.

'And what is that supposed to mean?' questioned the artist, now bristling slightly.

'Just wondering. You know. There's lots of 'em in Pommieland I believe so just thought yew'd be comfortable with a few yewz on hand, or wherever. That's all.'

It was time for another of Chauncy's soliloquies 'Young man. I am comfortable amongst all creatures of this world for I am an artist, a gifted being who can see far more in any given scene than most others on this earth could ever imagine,' he paused before adding 'including you, dear Barry.' He puffed out his chest.

'Bruce.'

'Whatever,' the clarification was dismissed as he continued 'so just you wait Mr. Dizzy from Brizzie, or wherever it is you hail from. I shall make sure you get fleeced in a very special way come the Year of the Sheep, no matter how much sheep-dip you drink, and that's a promise.'

He paused for a deep breath before ending the monologue on 'So there.'

'Rightie oh cocker,' accepted Bruce 'then I'll be seeing yewz in the school farmyard most nights of the week from now on then?'

'Quite,' A statement of fact, and he was off, a blurred vision in black and white sailcloth which billowed nicely as he raced up the stairs. A passing breeze caught his top and sped him to safe harbour in the second floor art room, at least they hoped it would.

'Wow,' sighed Bruce 'bit of a caution that one,' as he dug into his lunch.

'Never dull. He's always like that and usually a great laugh, just a bit fraught today it seems. Don't worry, you'll get to like him as he plays everything for laughs…always.' One could tell from the pained look on Bruce's face that he needed convincing on that point but was willing to hold back final judgment for a while.

The evening gathering back at Number 8 came together as planned with the girls bringing in copious amounts of food and the boys enough booze to float the Australian navy – twice. Well it was the weekend and they had serious business to discuss.

'Roight oh, this meeting of the Trent Way Teachers Travel Club is called to Order,' announced Sheila Three, using the name of their street in the official title, as each got comfortable on the hardly-polished, well-worn wooden lounge floor. Bottles of Aussie wine, well chilled and welcoming, stood before the ladies and stacks of almost-frozen cans of beer beckoned the gentlemen delegates from within a freezing eski sitting handily by the settee.

'Hear, hear,' Cazza advised the gathering.

'We haven't started yet,' Sheila One clarified in mock admonishment.

'Sorry, but I agree anyway. Need another slurp. Excited.' Caz announced with a giggle as Sheila Two did the necessary from the bottle of Blue Stripe White Burgundy closest to her.

'I now call on Mr. Tyrone of the Tasmanian pole-vault team – motto *'Our plans are always up in the air'* - to inform us of his findings in regard to the intended Chinese New Year travelling extravaganza featuring seven Aussies and their bathing cozzies.'

Everyone applauded …

'Give 'im the clap he deserves,' called Bruce to groans all round the plates of paté and biscuits which were being attacked rather aggressively.

'Let's hope his jokes get better, and newer, as the evening goes on,' Sheila One wished out loud.

'OK. Quiet please,' requested Tyrone, consulting his notes and laying out numerous brochures before him. 'The options we have are not that many,'

They groaned.

'But there are a few,'

They cheered and took comforting sips to ease the tension which was building. 'First of all let me tell you what's out,' they looked at him.

'Lombok,' silence 'Manado,' heavy silence and puzzled looks then a quiet questioning 'Where?' came back to him from Sheila Two.

'Knew that'd get yer,' Tyrone claimed 'Bruce, Mr. Geography master, can you take that one – for double points?'

'Indonesia. Famous for diving,' Bruce scored bonus points for added information.

'Anyway it's out. All full up,' Tyrone dismissed it.

They looked at him in surprise as Cazza asked 'How can it be full if no one's ever heard of it?'

'Suppose some have,' Sheila Three answered for her companions who could not speak at that point due to a heavy intake of cheese, biscuits and wine. Cheddar and Jacobs plus Jacob's Creek…in that order.

'Penang. Langkawi and Tioman are all full too,' he ticked them off his list 'and that's about the lot from the No-No stable.'

'Anyone would think it was Chinese New Year,' Sheila Three thought out loud as the audience applauded the presentation which they felt was well put together, if totally negative.

'And now for the good news, the following are available,' Tyrone supped on a fresh coldie and moved on as his audience sat up in anticipation 'Bangkok,' he paused.

The lads gave a 'Wheh-hey,' the girls a 'No way.'

'Filth, that's all you are,' Sheila Two informed Bruce, squeezing his toes tightly to make the point.

'We agreed on that previously,' Sheila Three reminded the delegates.

'Malacca,' silence 'and Phuket.' He looked around the circle as he chugged back the contents of his tinnie. He did not want to get left behind by his fellow beer-suppers who did not have to speak much so they had more time to take in the amber liquid.

All seven of them sat in silence for a moment.

'And that's it?' asked Simon quietly.

'That's it,' the confirmation came back from the Chairman who was actually lying on the floor propped up on an elbow, not sitting in a chair at all.

'Well Phuket sounds OK to me,' said Cazza 'though I did fancy Malaysia.'

'Well we can go to Malacca if you want but it's a drive and the traffic will be heavy and we'd have to hire a minibus and it's all a bit of a slog.' The reasons not to go with this option were quite strong.

'Any details on the Phuket deal?' asked Bruce, standing to replace three fast-moving cans of Anchor beer.

'Yes…an early-evening departure on the Wednesday, an hour and a half flight, four star hotel just off the main beach – Patong – accommodation, transfers and breakfasts included. One triple and two twin rooms for four nights…$ 559 each. Whad'ya think?'

Tyrone the pole-vaulting tour-guide put it to the floor… and the six other people sitting on it.

'I say bloody beauty mate. Sounds great,' announced Sheila Three.

'Well said,' endorsed Simon to supporting nods elsewhere.

'Well if it's ok with yewz, I have a tentative booking on 'hold' for us. We'll be staying at the Phuket Paradize Hotel and we have to pay a deposit of a hundred dollars each by noon tomorrow to confirm it. If yewz want to go with it, that is.'

'Well done that man. Ten bonus points,' commented an applauding Cazza and the girls as a bottle of Pinot Noir was opened.

'Lock it in,' agreed Bruce as they clapped a job well done by the elevation expert from Hobart. The evening descended into raucous revelry thereafter as deposits were passed over to Tyrone who kindly agreed to see the travel agent – Famous Ever Tour and Travel – the next morning. Hangover permitting.

A rather fragile Simon went with him as the monetary bodyguard the next day. They met up with the travel agency manager just after ten and had soon sorted out all the details. The fellow, whose name was Wally Ho, told them that he mainly sold China tours but was now branching out into other areas such as Thailand.

They promptly renamed him the Great Wal of China and asked where else he'd started selling, other than Phuket of course. He said he'd been trying to get some groups going to Turkey but there didn't seem to be much interest, even though it was Chinese New Year. They consoled him and advised that they felt interest in turkey would usually increase around Christmas time and that he should stick with it.

All Phuket arrangements were in place by the time the two tucked into a greasy lunch at a nearby chicken fast food outlet. Low calorie drinks at the double were supped in a token attempt to negate much of the previous nights somewhat excessive calorie intake. Such is life, the gestures of the guilty supposedly settling subconscious shame.

The afternoon was spent sleeping things off by most of the household and by evening a few gentle sips of a light white wine was about the most anyone could manage.

On Tuesday evening of the following week Simon was sitting

in the kitchen marking some English Language homework from one of his classes. He couldn't help but overhear what seemed like a rather extraordinary conversation going on in the lounge.

'My mother's a cow,' Sheila Two informed the others 'and my father's a rat.'

He sat up.

'So is mine,' Sheila One shared the fact 'and my brother is a pig…and my sister's a dog. Actually a bitch if you ask me,' roaring laughter accompanied the comment

Interesting, he thought. Could this be a new version of Family Favourites?

'Well my dad's a snake, my sister's a dragon and as far as I'm concerned my brother is a prat,' Cazza chipped in.

'My sister had three kids in five years and goes like a rabbit, though she's actually a monkey, and a cheeky one at that,' Sheila Three shared her family history.

Simon moved quietly towards the door to take a closer look at the scene.

'What do you reckon these three are?' Sheila Two asked conspiratorially pointing upwards towards the top-floor rooms occupied by the males in the household.

'I'd say,' certain thought followed 'Bruce is a cock, Simon a snake and Tyrone a dog, though he could be a rat,' Cazza's line-up thoughts were submitted.

'I'd go for two cocks and a snake,' Sheila One announced.

'So would I…any time,' agreed Sheila Two at which stage Simon moved into the room from the darkened doorway…curiosity getting the better of further silence.

'So am I a cock or a snake?' he questioned the giggling quartet who had long forgotten that he was in the kitchen quietly marking homework.

'Well are you, what year were you born?' came the response from Sheila Three who had a chart of Chinese birth-signs, their characteristics and meanings laid out on the floor before her. All was now clear.

'Oh I see what's going on. I thought you were having a go at quite a few defenceless people, but now I understand.'

Much discussion on Chinese year signs followed. It was then decided that in keeping with the upcoming occasion all residents would enter a competition to guess the Chinese birth sign of the other occupants in the house. Entries had to be submitted before the nine o'clock news and a winner declared before half past ten the same evening.

The two absent Signs in the form of Bruce and Tyrone arrived soon after the rules were spelt out to contestants and both readily joined in the competition.

Entry Forms were passed round by Sheila Two who had produced an old abacus on which to count the submissions. Careful thought went into final choices and it took quite some time before all papers were dropped into the Official Entry box which happened to be an empty six-pack of Anchor beer.

The final totals under the 'Chinese Signs Of The Times' competition came up as the following ….

Collectively there were - 5 Dragons, 4 Snakes, 12 Goats, 6 Monkeys, 10 Cocks, 3 Horses and 2 Dog entries.

No one had a completely correct entry, the main mistake being in forgetting that the Chinese New Year usually starts in February, not January. The menagerie was a rather happy farmyard though considering the laughs that each submission generated when read to the resident panel of judges – the Three Sheilas.

The final result declared Cazza the winner even though she underestimated the actual number of cocks in her total count, a fact which surprised everyone. For her endeavours she was presented with a bottle of Merlot which she shared with the 6 runners up – a trait of one born under the sign of the Monkey, which was what she turned out to be.

'Did you see the invitation on the Notice Board in the Staff Room to drinks at the Aussie High Commission on Friday?' Sheila Two asked the three ladies sitting alongside her on the downstairs long seat of a crowded Number 14 bus.

'Sure,' answered Sheila One. The others nodded.

'Going?' asked Sheila Two.

The response was another all-round 'Sure,'

'Need you ask?' Cazza questioned 'Free Aussie grog. Get some of my tax money back for a change.'

The three lads had also seen the Notice and made note of the starting time of 5.30pm. The evening was to be sponsored by a well-known Aussie winery with Australian cheese, pasties and pies also on offer. Heaven on a stick, they all agreed.

The evening finally came around and the group duly made their way by bus to the Australian High Commission carefully timing their arrival for 5.45pm, not wishing to seem too keen. At the same time they didn't want to miss out on too many of the good things on offer, especially the meat pies. Nothing wrong with fried rice…but Aussies are Aussies and meat pies are in the blood. A simple fact.

The High Commissioner and wife welcomed guests at the entrance, as did the local Sales Manager for the winery involved and the Managing Director of the company importing the Australian food. The large ground floor of the building was used for the occasion and the squad made their way into the welcoming green and grey toned area, collecting glasses of wine as they entered.

Gazing up at the long vines trailing from the upper floor landings the team took in the smart beauty of the setting and were suitably impressed.

'This is the best way to end the week, for sure,' commented Bruce slipping into a cool Aussie tipple.

'You're not wrong there,' agreed Tyrone in his best patriotic colours as usual. Simon nodded in agreement as he gulped down his own particularly cold Riesling.

The girls wandered off towards the loos to tart themselves up a bit in the hope no doubt that they might end up with some nice diplomatic immunity on their arms come home time.

'Hello, I'm Andrea Dimple, Chancery and Visas,' a rather large lady appeared right in front of Simon. She was in her late forties, he guessed, had rather too much make-up on as well as a bouffant hair style and black mascara that made him think she must be a Dusty Springfield fan.

'Oh, hello,' he responded 'I'm Simon Skeer from the Antipodean Academy.'

'How lofely for you,' his new companion declared in a posh bay-window voice

'We have some half dozen international schools coming in here tonight,' she announced before adding 'I just hope I'm not kept in detention for being naughty again.' The lady giggled happily at her scholarly comment before mentioning 'Mind you if it were you keeping me in the corner I'm sure I could suffer in silence.'

She flashed long black eyelashes in front of her large black eye-shadow base and offered a knowing smile. Simon thought she looked rather like a panda.

He let her comments land beyond the response zone and asked 'Are you Australian?' obviously puzzled by her very Pommie accent in such an absolutely Australian setting.

'Oh no, I'm British my dear,' she beamed at him regally 'but I lived 'down under' for a while before coming to Singapore some time ago. And so now here I am, keeping an eye on things for Queen & Country...and Australia,' she again gave maximum exposure to her flashing eyelashes.

'Dahling!' the cry came zooming in across Simon's left shoulder scoring a direct hit on the base of Andrea's upturned wine glass. He didn't need to turn around to see who it was.

'Dahling!' she responded as if she were taking the lead in a Noel Coward play and making sure her voice reached the back stalls, or in this case the swing-door entrance.

'Kissie…kissie…mmmm…mmmm…' she pouted into empty air over the assaulted shoulder.

God save me from the queen …Simon thought and turned to see a beaming Chauncy moving in fast. The artist rushed forward and received a gushing three-cheek welcoming kiss from Andrea before stepping back and holding hands with her as though they were about to burst into a duet from The Sound of Music.

'I see you've met Simon,' Chauncy stated with gushing delight to his fellow country-woman, grinning excessively at Simon as an afterthought. Andrea smiled knowingly.

'He is my FAVourite amongst this year's new entrants, dahling,' he advised, quite in his element 'DIvine…absolutely DIvine. Mmmmmmmm…' he finished off the exposure of his opinion with the usual rising hum.

'I know,' Andrea caught the flow as well as a passing drinks waiter 'such a young gentleman, and so handsome…' she smiled as she lifted two glasses of red wine from the tray.

Oh God…please rescue me from these two …Simon sent up an urgent request.

In either immediate answer, or perhaps pure coincidence, Bruce appeared at his shoulder.

'The Poms bothering you mate?' he whispered, smiling at the two people from the mother country.

'Brendon. Hiiiiiiiii…' Chauncy fluttered.

'Bruce,'

'Whatever. Look how's your drink?' asked the arty-farty master stopping another passing wine-waiter and replenishing his own supplies first.

'Fine, how's your sheep?'

'Great, how's your goat, Billy?'

'Bruce,'

'Whatever,'

'Now then boys…please behave…' the request came from the rather puzzled Chancery & Visa Section black-eyed staff who Simon expected to burst into *You don't have to say you love me* at any minute.

'This is my friend and colleague Bruce,' Simon said to Andrea who smiled glowingly at him from her black and white background as they shook hands.

'Andrea,' she whispered 'I look after applications.'

'For what?'

'That's for you to apply for and me to check your insides out. Put your name down and you may just find out,' she advised with a darkened flutter.

'Oh I say!' Chauncy admonished 'Now you two just stop it! Who knows where it will all lead.'

'We have to go, the girls have returned,' Simon was giving his 'excuse us' smile before steering Bruce away from the two kissie-kissie kiddies and into calmer waters.

'I don't know what wine she's on but try to get a few bottles of the same for me can you?' Bruce asked. Their little group came together for a Movements Meeting.

'OK folks, down to basics then - weez here for the laughs…and the booze and the pies…so let's get stuck into it and circumnavigate the room,' Simon advised the troops as Tyrone and Cazza joined the circle.

'This thing goes until eight or so, it seems, so if anyone wants to meet up at the end and maybe carry on somewhere afterwards, or just go home, be by the revolving doors by quarter past, latest, and we'll take it from there. OK?' they nodded 'So we'll see youz later then,' all agreed on the arrangements and cast off in varying social circles.

During his rather pleasant meanderings Simon managed to

score quite a few party-pies as well as one or two nicely burnt sausage rolls - his favourite. He got into conversation with an elderly lady from another overseas school for a while who told him she had founded the school in question many decades ago.

'Sort of a founding father eh?' he asked before correcting himself with a 'Sorry – founding mother might be a better description,' she smiled at him and took her leave as he wondered if she'd been slightly miffed at his joke. He then spotted some rather appealing hot-dogs against a far wall and was heading that way when a voice from behind said 'Hello,'

He turned, wondering if the greeting was perhaps misdirected as he knew so few people in Singapore, and there she stood, the very one - Miss Bookstore of the Year.

His eyes opened wide in surprise 'Oh, hello. It's you.'

'Yes it's me,'

He gulped and took in the vision of perfection now once again standing before him, wondering what to say next as his mouth dried up.

A silent 'Oh please God, let me say something smart, funny, witty, stunning and totally appropriate,' went upwards as an urgent request. Unlike in the earlier Chauncy-Andrea case there was no immediate answer so he settled for the mundane.

'Fancy seeing you here,' it can only get better he thought.

'Yes…well, here I am, and I thought I recognised you…so…'

'You're not Australian though, are you?' he asked, wishing he wasn't so thick.

'Oh you noticed,' she smiled before adding 'No I'm not but my boss is, the fellow who owns the bookshop, and he invited me and so here I am.'

'And here I am too,' Simon stated the obvious. At this rate she'll think I'm simple, he told himself, seeking scintillating words from somewhere. 'Can I get you a drink?' he settled for the good old basic Aussie question when in a dither – get the drinks in.

'Sure, but I can't drink much,' Miss World explained.

'Which confirms the fact that you're not Australian then.'

They both laughed and Simon felt a slight easing of the tension levels in muscles around his neck, shoulders, mouth, eyes, toes, nose and ears.

'Can I ask your name?'

'You can, it's Siew Moi,' she informed 'and you?'

'Simon,'

'Hello Simon,'

'Hello Siew Moi,' he wondered if he should add *Will you marry me?* Perhaps not just yet…maybe after another five flagons of wine…stay tuned and keep talking he told himself 'Does your name have an exotic translation into English?'

'Well it translates but I'm not sure if it's all that exotic.'

'Try me,'

'Actually it comes out as *Elegant Sister.*'

'Wow,' he gave the verdict 'that is very nice indeed.'

'And you, do you translate well?' she was teasing him, even though he didn't cotton on right away.

'Well, my full name is Simon Oliver Skeer – or SOS – so you can take it that I'm a walking disaster or distress area.'

'In need of immediate rescue?'

At this moment, yes, he thought silently 'Most of the time,' he answered 'though the rumour that I once went out with a girl called May Day isn't true.'

His heart began to palpitate and he thought he'd better finish his wine before he fainted or dropped dead, not wishing to waste it. 'The story isn't true,' he clarified, adding 'though if you want an imaginative translation of my name from an Aboriginal dialect I suppose it would be *Boy-Scout Who Could Never Light The Fire Because His Matches Were Always Soggy.*' He smiled at his Outback creativity.

'Oh, that's nice,' she pondered the options, wondering what

he was going on about 'so where in Australia are you from?'

'Perth.'

'And you teach?'

'Yes. English.'

'Not 'Strine'?' she referred to the Australian term for their own way of speaking English.

'Oh God no,' he laughed 'that would be like the teachers here teaching Singlish.'

It was now his turn to refer to the local Singaporean way of English-speak.

'Don't knock it till you try it, lah, before you know it you'll be speaking it too…lahs and all.'

'Oh I've heard all about the Lah word,' he confirmed. I should get five bonus points for that one from Miss Book-Of-The-Year he thought to himself. 'Have you been to Australia?' he was getting geographical.

'No. Which would probably make me the only Singaporean who hasn't.'

'Probably,' he agreed and caught the eye of a passing carrier of cheese and biscuits. They shared them over hard-to-control napkins, neither of which caught anything. The talk began to flow more easily as Siew Moi slowly sipped her wine and Simon got stuck into his in earnest and finally calmed down somewhat.

Neither of them seemed bothered about circulating any more, being quite content to chat to each other in the pleasant surroundings. Before very long he noticed it was close to eight o'clock and a much fortified, and more confident, Simon asked if Siew Moi would care to go for dinner with him.

'I'd love to but my mother has already cooked my dinner so I have to go home, and I'm already late so I'd better go soon.'

'Oh,' the disappointment was tangible 'what about tomorrow night then, are you free?' He went for Plan B immediately, well supported by two bottles of Verdelho.

'I am, that would be nice. Thank you.'

'OK great. I don't know the city very well so could you suggest a nice place we can go for a meal? Your choice…Chinese, Malay, Indian, Western, fish and chips, hamburger, egg sandwiches…whatever.' He was starting to ramble. She chuckled…

'Sure. I will meet you at say seven forty-five by the clock tower on the corner of Orchard and Scotts Roads. Is that OK?'

'Fine. Great.'

'There are actually two towers so make sure you go to the one on the Orchard Road side of the junction. That one has five brass bells in the upper part, the other one round the corner has chimes. I'd better say my Goodbyes to the hosts and my boss, if he's still here…nice to see you Simon. See you tomorrow then.' And she was gone.

'Beauty Newk,' a voice suggested from his right. It was the patriotic Tyrone though his bright red face clashed somewhat harshly with his green and gold jacket.

'I'll say,' agreed Simon.

'Havin' a good time?'

'Perfect,' came the response as he knocked back more of the soothing wine. 'One more and we'll adjourn, I think. It's around eight isn't it?'

'Yes it is, and a few revolting girls are at the revolving door already, waiting for us. That was a joke mate. I didn't mean it. They are all there except Cazza it seems…though Bruce isn't around either,' the group checker advised…wondering where the absent friends had got to.

Between them they took a couple of taxis home and Simon went to sleep wondering if he should call her Siew Moi or Elegant Sister tomorrow night. He finally settled on the first option as they weren't related anyway.

He slept well and dreamt of an Outback barbie at which he and Siew Moi were served steak and salads by Arthur the dingo.

The occasion went well even if they did have to send out for a packet of firelighters and a flint to get the fire going as the boy-scout who had been hired to start the fire failed abysmally to do so due to soggy pockets.

The Saturday morning summary of the events of Friday night went on for some time in various parts of the house.

Cazza and Bruce had seemingly gone off for dinner with a few people from another school, after which they went drinking at some supposedly trendy bar and finally got home at around half past. When asked 'Half past what?' neither could provide the missing number.

During breakfast Simon was questioned intensely about his 'lovely' by the girls and answered all questions as honestly and directly as he could. He had no other choice actually when four pairs of peering eyes and a quartet of knives covered in various flavours of jam hovered close to the face. He laughed away the accusations of letching and finally managed to escape his captors when someone with a keen sense of smell announced that the latest batch of toast was burning.

The day was hot and muggy, as it often was, with rain threatening in the afternoon. After the indulgences of the night before everyone felt guilty and swore never to drink again, unless it just happened to be courtesy of the Australian government of course.

Simon dozed much of the afternoon away before preparing himself for the evening. Not wishing to be late he left the house around half past six to raucous cries, comments, cheers and advice of housemates. After late afternoon rain the air was much fresher and things seemed pleasantly cooler than usual.

The air-con bus arrived and meandered slowly into town which didn't matter as he had plenty of time. It was not much after seven when he alighted along Orchard Boulevard and decided to take a wander around Wisma Atria shopping centre before crossing over to meet Siew Moi at their rendezvous point at a quarter to eight.

An empty street in Singapore would be somewhat of a rarity he thought as he dipped and dodged his way between crowds of young Singaporeans and older tourists excitedly going about their business on a hectic Saturday night.

Come twenty five to eight he slowly made his way via the network of underground passages to the opposite side of Orchard Road. He emerged from his rabbit warren at eighteen minutes to the hour, according to the clock atop the four exposed bells he had been told to look for. She wasn't there so he stood watching the traffic lights change and people scuttle across the road as he took in the darkening tropical night.

'Hello,' the voice again surprised him from behind. Turning, he gazed into her smiling bright eyes, a sight that left him rather breathless as her whole being was illuminated by the lights around them.

'Oh hello. Sorry, I didn't see you.'

'That's ok,' she smiled. Her hair was different, pulled to one side and falling over the left shoulder with a fanlike finish. She wore a black fitted dress that ended midway between knee and ankle set off by a thin gold watch, gold-link belt and a slim gold necklace. A small black bag completed the ensemble. Simple and at the same time rather classy, he thought.

'Great, and you have to decide where we are going to eat,' he reminded her 'so where do you think?'

'Well let's find out what you don't like in specific terms first . Do you like fish-head curry?' his eyes widened 'How about laksa?' a puzzled look took over 'Or mee rebus?'

'Is that like the Number 14 bus, but boiled?'

She giggled on cue and explained 'That's OK, I was setting you up somewhat. Just testing really,' he looked relieved 'We shall go to a nice Chinese restaurant I know not far from here, where the food isn't too hot and I am sure you will like what they have to offer.' And in so saying, without waiting for an answer, she pointed them in the direction they should take.

Talk came easy as they strolled along, neatly dodging rushing people. The subjects which came up for discussion were both the obvious and natural.

'Where are you from exactly?' - 'How long are you here for?'- 'Have you worked outside Australia before?' - 'What is the most difficult thing you have encountered here so far?'…from her.

And from him…'How many languages do you speak?' - 'How long have you worked in the bookshop?' - 'Where should one be sure not to miss seeing in Singapore?'

The answer to his question about languages was 'Two and a half, plus three dialects,' he looked puzzled 'Well, Mandarin and English fluently. Plus some Malay – that's the half – as well as Hokkien, Teochew and Hakka dialects.'

'God,' his mouth dropped 'all that and I'm still struggling with English,' he was suitably impressed 'but how come you speak the Maori language?'

Siew Moi looked questioningly at him 'Maori?'

'Yes, you did say Hakka didn't you? Which is what the New Zealand All Blacks rugby team chant before they start a game - in Maori.'

'No, no,' she laughed 'in this case Hakka is a Chinese dialect, not a New Zealand chant or language. My grandparents are from Guandong province in China where they speak Hakka, so rather naturally I speak it. I also speak a little Cantonese which is spoken in the same area, though I'm not fluent.'

'Wow,' he gasped 'I am suitably impressed.'

'Let's hope you'll be suitably impressed by the food within,'

They had arrived. She steered him into the doorway of the 'Golden River Lotus Restaurant' which was waiting to welcome them.

The place was packed but an attentive waiter about half way into the restaurant captured their attention as they stood in the entrance. Signalling with two fingers to confirm the unspoken question 'Two persons?' they nodded and followed him across the room as he beckoned them forth. He sat them in a far corner and they settled contentedly to look through the large gold and black menus which had been thrust before them.

'Any drinks?' the waiter asked. He stepped back as an attentive lady placed a dish of peanuts as well as a pot of Chinese tea on the red and white checked tablecloth and began pouring out two small cups of the light liquid.

Simon looked questioningly at Siew Moi for an answer about the drinks.

'Barley water please,'

'And I'll have a beer, please,'

'Anchor, Tiger, Carlsberg?' the choices were offered.

'Anchor, please,' he nodded and was gone.

Siew Moi took control 'OK, now what do you fancy out of this line-up?' she asked as they looked through numerous choices on the menu.

'Well maybe you should choose as you are the local representative of the party here.'

'Right,' she readily took on the responsibility and went through a small questionnaire with him as to his knowledge and like or dislike of certain dishes. Following the quiz the order was passed to the returning barley and beer-carrying waiter, in Chinese.

'So were you speaking Hakka to him?'

'No, Hokkien as Hakka isn't spoken by the majority of people here.'

'And Hokkien is?'

'Correct.' He was so impressed.

The decor of the restaurant was mainly red and yellow, the noise level high and the general ambiance fine. 'Nice place,' he commented as they saluted each other with their drinks. She smiled back.

'Are the people always so loud?'

'Of course, Chinese like noise, it's everywhere you turn. You'll get used to it. Are you OK with chopsticks or should I ask for a spoon and a fork?'

'I'm fine,' he confirmed confidently passing the test with full marks.

The two people sitting at the next table were both speaking into mobile phones. They each noticed this at the same time and Simon looked at Siew Moi questioningly

'He's asking her what she'd like to eat,' she said it with a straight face

'You're kidding.'

'Yes I am actually,' she agreed 'but everyone here loves mobile phones, as you can see. They are everywhere, they like all the ringing lah.' Their first lah of the evening had been shared.

Dishes arrived at regular intervals as the teapot lady now slid numerous plates of gastronomic delight across the table. A bowl of steamed rice was placed before each of them as the other dishes lined up around the centre of the table. He sat back watching, taking it all in. The young lady took the lead again in regard to what was what.

'This one is sweet and sour pork,' Siew Moi pointed.

He looked at the array of meat on the plate in question 'How do I know which is sweet and which is sour?'

She sat back, surprised, looked at him and started laughing. His eyes questioned the laughter.

'They are all the same, it's the sauce that's sweet and sour,' she advised, realising that he really didn't know.

'Oh, sorry,' he answered, rather embarrassed.

Moving on, she continued 'This one is scallops with asparagus, the one next to it is beef in oyster sauce and the vegetables are spinach and baby kai-lan. Not too hot,' she added, thinking of his perhaps delicate Aussie stomach.

'Well, it all looks great. Shall we have a go then?'

She took the lead, he followed. As anticipated, the meal was indeed enjoyable with only the company being better Simon thought to himself.

'Now, would you care for a nice Bubur Cha-Cha to finish off with?' she asked after most of the plates had been cleared of their contents and both diners were obviously slowing down.

'I can't dance,' he informed her 'and never on a full stomach.'

'It's not a dance, it's a desert,' she filled in the blanks once more, trying not to laugh this time.

'Oh God, here I go again,' he groaned 'it's a desert?'

'Yes, made of cubed yam and sweet potato cooked in coconut milk.'

'Sounds awful,' he was pulling his face.

'No it's wonderful. Try lah!' she assured him and he agreed to sample it, though with certain hesitation.

All in all it took them a good hour and a half to wade through the meal, including the dancing desert which he agreed in the end was quite pleasant if a little unusual for his taste. During the general chit chat it came to light that Siew Moi had done a Librarian course which had led to her present position in the bookshop. As they both enjoyed reading this brought on a rather lengthy exchange of 'Have you read…?' and 'What did you think of…?' and 'The film was nothing like the book….didn't you think?' questions relating to certain books each had read.

'We have a Librarian in our school, and house,' Simon informed, adding 'but she's not very much like you,' as his departing image that evening of Cazza standing on the verandah in a flimsy '*See-through and see the wobbling jellies*' pale green blouse came to mind. Together with the Three Sheilas her farewell advice could not be repeated in good company, or bad for that matter.

'I'd like to meet her sometime.'

'I'm sure you will,' the ponderous response was delivered.

The meal was over by just after half past nine and they made their way slowly back towards where they'd met, stopping for a drawn-out coffee at a handy Bun In The Oven along the way. Around half past ten Siew Moi said she had better go as she had to visit an aunty early the next morning and didn't want to oversleep. She was heading home on the underground train network so they parted under the bell tower clock.

'Well, thank you for a lovely meal and evening,' she said 'I hope you didn't feel I was setting you up with the sweet & sour pork, I really wasn't.'

'No, no, not at all,' he confirmed, laughing at his lack of familiarity with Chinese cuisine, which could only improve in future he thought.

'Here's my card,' she offered him a business card using both hands 'my mobile phone number and office number are on the front, my home number is on the back. Call me,' she instructed.

'Oh I will,' he promised, and with a quick peck on the cheek she was away, down the escalator and into the underground tunnels that lead to Orchard MRT Station.

Chapter 4

Baa Baa Black Sheep

Chauncy lay flat out on the tatty old settee in the Academy Staff Room. He was lying with his head on one of the arms, a pair of eyeshades in place, as his bare feet dangled over the far end of the piece of rather forlorn furniture. The hair was now blue and he wore a billowing pale blue and black striped smock which covered most of his being.

Bruce entered the room and had walked past Chauncy towards the ever-bubbling tea and coffee pots before he stopped in mid-stride as the identity of the being to his left registered. He paused and looked back at the prone artist.

'What's up with you Charlie?'

'Nothing is UP with me Benjamin, I am meditating.'

'Bruce,'

'Whatever,' the eyeshades never moved 'I do not wish to look upon creatures of the world such as you at this moment in time. And the name is Chauncy IF you don't mind,' he pontificated rather.

'Fine, good night to you then. Go back to sleep,' Bruce pulled a face at the non-seeing body.

Simon arrived as the exchange heated up and stepped between Bruce and his fallen foe indicating that the former should just continue with his quest for coffee.

'You look different Chauncy.'

'It's the hair dear bois,' came the unseeing answer 'I'm now blue, to reflect my mood.'

'Oh yes, so you are,' Simon cottoned on 'why?'

'Because it's all TOO much,' he was building from behind the barricades 'just HOW can I arrange an art competition for seven hundred kiddie-winkies? Make enough Chinese lanterns to cover the Great Wall of China – on both sides - AND find a flock of sheep who will allow me to give them a short back and sides? All in two weeks! Tell me – tell me! Somebody please tell me,' he wailed. The churning blue lagoon twitched alarmingly.

'Oh you can do it Chauncy,' the words of encouragement came easy 'you are so talented and it's all dead easy for you. The more you have to do, the more you can do.'

The left side of the eyeshade moved upwards and a watery blue iris focused his way 'Do you think so? Really? I mean…Really?' the poster painter was being stirred.

'Sure. Piece of cake, mate,' Simon assured him in his best okker fashion.

'Oh, OK. I'll have a go then,' he was feeling better already as the other eye became exposed 'By the way Simon, how do you like my 'blue look'?' he preened himself somewhat.

'Well it's fine but I thought red was the predominant Chinese colour so shouldn't you be in that for the New Year?'

'Quite correct, quite correct dear bois. And I will be red come the time, it's just that for now I need to be cool so it's blue. Mmmmmmmmm…' he reclined once more.

'Very nice,' confirmed Simon as he turned to take the offered coffee from Bruce who had rejoined the scene, nodding his thanks.

The door was flung open and Matilda Wilson made a grand entrance into the room. She moved fast in what was more of a quickstep than a slow waltz and her face indicated trouble. Those in situ looked up in surprise as it was an unwritten rule that she stayed in her own rooms on the top floor and was never, ever, seen 'below stairs'. Yet here she was, it was the once in a blue moon to match Chauncy's outfit. She looked grim.

'Mr. Chauncy,' she trilled standing just below his bare feet.

'Ma'am?' the horizontal body responded without moving.

'I need to see you in my rooms at two this afternoon to discuss the Chinese New Year projects. In full,' she ordered.

'But I have a papier-maché beginners class at that time,'

'No you don't. I've cancelled all the papers for today, nothing in them worth reading anyway. I'll see you then at two o'clock.' Her turning circle was smaller than that of a London taxi and she swept toward the door, pausing as it opened to fire a parting shot 'Mr. Chauncy,' he looked at her questioningly across a sea of blue 'your toe nails need cutting, and I don't think blue suits them…red was much better.'

The lady vanished.

Chauncy lay back gasping, practically speechless. Finally he turned to his inattentive audience 'Did you hear that? Did you, did you?'

Only Simon took any notice and nodded in response, others concentrated on their tea and biscuits.

'That woman,' he exclaimed 'will have to be sent back to Ayres Rock if she continues like this. And quickly. Doesn't like my blue indeed. Well I do, so there.' With that he rose regally from his couch, slipped into blue plastic see-through sandals and glided silently out of the room, a creator crushed. For five minutes.

Cazza wandered into the house not long after six that evening with a smiling Chinese lad on her arm. Two of the three Sheilas were in residence and both looked up questioningly as the couple made their entrance.

'Coooeee,' their stick-thin cohabitant cried 'this is my friend K.C. – or Kings Cross to you,' she introduced the young man.

'Kings Cross - as in Station and Monopoly?' queried Sheila Three.

'No, as in Sydney actually. He knows it well and loves it,' Cazza explained.

'So he doesn't pass Go and collect $200 very often then?' confirmed Sheila One.

'No, not very often. At least not while I've known him. Which is about two hours and twenty three minutes,' Caz advised checking her Barrier Reef watch which the makers claimed was coral resistant if scratched while diving at 600 feet – not that she'd tested it. Hadn't even worn it in the shower yet.

'Hello,' Kings Cross smiled at the Sheilas 'call me K.C. if it's any easier.'

Cazza gave Sheila Three a triumphant look as she settled him in a chair close to the telly before heading off to the kitchen to get some drinks. Her two companions followed after her at the trot.

'And just where did you find him?' demanded Sheila Three.

'In Takashimaya Shopping Centre. Nice eh?'

'Doing what?' the interrogation continued from Sheila One as they positioned themselves on either side of the smitten kitten.

'Well I was going up the escalator and he was going down the one next to it…and our eyes just sort of met…and then he pursed his lips at me and made a rather sexy squeaky sound as we passed each other…and that was that.' Her eyes clouded over.

'How bloody romantic,' surmised Sheila One.

'And then?' asked Three.

'Well then he jumped on to my escalator and we ended up at the top just looking at each other. I think it was the green stripes in his hair that grabbed me…just before he did.'

'He has green stripes in his hair?' Sheila One gasped. 'Why?'

'Fashion. He's very trendy.'

'And he grabbed you? In the middle of a shopping centre?' Sheila Three checked the events.

'Aren't you being somewhat of an easy pick-up?' Sheila One was setting her moral code out for display.

'Well it's a good job he did as I fell off my new eight-inch cork heels when they got stuck in the top of the thing. My fault entirely as

I wasn't actually looking where I was going. In fact I was looking back at him and he saved me from landing in the cleaner's bucket that was close by; my hero.' The mists set in…the eyes fluttered…the subject was all gah-gah.

'God! Green hair and eight-inch high heels…Romeo and Juliet had nothing on these two,' Sheila One muttered to herself.

Cazza continued the romantic tale 'So we went for coffee and then he asked me to go to the movies with him and so here I am about to get changed and then we're going to see some Chinese film he's been waiting to see for ages.'

'A Chinese film?' Sheila One was stunned.

'Hmmm, hmmmm,' confirmed the blonde.

'And do you think you'll be able to follow it if it's all in Mandarin?' Three questioned.

'Sure…it's a love story and the language of love is universal and anyway I now know three Chinese words so it should be OK,' the multilingual member of the household claimed.

'You know some Chinese?' gasped Three, sitting down in shock 'Since when?'

'Yes - *Wo ai ni* - since about five o'clock,' she grinned at her linguistic triumph.

'Which means?' Sheila One dug deeper at the in-house Terracotta Warrior.

'I love you,' the eyes misted again.

'Oh God, was this before or after the cappuccino?' One probed.

'Actually it was latte…and afterwards, as we needed a little time to get to know each other. About ten minutes actually,' Cazza was truly enraptured.

'What does he do?' Sheila Three took up the further questioning.

'He's a computer programmer in his father's company and has a degree in computer science,' Two pairs of eyes popped open wide.

'Greenpeace out there has a degree in computer science?' gasped Three.

'To go with his green striped hair?' gulped Sheila One.

'Yes and his tattoo,' the information data expanded.

'Where?' Three asked.

'On his bum,' another giggle.

'He told you, or you've seen it?' Three again.

'Not telling,' she left them somewhat stunned as she picked up two of the four glasses of Diet Coke she'd been pouring during the inquisition and tottered back into the lounge.

'Love at first sight,' Sheila One commented.

'Well she certainly fell for him, it seems, and just missed the bucket,' came in Three. They wandered back into the lounge and turned their interrogation tactics to the guest 'Been to Sydney then K.C.?' Sheila Three started slowly.

'I studied there,'

'Like it?' One came in from the dark area to his left playing the element of surprise.

'Beaut.' he declared, sipping his drink slowly and playing the Aussie word card for familiarity sake.

'I come from a town quite close to Sydney. Wheredyalive when yewz was there?' the questioning Sheila One came in from the dark side of the room again, slipping into the vernacular somewhat to test the recipient's familiarity with Strine.

'Randwick,' the answer galloped back at them.

'Back a winner or two did ya?' Sheila Three asked, referring to the racecourse in the same suburb.

'Sometimes,' he smiled as Cazza giggled and sat on the arm of his easy-chair for another close encounter of the green kind. K.C. was about five foot ten and slim. He wore fawn trousers and a black chest-hugging t-shirt that gripped his upper body emphatically, when his new lady-love wasn't doing the same. The shiny black hair was streaked green with a layered look framing his thin face. Cazza slipped quietly down the corridor towards her room, leaving K.C. to face the music and the questioning for a little while longer.

'Howdyagetthenamethen?' Sheila Three posed the question.

'Well I always wanted to live in Kings Cross when I was there but never did so took the name in tribute anyway. Seeing as I had the initials too,' the answers flowed easily, perhaps he wasn't as daft as he looked after all, they thought.

'So what's your real name?'

'Chai Kian Choo. Chai is my surname, Kian Choo are my given names – or K.C. for short you see - and I'm a Teochew,' he gave the full explanation. That last bit floored them.

'You're a what?' Three asked.

'Teochew.'

'Is it catching?' Sheila One questioned medically.

'No it's my dialect. My grandfather and grandmother came from Swatow in China which is the region where the Teochews originate,' they were now getting into districts and dialects.

'I thought everyone here was Hokkien,' Sheila One stated.

'In Singapore many are, but not all,' he grinned at them knowingly, enjoying the history lesson.

'How long have you had your hair like that?' Three took the questioning in a colourful direction.

'A few weeks, it use to be red but I didn't like it after a while so changed.'

As Cazza had changed in two minutes ten seconds flat she now appearing in a red dress and lower level shoes 'Green is my favourite colour anyway,' Cazza informed the courtroom as she sat down and stroked his hair.

'Since your mother came from Cairns via Cork in Ireland, which explains how you got your fetish for cork heels?' asked Sheila One somewhat sarcastically.

'No, since her daughter got her new cork shoes stuck in the escalator today.'

'That'll teach yew to go out looking like a bloody stilt walker.'

Cazza giggled and ruffled K. C.s hair. He responded by nibbling her fingers. The non-nibblers in the room groaned at the explicit examples of affection.

'How old are you?' Asked Sheila One. He looked about eighteen but like most Chinese was probably older she thought.

'Twenty five.'

'Don't look it,' Three informed him.

'I know, put it down to clean living.'

'Oh I hope not!' Cazza reacted. She and her green dream giggled and had another quick grope of each other.

Bruce and Tyrone came through the front door as the grabbing moved into overdrive.

'G'day,' they echoed automatically as they walked in, before spotting Cazza and her Chinese Casanova 'So who do we have here Miss Caz?' asked a green and gold Tyrone, grinning expectantly.

'This is Kings Cross Choi,' she informed them before turning to K.C. and telling him 'and these two gentlemen are Bruce and Tyrone,' K.C. stood and shook hands with both.

'Sounds like a takeaway deli. at the top of William Street in Sydney,' Tyrone thought out loud.

'Been rolling about on the lawn have yewz?' Bruce asked as Cazza looked at him questioningly 'Well he's got grass all over his hair.'

'No he hasn't,' she responded 'it's the colour, he has green stripes in it.'

'Green stripes?' Bruce gasped.

The two lovebirds nodded.

'God!' He sat down, adding 'I think I need a drink.'

'Should be green and gold if you ask me,' felt the patriotic Tyrone 'then maybe you'd qualify as a real Aussie battler.'

'I don't want to be an Aussie battler, I'm quite happy as a Singaporean superstar,' Kings Cross's train of thought pulled out of the station with a resounding blast.

'Whoooooooooooooooo....' all five residents of the house chorused, readily applauding his quick wit.

'OK, enough questioning,' Ms. Cairns announced 'we're going to the movies so come on Mr. Wonderful,' she turned to yank K.C. out of his chair.

'There's a bus in five minutes,' Bruce advised the departing duo as he glanced at his watch.

'That's OK we have K.C.'s sports car outside,' Cazza countered.

'Four on the floor?' questioned Sheila One.

'Or two on the door,' added Sheila Three as the two fled in a rush of green, red and black.

'The back row of the Lido cinema will never be the same again,' The two lads looked at them, wondering what it was all about.

'Later,' One announced 'after we get into a bottle of Shiraz. Don't know about yewz Sheil but I need a drink – badly.'

'A double darls,' confirmed Three.

By the time Simon arrived home all five remaining residents were feeling no pain. Sheila Two had turned up just after the departure of the stilt walker and her railway station to be filled in on all the rich details of the visit.

Simon had met Siew Moi after work for coffee and cake at the Bun In The Oven near school and was feeling rather relaxed about things.

'So what's the occasion?' he asked spotting the wine bottles, people and glasses scattered about the floor.

'Oh Cazza's just departed from Platform 1 with Kings Cross,' advised Sheila Three to various ribald comments from around the floorboard sidings.

'And he should be chugging along quite nicely just about now,' claimed Tyrone.

Sheila One clipped him across the head 'Smut doesn't get you anywhere…especially if you're on Platform 5 and your train just left from Platform 8.'

'Maybe she'll join a gardening club soon, specialising in greens as they are supposed to be good for you,' One suggested to the floor and those lying on it.

Accepting the offered glass of red wine Simon asked 'Just what is going on? Why is Cazza at the railway station and why is she now interested in gardening?' He also sat on the floorboards, realising there was nothing worse than joining a group of well-oiled people when you are stone cold sober.

Sheila Two carefully filled him in, to raucous punchlines from the assembly.

'Well good for her, and a BMW Sports to boot eh? Can't be bad,' the rough red hit the right spot.

'And as he's a computer whiz with all the hard drives she ever wanted it seems,' added Bruce…at which his audience dissolved into hysterics.

The following Wednesday Simon found a dark blue envelope in his box at school. It was addressed to him in rather flowery calligraphic script. He opened it, somewhat puzzled, and read…

Ms. Andrea Dimple wishes to invite:
Simon Skeer & Guest
To a Garden Dinner
Saturday 25th January 'At home'
16 Trage Drive Singapore 482996
7.30pm for 8pm

RSVP: 6496-8105   22 January

How nice, he thought, but then wondered *Why me?*
Chauncy appeared silently beside him 'So can you come?' he

asked of the English teacher, beaming brightly.

Simon looked at him 'You're going too?'

'Naturally. For I am the co-host dear bois,' he announced 'so it will be a simply marvellous evening and anyone who is anyone will be there.'

'Then why am I invited?'

'Because you are not just anyone!' announced the rambling Rodin 'and you will LOVE it because it will be so YOU – and you MUST bring that lovely young thing I saw you with at the Australian High Comm. So do, do, do, do, do come. Mmmmmmmmmmmm… oh do!'

'I'll try,' was the response before he hurried away for an afternoon class, thinking he'd call Siew Moi and check out her interest level. She hesitated at first as she was concerned that they wouldn't know anyone there.

'Don't worry, that doesn't matter. It'll be great, and if it isn't we'll just play it for laughs anyway.' Simon had decided this would be the best approach and she went along with it.

The date in question duly arrived and just before eight in the evening the rather edgy, though very smart, couple arrived by taxi in front of a most resplendent house in one of the 'right' districts in Singapore. The door was flung open just as Simon reached out to knock and there stood Chauncy. A sweeping rainbow coloured shirt bid them a colourful welcome above billowing khaki calf-length pantaloons. His head was covered in the same rainbow material as the shirt, pulled back pirate style with ribbons dangling down his back. Different, thought Simon, adding 'never dull'.

'Simon,' Chauncy gasped dramatically 'and Vision of Delight. You made it!'

He beamed and bowed to Siew Moi 'Enter, do…a world of wonders awaits you,' his right hand rotated in the direction they were to go as he guffawed rather hysterically and sipped on a glass of red wine. Probably started on the turps quite early, thought Simon.

They passed over a box of Singapore Sling bought earlier in a supermarket near their usual rendezvous point at the Orchard and Scotts Roads five-bells clock tower.

'Oh you shouldn't have!' Chauncy admonished, but after seeing what was in the bag added 'Oh you should have…you did…how wonderful. Mmmmmm………' he was in his element. Hysteria probably ran in the family thought Simon.

They moved down the hall and entered a large room on the left packed with Chinese furniture and people. Andrea hove into view across the landscape, waved and rushed over to them.

'Dahlings…' she gushed as she arrived, kissing both on each cheek. The black eye-shadow was now a thing of the past, the panda had presumably been saved.

'Andrea, this is Siew Moi,' Simon did the introductions.

'Delightful,' Andrea voted with her smile 'how lovely you look my dear, and what a perfect partner you have for the evening,' she grinned knowingly at Simon.

Siew Moi was in an ankle-length off-yellow dress with a white choker made up of three rows of pearls. White shoes and bag kept things simple. Andrea continued smiling at them 'Look, make yourselves at home. Circulate, cultivate, gravitate, fumigate – oh no, that's Chauncy's job – and just make sure you have a good time.'

She turned and headed off towards the well-lit back garden in the wake of a passing tray of hors-d'oeuvres. Another tray appeared in front of them, this one offering drinks, and Simon duly collected two glasses of white wine. Passing one to Siew Moi they silently signalled 'Cheers' to each other and sipped the well-chilled liquid.

'Have you ever noticed how the English become more English as soon as they leave the place?' He was thinking out loud and speaking to no one in particular.

Siew Moi smiled back at him without comment and as if to emphasise the point an obviously British lady pulled up alongside them and started chatting.

'Do you know darlings I always say that listening to the BBC World Service is all I live for nowadays. There's so little else. How about you?' The opinion-giver had seen some sixty odd summers, was tall, grey and straight-backed. She was wearing a 'sensible' blue cocktail dress that had a pink orchid brooch covering much of the upper left area. Your typically British expatriate wife, Simon thought as the lady's presence silently sang 'There'll always be an England'.

'Well I don't listen to it all that much actually,' Simon answered. Siew Moi just smiled.

'You don't?' she was shocked 'Then how can you possibly COPE?' she was most surprised. 'By the way I'm Mimi Huntingdon-Wallace. My husband's in Oil.' The lady shared her family C.V.

'Is he?' Simon responded, eyes opening wide with interest, 'Castrol?'

'Charles actually,' she corrected. They both smiled.

'Castrol is our son,' Mimi continued 'he's also in Oil – of course. Lives in The Gulf where he's in charge of accommodation and catering Out in the Field for a few thousand or so. Or maybe that should be Out in the Desert given the terrain,' she thought about the location.

'Sort of caring for the Bedouin and breakfast,' confirmed Simon.

'Quite,' she thought about that before crying 'Bertie! Ho there darling…wait for me…' and chasing after a tottering fellow of similar vintage who seemed to be heading towards the back garden. He could though easily end up in the library opposite given the angle of his gait.

'They're all Poms,' Simon mentioned to Siew Moi who looked at him rather puzzled. 'English.' he clarified the term.

'No they are not,' a new arrival with excellent hearing contested the claim, adding 'mate' in a rich Aussie twang. Thank goodness, thought Simon, we are not alone.

'Charlie. The name's Charlie Jackson, from Toowoomba,' the fellow shook hands expansively and expressively with them both as they exchanged reassuring and satisfying 'G'day's,' all round.

'I'm in insurance. Bloody boring but it's a living,' he laughed heartily 'but when you own the company you have to keep at it, never any time for a break.' Charlie was letting them know his position on the insurance policy tree rather discreetly.

'I'm Simon Skeer and I'm a teacher at the Antipodean Academy. Siew Moi here is a bookworm,' Simon exchanged their data on their personal roles in Singapore society.

'A bookworm eh, wriggle about a lot then do you then?' Charlie chuckled, gazing at the lady with knowing eyes.

'Only when I have to.'

'Lots o' bloody old things about the place aren't there?' Charlie commented, looking around the large room.

'Are you referring to the people or furniture?' Simon deadpanned back.

'Both I suppose,' Charlie considered the entrants under both headings 'you having a beer with me or what?' he asked of Simon 'You don't have to stick to the wine you know, weez Aussies after all aren't we? So weez gonna drink some proper bloody beer!' He had stated the obvious and grabbed two glasses of beer from a passing table.

'Thanks,' Simon smiled taking the one offered, offloading his empty wine glass on a nearby tray.

'Yewz ok darlin', need anything?' Charlie checked the state of play with Siew Moi.

'I'm fine thanks. I'll let you know if I need a wriggle.'

'You do that, you might just need some help,' he winked at her 'God that's good,' he gave the verdict on his cold beer.. 'Well, I suppose I'd better look for my wife Beryl and see what mischief she's getting up to while I'm not keepin' an eye on things.' He looked around the room slowly 'Could be off with that bloody milkman again for all I know – quite keen on his clotted cream she says,' Charlie laughed, knocked back most of the amber brew, smiled at them and with a 'See yewz later,' wandered away in search of wifey, the apprentice milkmaid.

'I supposed we'd better circulate,' Simon thought out loud as they started to meander around the room in a clockwise direction, smiles in place.

'Siew Moi!' the shout came from a doorway on their right.

'Gail!' Siew Moi responded happily as a Singaporean couple headed their way.

'Hiiiiiiii, what are you doing here?' asked the new arrival, beau in tow.

'I could ask you the same,' Siew Moi responded as all four people smiled happily at each other. She turned and explained to Simon 'This is Gail. She and I did a course on Modern Literature Styles together not so long ago, which is how we know each other.'

'Hello,' the boy friend greeted them both with outstretched hand.

'Simon,' the Aussie shook hands with both the fellow and his companion.

'I'm Sonny and this, as you've just heard, is Gail,' the name exchange was complete 'I know we sound like a changeable weather forecast,' Sonny commented 'but we are actually always bright and breezy,' They both grinned at the presumably often used description.

Simon worked it out silently 'Quite,' he smiled, taking another sip of his beer and wondering what storm clouds would come their way next, and from which direction.

'Mmmmmmmmmmmmm….' the question was answered.

'Hiiiiiiiiiiii….' Rainbow Warrior was at hand 'Isn't it all just too yummy? Have you tried the oysters and caviar seaweed biscuits?' Chauncy gasped at the thought. He didn't wait for an answer before informing them 'Divine…mmmmmmmm…just DIvine…' eyes revolving around all four of them. The optical spinning stopped long enough to focus on a nearby movement 'Samantha!' he cried to the passing lady.

His target spun round on sizeable heels – Cazza would have been envious, thought Simon – arms outstretched 'Chauncy, dahling,' they fell into each others arms exchanging air-flown kisses in quadruplicate.

'Come, come, come, come,' Chauncy brought his once passing, now parked, friend to their little group.

'Everyone, THIS is the one and only Samantha Anderson, a musical lady of the tropics,' he announced then paused before starting the reverse introductions.

'And this is Simon, and Siew Moi and……????' he left two blanks for the other couple to fill in, which they did by claiming they were 'Bright and Breezy.'

'Sounds like a Yorkshire Holiday Camp,' the rather puzzled artist commented, his open mouth sagging at the sides at the thought. Not put off for long though, he continued 'Sammi here is the absolute BEST harpist in Singapore. No, no – in Asia. No, no - in the World I'd say.' He qualified, throwing his arms out to encompass said world 'And as such she plucks her way around the region with her very own personalised travelling harp…as guest player with various Symphony Orchestras here and there…so there.' He gushed, then clarified 'I mean here…for here she is,' He held hands with the travelling plucker and beamed excessively at her.

'Well, not quite, but sort of,' his wandering ward commented, somewhat embarrassed 'and I will be playing later on, out in the garden, so if you can stand it do stay.'

'Oh you will?' Chauncy feigned surprised 'Oh HEAVen. I shall curl up in a small ball and sit at your feet oh angel of the lyre. For I am known as the 'little liar' amongst certain people in certain areas,' the eyes fluttered.

'I think we'll head for the garden,' Simon suggested to Siew Moi, guiding her towards the open doors.

'Oh yes, let's,' the artist in-somebody-else's-residence latched on to them.

When they stood on the steps to the garden they both gasped, before them was a scene of excessive splendour. The lush tropical area stretched way back with palms, plants and stone carvings of an Asian theme dotting the landscape. A network of slate paths wound their way between lawns, bushes, tables and benches as numerous flares lit the plants and night sky with their leaping red and yellow flames.

'It looks like a film set.'

'Amazing,' Siew Moi agreed.

'Chauncy,' Simon asked quietly, leaning his way slightly 'just what is the occasion anyway?'

'It's Andrea's anniversary.'

'Of what?'

'Oh I don't know, getting her first two-wheeler bike or issuing her ten thousandth visa, something like that,' he laughed 'any excuse will do.'

'Obviously,' Simon took another slug of his beer as they strolled down a meandering path 'can I ask though how you come to be the joint-host?'

'Ah well, you see, that's the question all newcomers ask. Well,' he was starting to wind up again 'ever since Andrea and I met over a visa application quest for Australia by an English friend of yours truly, with which I assisted, we have been inseparable. In fact it was love at first chop,' he used the local term for a passport stamp.
'Mind you I let her, and the High Commissioner, know what I thought about us Poms needing visas to go to Oz when your lot don't need them to go to England,' he looked pained at the obvious injustice.

'I'll bet you did.'

'Oh yes,' he quivered in recollection before letting out another 'Mmmmmm…'as they moved towards the centre of the garden where tables heavily laden with food of almost every imagination beckoned.

A trio of musicians in black, white and gold Chinese silks sat near a small fishpond playing Chinese instruments. On the other side of the pond a wide bar-b-q sizzled away under the attention of three white-outfitted chefs.

'It's like a tea-party at the Governor General's place in Canberra, but probably better,' commented Simon.

'Of course. It would be,' confirmed Chauncy haughtily as an exotic looking lady in flowing pale-blue chiffon drapes wafted into immediate range. She was wearing at least a dozen or so layers of whatever it was she actually had on, presenting an overall whispish and mysterious veiled effect.

'Contessa,' Chauncy bowed extravagantly before her. She smiled regally 'so nice to see you. Look, how are you?' he took her hand and stroked it, head to one side, much like a doctor awaiting her medical report on the bunion treatment he'd prescribed the week previous. She must have been over seventy but seemed to be wearing well, bodily if not clothingly.

'My dollink. I am, as alvays, schplendid,' she confirmed in mid-European accent. Passing her smudged lipstick smile on to Simon and Siew Moi as as she detailed her state of well-being.

'Oh sorry. Naughty, naughty Chauncy,' he admonished himself, slapping his limp left wrist with the right hand 'this is Simon and Siew Moi – my DEAR friends – and this wondrous lady,' turning to his newly appointed DEAR friends 'is La Contessa Katarina von Pumper und Nickel,' he gave another bow to add a suitably courtly effect to the introductions.

They shook hands and chatted easily for a while.

It seemed that the lady came from Romania, had been in Singapore for some fifteen years and ran her own crystal import and export operation out of eastern Europe, serving the Southeast Asian region. Chauncy nodded and smiled along the information trail, soaking up every word being exchanged. The two minutes silence which he endured in doing so was too much for him though and he soon burst back to life by asking 'Contessa where is your smart assistant, didn't I see him hovering by the charcoal grill a moment or two ago?'

'Probably. He's always after zee hot stuffen und cooken zat one,' she smiled knowingly before adding a chuckling 'Zank Gott.'

'Oh I know,' confirmed Chauncy conspiratorially, winking at Simon as he did.

'Ah, zere he is,' the Contessa announced, looking past the barbie and waving at her target 'I must talk to him about somezing. So Farewell and Guten-Bye dear peoples all.' She wafted off in the direction of a Chinese man who looked about half her age.

'Well, you certainly do meet them Chauncy,' declared Simon.

'I know. But don't believe a word of that Balkan gypsy story, as romantic as it may sound,' they were all ears 'her real name is Katie Crabtree and she's from Runcorn not Romania. The present incarnation came from a Romany Gypsy she met on a seven day Thomas Cook tour of Eastern Europe, donkeys years ago.

Anyway said gypsy seemingly showed her his donkey, caravan, golden earrings and crystal balls …and that was it. She was captivated, with him, his caravan, his balls – everything. Even liked the donkey it seemed. And after that she never went back to good old England.'

Chauncy took a lubricating sip of his white wine as Simon and Siew Moi stood transfixed with the tale.

'As luck would have it he was then made Roving Romany Ambassador-at-Large to Asia under one of those daft, well-meaning, UN arrangements in which nobody quite knows what such people do or why they are there in the first place. But there is a budget for such things so someone has to do it…' he paused for another sip of wine 'and so, dear open-mouthed duo, here you have our Diplomatic Exhibits A and B — Katie and the Count.'

Another sip. More data. 'And so since then they've been travelling the East, and having a great old time of it too. All thanks to the UN, which is why she always wears veils in the UN colour of light blue - you may have noticed - in recognition, and appreciation I would think, of where all the dosh comes from. Can't be bad eh?' He smiled and took another sip of wine. Simon and Siew Moi gasped, quite speechless from it all.

'So, the accent and the exotic air?' Siew Moi finally asked.

'All show my dear. Perfected over the years and over lots of bowls of steaming borsch. But she's good at it and she does sell crystals and makes a profession out of being on the 'A' List of most of the Cocktail Circuits. That way she meets all the 'right' people who she then sells her crystals to at high prices. She also adds to her income by giving personalised fortune telling, via her favourite crystal ball. Also not cheap, I can tell you,' more vino 'nice eh?' he asked 'Not a bad living actually.'

'And the husband, where is he then? Is he really a Count?' Siew Moi presented the questions.

Chauncy shook his head before taking in more juice of the grape 'Well a self-appointed, though permanently pickled, one. After about nine in the morning, usually. This Count couldn't even count to ten these days. Rarely turns up at this kind of thing, well out of it by now. Hence the toy-boy in tow. Not bad at all.' Chauncy paused to let it, and more wine, sink in.

'The story or the toy-boy?'

'Both,' and then he too was off, with a wave. Grabbing the arm of a passing lady and chatting intently to her as they headed in the direction of the bar-b-q.

'Being the perfect host,' Siew Moi commented.

'I think I need another beer after that little lot,' Simon quietly announced, swapping his empty glass for a full one from another passing tray and scooping up a glass of wine for Siew Moi without being asked. 'Shall we eat?' he instructed more than considered, guiding her towards the food.

The buffet was both glamorous and expansive and they joined a queue by the salad displays before moving on to the meats, prawns and numerous types of fish. There were tables of various shapes and sizes around the garden, all laid out attractively. They managed to find an empty four-seater and were just settling down on wooden directors chairs with their collection of gastronomic delight as Bright and Breezy blew their way.

'Taken?' Gail asked with a questioning turn of the head as she touched an empty chair.

'No. Come, join us,' Siew Moi welcomed them. They sat and the chat was easy and pleasant for the next hour or so.

It seemed that Sonny worked in an investment bank and Gail in the National Library. Hawk-eyed waiters flitted about with bottles of wine, topping up half empty glasses without being asked.

Very impressive, must have cost a fortune, thought Simon as they got stuck in to the delicious offerings in the most pleasant of settings. The haunting background Chinese music provided the perfect touch. He couldn't help though but overhear the 'bay-window' conversation going on between two middle aged English ladies of the blue-rinse set at the table next to them.

'How are you coping with your maid these days, Clara?'

'Dreadful darling, just dreadful, so many problems. She has this thing about the dustbinman you see.'

'I know, oh I know. It's always the same,' her companion sympathised as her dentures got stuck in a bread roll and had to be tugged out rather forcibly.

'You see,' Clara continued 'when I remind her to take out the rubbish in the evening she'll take the bags out around ten and then we won't see her again for days.' The exasperated lady sighed into her wine glass.

'Why, what happens?' Blue-rinse leader led the enquiry as she nibbled carefully at the clinging dough.

'Well she does a home-delivery you see. Instead of leaving the bags in the rubbish bin she takes them round to his place and then, well…you know, stays there. All of which means we don't see her for a few days, until he finally brings her back packed in a spare dustbin and drops her off at the gate.' Clara sipped her Chardonnay in despair 'And by then the rubbish has built up once more so she's off again that night, and so it goes on, week after week. I don't know what to do.'

The Perils of Expatriate Living, Simon thought.

'That's terrible darling, where's she from?' her companion asked, knocking back her glass of Sauvignon Blanc to help cope with the detailed trauma.

'Oh I've no idea, somewhere.'

'Quite. They're always the worst.'

'How's your maid then?' Clara started her own Question Time.

'Well all this new one wants to do is play in the paddling pool in the back garden with my son Jeremy all day long.'

'Aw, that's nice,' she sighed, images of a water-winged youngster and caring maid flashed before her 'I haven't seen him for ages, how is the little darling?'

'Oh fine, growing fast.'

'I'm sure he is, they always do. How old is he now?'

'Seventeen,' the smiling mother advised 'heading off to university next year. Says he doesn't really want to go, would rather just stay at home and play in the pool with the maid.'

'I wonder why.'

Over in the musical activity area of the garden, close to the bar-b-q, Chauncy appeared on top of a stepladder. Framed in an ethereal glow from the fire below he dramatically rang a gong and spoke to the hushed gathering of what must have been two hundred or more people.

'Ladies and gentlemen, special friends all,' he was expansive 'may I bid you a very warm welcome – though perhaps not as warm for you as it is for me right now,' he added, wafting his face which also fanned the bar-b-q flames below. 'Welcome on behalf of Andrea and myself to yet another one of our '*Any Excuse Will Do*' evenings where all we ask is that the food and the company are equally splendiferous.'

He grinned lavishly at his audience who smiled back and clapped endorsement of his thoughts 'As most of you are now settled into the food may I draw your attention to the beautiful and talented Sammi Anderson who will provide some rather special musical entertainment for us this evening,' he beamed at the lady in question who was now seated in front of the musicians.

'Sammi has now taken to the small stage with our musical trio,' he paused while a spotlight lit up the lady and her backing 'and will, as usual, DElight us with her wonderful, exquisite and quite beautiful music from the harp.' He paused and smiled warmly at the musician from atop his ladder.

'May I ask then that we all give an appropriate welcome to our soloist for the evening.' His right arm waved in the direction of the elegant and smiling lady perched alongside her harp and in so doing he lost his balance and fell.

He quickly disappeared from view and the resultant sounds of crashing crockery and breaking wood confirmed that his landing had been on one of the cutlery tables.

The concerned gasp from his audience was responded to by out-of-vision assurances of 'It's OK. Really, I'm OK. I'm all right. Leave me ALONE – I'm fine. Truly. Get OFF me...please!' from deep amongst presumably non life-threatening splinters, knives and forks.

The clear, flowing, gentle music of the harp began. Idle chat hushed as people sat back and absorbed the captivating sounds which, together with the muted backing and pleasant wines, was the highlight of the evening. Guests were absorbed with the blend of musical cultures and showed their appreciation of the talents in the appropriate manner at the finalé. Their cheers and applause demand two encores from the harpist and her musicians…who smilingly obliged.

It was midnight before they knew it and Siew Moi said to Simon that she had better be going soon.

'Do you know, I don't even know exactly where you live.'

'It's no secret but seeing as you don't have a car you couldn't drive me home anyway, could you?'

'I was actually thinking of taking you to my home, not yours,' he grinned rather wickedly in response, testing the waters at the same time.

'We'll have none of that,' she admonished, hitting him lightly on the upper arm with the small fan she had produced during the musical performance 'you don't know where I've been.'

'True, but if I took you back I'd know where you were going.'

'Simon, I think you've had too much to drink.'

'Would you care to make an old man happy?'

'Who, Chauncy?'

'No, me! I somehow don't think you're his type.'

'Probably not,' she agreed. 'some other time, kind sir.'

'Promise?'

'Maybe,' she giggled 'now see me off the premises, please.'

They said their farewells to those around them and made sure that Andrea and Chauncy both knew they had enjoyed themselves immensely.

'Pleasure, dear bois,' confirmed the now slightly rocking rainbow 'so nice to see you both.'

'Did you get hurt in your fall?' Siew Moi asked.

'No, no, of course not. What's a knife in the back amongst friends?' He grinned a grimace.

'Thank you Andrea,' they both thanked their hostess effusively.

She was grinning and gushing her goodbyes left, right and centre as quite a few people took their leave at the same time.

Two taxis later, travelling in opposite directions, and the night was over for both of them though the memories would last a great deal longer. Perfect, they both thought.

On February 1st bright red lanterns appeared all around the Academy. The Hall was bedecked with them, as was every class-room and corridor. Chauncy had been in overdrive with his art classes and had claimed, to anyone who would listen, that this would be definitely, certainly, unequivocally, the LAST time he would let himself be talked into such an exercise.

Oh yeah, they all answered. Heard it all before.

On the Monday of the following week painting competition entries were displayed in The Hall, the Canteen and outside class-rooms. The students had been given the simple theme of 'Chinese New Year' and left to it. There must have been many hundreds of entries as most walls in the school seemed to be covered in them. Each displayed entry carried the name of the artist, age and their class information. Simon's class had just eighteen pictures on dis-play that he noticed and he wondered why there were not more from his charges. Some were obviously not all that keen on painting he presumed, can't win 'em all.

Come the Friday of that week the Judging Panel gathered in Matilda's rooms to discuss the entries and select the winners. The Panel consisted of Matilda, Deputy Head Dot Com and Head of Art, Chauncy. It was agreed beforehand that in the unlikely event of a tie in terms of winners and place getters then the majority vote would decide, which translated as the one chosen by Matilda.

The paintings were stacked by class, year and age and duly laid out around the carpet for Panel consideration. Judging started at 4pm, after school closed, and if previous years were any example, it would carry on until after the pubs closed.

'OK then Mr. Chauncy,' Matilda opened the proceedings 'let's see if we can make this year's extravaganza quicker than usual as I would like to have the weekend free,' she said it with a straight face.

'Me too ma'am,' he concurred, looking slightly miffed.

'Ms. Dot Com, shall we start?' Head of School suggested, an air of urgency about her, and the website lady took up the cause.

'Roight. First year – six classes, 166 entries, as you see laid out before you,' Judging had commenced.

'Perhaps Mr. Chauncy would care to give us his choices and comments as the resident expert here?' Dot Com suggested.

Chauncy stood and began his presentation 'Ladies, I feel we have to be somewhat ruthless today. Otherwise not only will Head not have a weekend off, she will find that half of next week has also gone by and she's still sitting here looking at paintings.'

'Rightee-ho,' Deputy Head agreed.

'Let's get on with it then. Your comments, suggestions and thoughts Mr. Chauncy?' Head urged him along.

The floor was his, once he found enough room to stand amongst the hundreds of paintings. Head and Deputy Head sat side by side on chairs in front of the headmistress's expansive desk, Chauncy took to the carpet and turned to the first pile.

'We will start with Year 1. There is one outstanding painting in here which I think embodies all the feeling, the ritual and the history of Chinese New Year..' His enthusiasm was building 'For me it symbolises the dynamism of China, its past, present and future,' his eyes began to expand 'and to me it also says EVERYthing about this special occasion,' the head dropped in fatigued delight.

'Go on then, which one is it?' Dot Com was eager.

'Show us please,' Matilda urged, notepad at the ready.

With great flourish he produced a painting which was completely black. He gasped, clutching his chest in dramatic effect, eyes looking towards the heavens.

'But the paper is all black,' Dot Com stated the obvious.

'I know,' he admonished 'it's titled Tomorrow and was obviously painted around midnight, I'd say.'

The two ladies looked at each other.

'What has this to do with Chinese New Year?' Matilda wondered.

'It's all there! In many parts of China they don't have electricity so whatever day it is it's invariably dark after the sun goes down,' he rambled rather.

'Then why didn't she just paint a candle? Surely they had some in the cupboard,' Dot Com was being logical.

'Tripe. Next,' she ordered, instantly dismissing the Dark Night entry as one which would never see the light of day. Chauncy placed the black paper to one side, swung on his heels, picked out another entry and held it close to his chest.

He turned to the ladies with a huge smile and, gushing again, announced 'Year 2. To me THIS one says it all. You say 'Chinese New Year' and for me this painting is everything that these three words could ever mean,' his head dropped for effect once more. The two ladies looked interested.

'Go on then,' Dot Com ordered. Chauncy turned the entry around and gasped behind closed eyes. The ladies looked at it, and also gasped. The paining was of a brick. Nothing else.

'That's it?' Matilda asked quietly.

'I know. It's wonderful, isn't it?' Chauncy gulped, choking with excitement.

'A brick?' Dot Com questioned.

'As in the Great Wall of China. Don't you see? Mmmmmmm....' he raved 'it's all there!' he gasped as they gaped 'Brilliant. Absolutely simple but brilliant – nothing less. I LOVE it.' It was the turn of the two ladies to gulp.

'Shall we move on?' Matilda asked discarding it with a wave.

'OK fine,' he smiled, placing the brick on top of the all-black painting to keep it in place 'I also like this one from Year 4. For me it indicates the global interest and reach of the occasion,' he smiled again and turned over another.

'It's a bloody surfboard,' Dot Com failed to immediately see the Chinese New Year connection.

'True. And doesn't it then show how the celebrations have spread all the way from the Middle Kingdom to Down Under? And this painting was done by an Australian student, which I think is so appropriate and telling.'

'Bloody rubbish. I'm telling you,' Matilda summarised regally 'more likely to have been thinking about going surfing than to a lion dance, if you ask me. Ditch it.' Head of School sank the surfboard without trace.

Chauncy looked miffed and sniffed accordingly. He carried on as slightly damaged goods 'This one I also love…it says it all to me….though to you…' the face was now expressionless.

'Let's have a look then,' Matilda requested and he turned over the paper.

'It's a red envelope,' Dot Com announced.

'Actually it's what the Chinese refer to as a *red packet* Ms. Comardy. The red envelope itself epitomises the occasion perfectly as this is what the elders give the children at Chinese New Year, usually filled with money.'

'Smart kid, going for the money. Who did this?' Matilda asked.

'A Taiwanese girl actually.'

'Must be taking after her father's business. Is he a banker?'

'No, a postman, as far as I know.'

The two ladies glanced at each other, each thinking they'd need a drink soon.

'Any more worthy of *special mention?*' Matilda wondered.

'Ooohhhhh, many!' he exclaimed 'Look, look, do look at this one from Year 5,' he requested, producing another bright entry.

'Looks like a Christmas cracker,' Dot Com stated the obvious.

'Well it is but you see this artist is from South Africa and as far as he knows they have crackers in China at both Christmas and

Chinese New Year so he's painted a Christmas cracker. Very imaginative and cross-cultural, I feel,' Chauncy gushed.

The ladies sat in silence, missing the point completely. Chauncy put this one aside and reached into another stack.

'Well this one is the ABsolute best as far as I am concerned,' he turned it over.

'It's a mobile phone.'

'Correct. And isn't that the perfect example of Chinese New Year?'

'In what way?' Matilda had a bad connection.

'Well this painting combines both the old and the new. The new is the mobile phone. The old is the fact that all the figures on the dial are Number 8. This exposes the ancient Chinese belief that the number 8 is lucky, soooo whoever you dial on this mobile phone you, and they, will receive endless good luck. Brilliant!'

He collapsed on the carpet, rolled over backwards and kicked his feet in the air.

'No,' Matilda had spoken, and not by phone.

By nine o'clock they were almost through, having settled on the winners and three runners-up in nine age categories as well as half a dozen 'special merit' awards for entries which showed creative imagination – as agreed by all, not just Chauncy.

'Mr. Chauncy,' Matilda brought the meeting to final order.

'Ma'am?'

'How are your 'New Year Show' plans coming along for the Wednesday morning?'

'If you mean my sheepskin coat line-up, it's not,' he answered, rather cool 'I am still trying to get the wool for the ensemble and have called on the Kiwi members of staff to help. After all, there are 70 million sheep where they come from so I'm hoping they will have a few good shearing connections,' the eyes flashed.

'So we can take it that the extravaganza will take place as planned, and will be as imaginative and as enjoyable as your usual presentations?' Dot Com checked.

'Of course, have I ever let the Academy down?'

The ladies smiled, any concerns quashed 'Good! Then let's have a tinnie or two in celebration of the fact,' Dot Com moved to the liquid part of the occasion. The resident human website then produced three freezing cold cans of Heineken from an eski she had hidden behind the desk.

'Angels,' Chauncy gasped 'you have saved my life,' he smiled benignly and accepted the offering. The ladies settled back and got stuck into their cans with certain gusto.

What the next few days leading up to the Chinese New Year events would bring was anyone's guess. And as most of them were in the hands of the art master they could only hope and pray that the show would indeed go as planned.

Chapter 5

Lunar New Year

Wednesday February 14th finally arrived, as it had been threatening to for some time. Certain folk within the Antipodean Academy had been quite apprehensive about the day but here it was and here it would remain, for all of 24 hours. The atmosphere in school that morning was one of relaxed casualness as teachers and students knew they would finish after lunch for a nice long break.

The full school gathered in The Hall at nine as usual and as the Assembly bell rang so did Matilda and Dot Com make their special Valentine's Day entrance.

'Gong Xi Fa Cai,' Matilda greeted her audience in the traditional Mandarin expression for the new year. Literally translated as *Congratulations on your prosperity* the wish was an example of the Chinese emphasis on achieving wealth. Dot Com smiled her greetings from behind the Head. Both of them were wearing red in recognition of the occasion.

'Let me also wish you all a Happy Valentine's Day, and thank my twenty five secret admirers for their cards,' she kept a straight face. This lady has style, Simon thought. Right on the knocker, another ten bonus points for she at the top of the tree in terms of the appropriate choice of words.

'Today is an unusual day as Chinese New Year is upon us,' she paused, smiled, then continued 'and school will finish after lunch and reopen next Monday.'

The students grinned in expectation and couldn't stop themselves from clapping and cheering at the prospect.

'First though there are a number of rather special pleasantries for us to share together. Let us start with the Winners and Special Commendations in the Chinese New Year Art Competition as conducted and co-ordinated by Mr. Chauncy, for which I will hand over to Deputy Head to do the honours.'

Dot Com moved forward. 'We had an extremely high number of entries this year and all those who put their brushes to work are to be commended for their efforts and imagination,' she beamed at the artistic audience 'As always in such cases it was very hard to select the winners but someone had to do it and I'm afraid that I was one of the Judiciary Panel,' she paused 'To those of you who have won a prize we say 'Well done' and to those who have not we also say 'Well done, and better luck next time.' Please remember that Participation is more important than any Prize.' She then set about reading out the names of the winners and runners up who were asked to come up to the stage and accept a 'Red Packet' as their prize from Head of School.

The audience gave them suitable recognition and cheers as first the painting and then the artist was revealed. The prize-giving took almost half an hour with the winners representing numerous nations and was indeed a fine example of the talented wide multi-cultural vein within the school. When it was finally over Dot Com handed proceedings back to Matilda.

'We now come to a very special part of today's celebrations in welcoming the Year of the Sheep. Mr. Chauncy from Art has worked long and hard – so he tells me – together with Miss Finn from Music to bring together what will be, as usual, an imaginative musical presentation of the highest quality.'

A glance to the side of the stage confirmed that all was ready 'The second part of today's programme then is the Lion Dance featuring students from the Academy. Let me ask you for a big hand to welcome the Antipodean Academy Lion Dancers.'

She stepped away and joined Dot Com at the side of the stage as applause rung out and the clash of Chinese music, gongs and cymbals filled The Hall.

Two boys hidden inside a large lion outfit made their way onto the stage. They twitched and turned to the beat of the drums, cymbals and gongs played by six schoolmates who followed, and took up supporting positions at the back of the stage. All of them wore bright Chinese red, gold and white silks as the occasion called for. The boy at the front of the lion held the head high above upright arms, it's beard and other trappings covered most of his face leaving him with little vision through which to manoeuvre.

The noise was extreme and the movements exotic, the costumes of the ensemble a combination of both. Chauncy and Miss Finn plus the eight 'auspicious' boys taking part had visited Lion Dance troops on a number of occasions to get both rhythm and movements right. The dance lasted some ten minutes and followed the correct format, even to the stage of the lead Lion Boy jumping on the shoulders of his rear-positioned partner for the lion head to then 'eat' a bunch of lettuce leaves offered on a high pole by one of the attendants.

The students loved it and cheered encouragement. For the newly arrived teachers it was quite an educational experience as they had never seen anything like it. Simon sat next to Tyrone and they soaked it all up with enthusiastic amazement at the professionalism of those on stage who had obviously practiced for many hours.

Rapturous applause greeted the finale as the sweating dancers, of various ages and nationalities, took their bows grinning in
delight at a job well done. Head and Deputy Head beamed at them in expansive pride as they left the stage before Matilda again took up the microphone.

'Excellent. Wonderful. The lion dancers and the lion trainers are to be congratulated on their presentation. That was absolutely terrific, marvellous. Very well done to everyone involved,' she gushed with obvious delight and applauded emphatically at such a good presentation.

'There will now be a 45 minute break during which Chinese tea and cakes from the baking competition arranged by Miss Winterbottom and her Domestic Science squad will be available in the canteen. Sincere thanks to the Cookery Team for their hard work and for the hundreds of cakes that have been freshly baked by numerous students since very early this morning.'

The Hall emptied as the human mass moved down to the ground floor trekking towards the canteen where the freshly baked food awaited them.

Three quarters of an hour or so later, when most had had their fill, the assembly regrouped for the final part of the show. Matilda awaited them.

'We now come to the third and final part of the celebratory programme. As tomorrow sees the first day of the Year of the Sheep what could be more appropriate than our very own Dance of the Sheep?' She smiled before continuing 'Arranged and choreographed by the multi-talented Mr. Chauncy, with able assistance from Ms. Finn, may I ask you then to welcome the Antipodean Academy Sheep Dancers.'

The audience clapped and cheered enthusiastically as she stepped aside to join Dot Com on a couple of chairs at the rear right hand side of the stage.

Three boys and three girls, each dressed in sheepskin coats, shuffled on stage in tune to typical Chinese New Year music which had started playing over the tannoy. In addition to a long white woollen coat every child had a large, grinning, cardboard sheep's head fitted over their own.

The three boys each carried a silver tray of lamb products with typical butcher's signs hanging beneath. The first read 'Lamb chops - $4 a kilo.' the second 'Lambs fry – 88 cents a packet.' and the last 'Leg of Lamb - \$5.' Farm-fresh offerings were proudly displayed above the price tags. The three girls carried trays of multicoloured wool and knitting needles.

The dancing half-dozen swayed and twitched to the music in animal-type movements before ending up in two lines of three on either side of centre stage. And as the rhythm of the music built Chauncy made a dramatic entrance through their midst, the audience gasped as he twitched into view in time with the clashing gongs and drums. He was bedecked from collar to ankle in a flowing woollen cloak of many colours with huge red ten-inch cork shoes on his feet.

The coat hem, cuffs and collar were decorated with balls of white wool above which his face was covered in a white paste – concentrated sheep dip in fact. The Art Master was totally expressionless, zombie like.

His once-again red hair was piled high with a pair of crossed black knitting needles sticking upwards through it, each needle pierced a ball of yellow wool at their inverted triangular top. Ever the one to recognise tradition Chauncy had chosen yellow wool as it was the colour of Chinese emperors, though whether or not his audience would know that was questionable.

'It's *The New Zealand Wool Board meets Lady Macbeth*,' Tyrone whispered to Simon whose mouth had fallen open at the apparition on stage.

'I was thinking *Geisha Gone Wrong* actually,' he responded, looking across the hall at Bruce who was falling off his seat with laughter. The three Sheilas were sat near him and seemed to be having convulsions at the display. Cazza was nowhere in sight, presumably rolling on the floor by now wondering where she could get a pair of those red cork shoes.

The sheep commenced a traditional Chinese dance movement which had been adapted for the occasion. The overall intention was for the meat on each tray to be exchanged with the balls of wool on the three other trays. All of which was supposed to take place while Chauncy twitched, skipped and danced about between the six sheep traders.

The exercise commenced with the boys on the left lobbing the chops, lambs-fry and leg of lamb across the stage towards the girls on the right. At the same time each girl knelt down and rolled their balls of wool towards the boys while Chauncy performed his own party act in the middle of things. Taking aim and keeping time to the music proved too much for most, including the lead dancer, as poor old Chauncy copped a chop across his chops when he rose high on a downbeat that had actually called for a dip rather than a skip.

A stray flying sliver of liver landed on his right knitting needle and slid slowly down to settle juicily on jelled red hair. It had to be said that the red, yellow and liver colour combination looked rather fetching to those on the front few rows.

As the music built a black and white sheepdog ran onto the stage and started nipping at the heels of the dancing Chauncy. The original intention had been for the animal to catch the balls of wool thrown his way by the twitching sheep-kids. Instead of doing as it was supposed to though, the dog concentrated totally on Chauncy's jigging feet, obviously thinking that they could provide far more juice than a dry ball of wool.

The audience was now falling about the place cheering both dancers and dog on to a rousing ending, which duly came about. The 'Gong Xi, Gong Xi, Gong Xi,' music built to a crescendo as Chauncy suddenly came down off his stilt heels and collapsed in a woollen heap, centre stage. The wildly rocking and rolling art master was now lying there shouting 'Get off me. Just get off me, you stupid mutt,' at his nipping black and white attacker. The dog though, like everyone else in The Hall, was being swept along with the music and managed to get a good grip on his left shoe and wasn't letting go.

Finally the music stopped as the dancing students ended their swaying and waving of trays and shuffled off stage. Chauncy crawled after them carefully herded along by a triumphant sheep-dog with a six inch piece of red cork in its mouth.

Dot Com hurriedly took the microphone 'And that concludes the entertainment,' she smiled rather hesitantly at the still laughing audience 'thank you all for your participation and time in connection with the excellent entertainment we have seen this morning.' She seemed to be rather concerned.

An offstage howl came forth and Dot Com looked worriedly in its direction before continuing 'On behalf of Head of the Academy may I wish all staff and students a very Happy New Year of the Sheep…and indeed a sincere Gong Xi Fa Cai to you all.'

Another wail came out from the wings, this one slightly different in tone to the first. More a growl than a howl and perhaps signalling that the art master was now using the flying leg of lamb to fight back.

Obviously alarmed Head and Deputy Head rushed off stage, each asking the other 'Who's dog is it anyway?' as they went. The audience stood as one and roared its appreciation of the entertainment, voting the show the best ever seen on the school stage.

It was almost noon and time for lunch when The Hall was finally cleared. Students and teachers trooped out in high spirits. The excited chat continued down the stairs and beyond as the seven housemates gathered at a table together in the packed canteen. The place was abuzz with comments and imitations of the performance they had just witnessed. As the still-recovering little group got stuck into the meal Chauncy himself appeared – sans woollen covering — and flopped down next to Simon. All eating in the canteen stopped as over seven hundred pairs of eyes gazed at him in stunned wonder and silence. The Academy had never been so quiet.

'Don't. Just don't – don't say a word,' he cried to no one in particular 'that is it. Kaput! Finito! No moreo! Never again! She can take her Chinese New Year and stick it where the sheep hide their golden fleece. It's all too much. Never again. Never. I have had it!' He groaned in deep inner agony and rolled forlornly about the table top. His audience could not be sure as to whether the pain was coming from within or from the canine attack on his now bandaged ankle.

The level of discussion around the room slowly built again as most realised their meals were getting cold while they watched the encore performance.

'It wasn't that bad,' consoled Simon.

'Oh yes it was,' confirmed Bruce.

'Thanks for the kind word Brynn,'

'Brian,'

'Whatever,' he looked at Bruce with certain menace 'That's it. Go on, hit a man when he's down. Just go on then, have a go Joe!'

'Brian,'

'Whatever. At least I got up there and DID something, unlike MOST around here,' he huffed and puffed in increasing dismay. and agitation.

'Sure you did, so why not have some lunch and then you can forget about all this and think about your nice Chinese New Year holiday break,' Simon suggested.

'What holiday? I'm not going anywhere,' they all looked at him in surprise.

'Oh dear. I didn't know that, you could have come with us to Phuket,' Simon thought out loud 'with your knowledge of things Thai it would have been a great laugh.'

'True,' gasped Chauncy 'but I'm really not in the mood, it's all been too much for me. I think I'll just stay here and kill myself – or that bloody dog.'

Sheila One pushed a plate of fruit his way 'Come on old sausage, have some rambutan. That'll soon get you going again,' she winked at him knowingly.

'What, like Tongkat Ali?' asked Chauncy referring to the

regional herbal root which supposedly '*puts lead in yer pencil*' as a proven male aphrodisiac.

'Could be, only one way to find out,' Sheila Two laughed as she chewed on a piece of melon, the red fruit matching her hair rather nicely.

'I'll have a double then,' Chauncy showed signs of certain merriment returning to his being. At that moment Matilda danced into the canteen, looked around the crowded area, spotted their group and headed over at some speed. All eyes followed her.

'Mr. Chauncy,' she addressed the recovering painter who stirred slowly from his wounded position next to a plate of noodles and looked at her. Nearby tables went silent 'I would just like to thank you personally for all your efforts this morning and indeed for all the many previous mornings, afternoons and evenings which you put in for the Academy,' she paused to smile on him. He responded with a blank look.

'And may I pass you this little token of appreciation from the whole school, especially me, for your outstanding work effort this Chinese New Year.' She handed him a traditional 'red packet'. Matilda smiled at everyone at the table before turning on her heels and heading out of the canteen as speedily as she had arrived.

Chauncy was totally stunned. He gasped at his fellow table occupants as he held the red envelope in both hands 'Did you see that? I have never been recognised like this by anyone in all my years of teaching. Oh my God,' he was in shock and looking slightly tearful.

'How much's she given you?' Cazza asked pointedly.

'I don't know, shall we look?' the face screwed up conspiratorially, and without waiting for an answer he opened the envelope and withdrew eight $50 notes.

'My God, all this. I can't believe it,' he looked as if he would faint, or cry, or both 'You see, with a red envelope one is supposed to put an even number of notes inside…and the number 8 is especially lucky, as you know.' He counted them again, slowly. 'Oh my God, how very kind! Now I really will have myself a nice break. So kind....' his voice was breaking, he was quite overcome.

'Can't be such a bad old bird after all then eh?' commented Sheila Three as they stood to leave. He smiled back at her through watery windows.

'Now yewz enjoy yerself, whatever it is you end up doing,' suggested Sheila Two from behind her ample molars.

'And we'll have one for you in Phuket,' Cazza confirmed.

'Oh do,' he endorsed the suggestion 'and if you find a spare one bring them back for me.'

The team gathered outside the Academy for their final logistical instructions.

'OK folks we all have things to do this afternoon so I just want to recap. the arrangements before we split up.' Tyrone called the travellers to order 'The plane leaves at 7.30pm – that's take-off, not check-in - from Terminal 1 at Changi Airport. You've all got your own tickets so are responsible for them. Don't lose them or otherwise yewz stuffed, OK?' All nodded.

'Those leaving from the house will be heading off at six exactly. Two taxis are booked. Anyone going directly to the airport, be there by half past six – no later. Roight?'

Bruce saluted, Simon smiled, the girls nodded. They were dismissed. The long break was at hand.

Six of them left the house in the taxis, only Cazza being independent as she was travelling by sports-car with K. C. as her chauffeur. Simon had spent the afternoon in a Bun In The Oven with Siew Moi drinking coffee. She was going to the traditional Family Reunion Dinner that night and looking forward to seeing all her relatives.

The happy half-dozen stood in a Check-in Counter queue in a state of quiet excitement. A great deal had happened to them since they had arrived at the same airport just seven weeks ago and here they were again, all ready to leave.

'Where is she?' Sheila Two asked no one in particular through clenched teeth as the queue got closer to the Check-In counter.

'No trace,' Bruce reported as he surveyed the busy horizon.

'Oh yes there is,' Sheila Three countered, announcing a positive identification 'here they come.'

The other five turned to look in the direction she pointed and sure enough Cazza and K.C. were heading their way, grinning and waving as they spotted the group. Both were dressed completely in yellow. Cazza was in a tight jump-suit and K.C. a loose yellow shirt and yellow pants that ended at the ankle in loopy knots. Completing the ensemble were two pairs of canary yellow trainers and yellow headscarves.

'Yewz look like a pair of bloody bananas,' Bruce greeted them.

'Hi,' Cazza giggled 'isn't this exciting?' her check-in baggage consisted of an ensemble-matching canary yellow bag with a side-lock. There shouldn't be many others like that on board Simon thought.

'It'll show the dirt you know,' Sheila Two informed her.

'What will?'

'The yellow thingi you're wearing,' she was informed by a grinning molar mouth.

'Oh that's OK, I won't have it on for very long anyway,'

'Why, is K.C. coming too?' Simon asked.

She punched him on the arm. 'Oh no, of course not. He has to go home and be the filial son and collect as much money as possible in red packets from his family and relatives. Then he can buy the new car he's been fancying,' K.C. smiled in agreement.

Whilst all the banter had been going on Tyrone had been doing the check-in and seat allocation. 'OK,' he announced, turning to face the party 'weez all in and locked. Here's your Boarding Passes and weez ready to go.' He handed the passes around the group.

'Great,' a collective statement from all six recipients echoed around the terminal as they then shuffled their way towards the Immigration & Departures area.

The two bananas lagged behind the main party somewhat. As the front-runners reached the policemen doing the documents check at the Departure Area entrance the bananas went into a somewhat strange series of movements.

K.C. first took Cazza in his arms, dipped his knees and tipped her backwards over his right thigh before bearing down with a killer kiss. He then repeated the movement across his left thigh, twisting her round in mid air like a spinning ice skater as she changed sides. What just moments ago had looked like two bananas had now merged into a single writhing mango.

The policemen checking the papers stopped their work, mouths agape as they watched the twitching yellow mass before them.

'Just look at them now,' declared Sheila One 'the bananas have turned into a bloody mango – that looks like it's doing a tango.'

'Amazing,' agreed the Sheilas Two and Three as the three lads also took in the yellow dancing display with certain wonder. Four passing Singaporean parents shielded the eyes of their six children and hurried them away from the scene before they got any bright ideas of their own.

'Do you think they've met before?' asked Tyrone, straight-faced.

'She's only going to bloody Phuket,' sighed Bruce adding 'anyone would think she was off to the moon for a month.'

The mango twitching became even more violent as Cazza now took over movement control and it was K.C.'s body which bent over backwards.

'Cazza. If you don't behave I shall throw this bottle of water over yewz. Then these policemen will make you mop it all up before you can go anywhere…and you'll miss the bloody flight,' Sheila One shouted.

'Now just cut it OUT!' Sheila Two ordered in her best school-marm voice as an X Rating Card was about to be held over them.

The over-ripe mango froze and moved no more. The two finally parted, adjusting their clothing as they did so, totally oblivi-
ous to their growing 'Adults Only' audience. 'Bye K.C.' she drooled,
blowing kisses as the gap between them widened 'Miss you.'

'You haven't even left yet so how can you miss him?' Sheila
Three asked 'Now just get on with it,' she ordered, pushing the
singular yellow submarine towards the Passport Check.

Effusive kisses were blown and thrown continually between
the separated Siamese bananas. These continued beyond the
Immigration desks, the inner fountain and duty-free shops until
Cazza was finally dragged by her yellow bandana towards the
departure gate by Bruce doing his caveman impersonation.

The flight was full but they sat together and had a few enjoyable tinnies on the way, in rehearsal for the good times they were
sure awaited them. An hour and a half later they were in Phuket
and as the local time was an hour behind Singapore they had much
of the evening still ahead of them.

The minibus transfer to the Patong Beach area took almost an
hour and they finally arrived at the Phuket Paradize & Delight
Hotel around 9pm local time.

'Is this the right place?' Bruce asked Tyrone.

'Guess so, why not?'

'Because the itinerary says 'Phuket Paradiz Hotel,' and this is
the 'Phuket Paradiz & Delight Hotel,' the detective in him
advised his tour leader.

'Oh yeah, dead right Brucie,' Sheila Two agreed 'well spotted,
five bonus points.'

'Never mind the official name, they've added some 'Delight'
for our visit perhaps,' Sheila Three suggested.

'Only one way to find out, let's see if we are booked,' Simon
moved the party forward and they trooped into the palm-tree-
sheltered entrance.

'Sawasdee,' a smiling Miss Thailand greeted them in a lilting

Thai accent, hands joined prayer-like before her in the traditional gesture of welcome 'Welcome in Paradize.' The young lady was dressed in a traditional Thai ankle-length gown of biscuit coloured silk interwoven with rich patterns involving red, orange, yellow and green. A sash of red and orange stripes trailed over her left shoulder. She looked absolutely stunning.

'You're not wrong there,' agreed an instantly-smitten Tyrone, passing over the documents as his role as tour-leader demanded.

'We have two twin and one triple room for you. Is it OK?' the lovely lady asked.

'Perfect by me,' he smiled back into dark eyes wondering if she had time to see him later.

'Moment please,' she asked 'don't mind. Please to sit down while I arrange,' she directed the party towards an area of seats opposite the Reception desk. All seven sat on low wicker chairs as a young fellow came over with 'Welcoming drinks'. He passed them around together with a cheerful smile.

'Nice start,' Cazza smiled, taking a sip 'Oooooh this tastes….'

'Gorgeous,' Sheila One finished off the opinion. Others nodded. 'It's all part of the package,' Tyrone informed them, mentally ticking it off his list of inclusions.

'Can't wait to try the rest of it,' Sheila Two smiled her race-winning grin from beneath fizzy red hair as the room keys arrived.

They were all settled, showered and changed in half an hour after which the super seven snaked their way out of the hotel on a discovery tour of racy Patong Beach.

'Fancy a drink 'ere?' Bruce asked the squad as they stopped to survey a group of square, open bars, each with chrome poles in the centre around which scantily-clad girls gyrated. An all-male audience sat captivated before them.

'No,' the ladies responded in quadruplicate chorus.

'It's rather basic,' commented Sheila Two 'let's find a nicer place…please.'

'That's OK,' Tyrone agreed 'could be a laugh here though.'

'Another night,' Sheila One gave the majority verdict as they moved on in search of a more acceptable location.

Moments later a much classier bar on the ocean side of the road came into view and all seven agreed that a few drinks by the whispering seashore, plus maybe a few spicy Thai side dishes for supper would be just perfect.

'Yest, please come in,' a smiling fellow standing at the entrance bid them …and they did exactly that.

The party meandered through the main bar and out into a leafy courtyard, finally settling by the low sea-wall at the far end of the complex. Mai-Tais were ordered for the girls and Singha beers for the boys. Copies of the menu were passed around the table for those feeling somewhat peckish. A small band played Thai songs back inside the brightly lit inner bar and the place was packed with what seemed to be a mix of both foreign and Thais tourists.

The team settled on a mix of chicken pieces, fish-cakes and pork in oyster sauce for their late-night snack and passed the details to the attentive fellow who had escorted them to their table. The waiter was both fast and pleasant with the drinks arriving quickly, just before the food did the same.

'Did anyone notice the prices?' Sheila One asked.

'No. Why?'

'Well they are about a third of those in Singapore.'

'Beauty Newk. Weez can have three tinnies for the price of one then.' Tyrone declared, wondering how the young-lady in Reception at their hotel liked the colours green and gold. No sooner had they settled down to drinks and snacks than two dark girls appeared in front of the boys. From where they actually came no one was quite sure but there they were, smiling seductively at the three males in the gathering.

Both were tall with long, flowing, though somewhat wild, hair.

One was dressed in a white see-through top which revealed her black bra in full detail. She also wore a black pleated schoolgirl skirt that barely came within sight of her knees, white calves led down to black plastic knee-high boots. Her face was pale with black lipstick adding to the overall zebra-crossing effect.

The other girl wore an orange lurex figure-hugging dress that also ended way above the knees. Orange hair framed a face of similar colour from which a jutting chin pointed the way forward. 'Hello. You like me?' the Orange one asked Simon in a seductive husky voice, moving closer to him than was perhaps expected. He was too stunned to answer.

'Big Boy farang, you be my friend?' the Zebra Woman asked Bruce. She used the Thai word for foreigner, whose reaction was far quicker than Simon's.

'Sure darlin' you can write to me in Brizzie any time you like, and don't forget the stamp,' he advised, egging the striped one on.

'You come wid me now,' she suggested wriggling in front of him rather seductively. She was obviously pleased with his opening response and was fast putting together a few animal moves that he hadn't seen recently.

'No thanks, weez lads are busy havin' a few tinnies and looking after our four ageing aunties 'ere.' Bruce informed Zebra Lady, pointing to the four gob-smacked girls who sat watching the impromptu entertainment in stunned silence.

'Is OK,' the Orange one advised 'so how about your friend?' she smiled and moved on to Tyrone.

Sitting on his knee she started stroking his green and gold striped t-shirt 'I like this orange colour so much, just like my dress,' she announced, reaching under the shirt and stroking his chest. Her chipped, uneven nails, the result of a few rough evenings perhaps, scratched him around the right nipple.

'It's gold, not orange,' he corrected her, adding 'anyway I just got engaged so no thanks and stop scratching me, it hurts.'

'You got engaged?' Simon asked, turning to him with open eyes 'to who?'

'Miss Paradiz Delight, that's who. Only she doesn't know about it yet so it's still an official secret and you are not to say a word to anyone,' five others took in the information as the rather dreamy faraway look returned to his eyes.

'Is OK, everyone can come and we all party together big time,' Miss Zebra Skin opened up the membership to the gathering in her most alluring tones.

'What is all this, a bloody gang-bang or what!' Sheila Three finally spoke, her shock now subsiding enough to allow speech. She turned to the Zebra Lady 'Listen love, weez just having a few quiet drinks together so you and your mate Orange-Ada there can move along please and we'll see youz later,' she suggested adding as an afterthought 'though not if we see youz first. So – Goodbye,' she waved them away.

The visitors both pouted, obviously deeply hurt, and moved off to focus on a table on the far side of the outdoor pond at which two newly arrived farangs were sitting down.

'Well there you go Brucie. Still got it eh?' Sheila Three asked.

'S'roight. Can't keep a good man down darls,' he agreed as the waiter came over with more drinks.

'Did the lady-boys bother you?' he asked as he transferred his precious cargo to their table.

'The what?' Tyrone was puzzled.

'Lady-boys,' he smiled knowingly and continued 'they not girls, they boys. Very pretty eh? You like…is OK, I fix for you, special deal, two for the price of one.' The background information on their recent visitors was enlightening to say the least. The real girls were now doubled up laughing at the shocked reaction of their male companions.

'Oooooh boys…now you know where your secret appeal really lies,' nodded Cazza knowingly.

'Which is OK with us, it takes all sorts. Don't knock it till you try it,' Sheila One nodded knowingly.

'I did think the Zebra Lady looked rather dark around the chin actually, but then I thought it was the light, or lack of it, around here,' Tyrone recalled.

'Gizzanother three beers mate, will yer? As quick as you can. And four of the same for the old aunties please,' a rather disturbed Bruce asked of the waiter who did as bid in double-quick time. The music and tableside tales increased in volume, as did the empty cans and glasses. And after a most pleasant couple of hours and lots of laughs they made their way back to the Paradize Hotel and called it a night – or morning, as it actually was by then.

All seven slept late and gradually appeared in the coffee-house around half-past ten for breakfast. By then all other Paradize Delight residents had long departed the premises which left the dining area to the not-so-super-but-working-on-it seven.

The food options were wide ranging and they tucked into final selections with great enthusiasm. The plan was to forego lunch as it was almost that time when they finished anyway.

Miss Paradize wasn't on duty so Tyrone asked the Miss Thailand runner-up in Reception when the lady of his dreams would be in.

'Moment please,' the response came back and after checking with various people he was told she would start work at two that afternoon. When he asked the lady's name, the answer was Pui. The little group finally got their beach gear and other accessories together and left the hotel at noon. The weather was roasting hot with clear blue skies and a light breeze coming off the sea. They lazily strolled along the busy, curved beach-front, fighting off souvenir sellers as they meandered towards nowhere in particular.

'Where are weez going to lob on the old beach and build up the bronzies then?' Bruce asked after a while. Certain locations were discussed and Cazza pointed to a spot where umbrellas were in plentiful supply, adding that they could soon be needed given the ferocity of the sun. The suggestion was accepted and seven soon-to-be-bronzed Anzacs quietly settled on warm sands within easy distance of a gentle surf. Aussie cozzies of varying sizes and designs revealed four bikini-clad ladies with Cazza leading the way in terms of a minimalist approach to beachwear.

Bruce looked at his fellow Queenslander with certain interest and asked 'What did yewz do with the rest of the contents of the box of hankies Caz?' The lady in question giggled in response which itself created much wobbling of the upper deck tissues.

The lads all wore Speedo bathers with Tyrone, as expected, sporting green and gold – this time in a striped format with tiny white kangaroos around the waist-band. Patriotism didn't stop for sand and surf it seemed.

'Drinks?' a lady of uncertain age appeared before them, clad from top to toe in dark blue clothing. On her head a bundle of cloth provided the base for the tray of drinks balanced above.

'OK,' Simon took up the suggestion and ordered seven soft drinks for the squad. They had agreed that there would be no alcohol before sundown as they wanted to enjoy the delights of the days fully. The evenings could then take care of themselves.

'You want massage?' Another question was put to them not long after the drinks lady had left. Two rather elderly and deeply brown ladies wearing wide straw hats, blue tops and black billowing cotton trousers that finished half way down the calf stood before them.

'How much?' Sheila Two asked, grinning at the ladies as only she could on the chance of a possible discount. She hoped that they would consider how much she would have to fork out to get those protrudinous teeth of hers seen to, feel sorry for her, and offer a special price. No chance.

'Two hundred and fifty baht,' head Hat Lady advised.

'No way. One hundred,' Sheila One joined the negotiation table. The smiling ladies giggled, having been through this hundreds of times and no doubt thinking 'Another bunch of daft farangs who think they can outsmart us.'

'Cannot,' she smiled back.

All seven of them added 'Lah' in deference to the usual Singapore response they had by now become accustomed to.

'OK, how much then?' Sheila Two asked.

'Two hundred baht,' came the reduced offer 'last price.'

'How much is that?' Cazza asked.

'About eight Singapore dollars,' the calculating Bruce informed the party.

'Well that's OK. What are we bargaining and arguing about for?' Sheila Three wondered before questioning the Straw Hat ladies herself 'For how long?'

'Forty-five minutes,' the blank space was filled.

'Ah…but how much for seven bodies? Very special price please,' Sheila Two threw down their ace card – there's bargaining power in numbers, she always said.

'Do you realise that these two will be here for around four hours if we all have a go?' Simon mentioned, wondering what time it got dark in these parts.

'No problem. Moment please,' assistant Straw Lady picked up his concern over the time factor. Whipping out a mobile phone from her bag of massage delights she made a hurried call. Within minutes reinforcements from the Beach Massage Squad descended on them from all corners of the sand.

'Looks like we're committed,' Tyrone summed up the situation as five more ladies of similar age and attributes as the first two joined the line-up 'How much though for seven?' Now he took up the costing cause.

'OK,' Straw Leader answered 'for seven peoples we cost you thirteen hundred baht – for one hour each. Last, very last, price. Finish.' the head massage momma presented her final offer.

'Roight oh,' accepted Bruce on behalf of the Singapore Sunlovers 'now where do youz want us to strip off?' he asked of the Head Lady. He was wearing just a skimpy pair of bathers and a straight face at the time.

The girls screamed with delight and the Straw Hat Ladies giggled as they laid out seven rattan mats under shady umbrellas on various parts of the sand. When they were ready the visitors were asked to choose a mat and lie face down. The pummelling, pushing and shoving commenced as the visually rather frail ladies proved in reality to have the hands of prizefighters.

Bikini tops were undone as they attacked the girls' backs and Aussie cozzie bottoms were pulled almost indecently down as they prodded the rear ends of the male members of the party.

'I can see a few ugly beach-bums from here,' Sheila Two quietly commented from her mat as three ladies went to work on male posteriors.

'Stop looking,' Tyrone told her without moving his head 'these are our hidden assets.' The comment caused a sit-up survey by all four girls, none of the boys noticing the four way full frontal boob flash as they gritted their teeth in agony from the pounding they were enduring. Necks, arms, lower backs and legs were treated with probing care and conviction and all seven subjects had certain difficulty in turning over after half an hour, when requested to do so. Due to their pulverised state movement did not come easy. Each of them kept their eyes closed as they were rolled over by the powerful ladies

'Forgot to tie-up the top did yewz?' Bruce asked Cazza through a half-open eyelid.

'S'roight. How did you know,' she played along — but quickly checked, just in case. Tyrone shot upright to check the claim, which in the event proved false.

Another half an hour plus a gallon and a half of massage oil later and they were feeling no pain, just a pleasant dull ache in all parts. The finishing head-scratch tipped each of them into a sea of floating happiness in which they happily wallowed.

The Straw Ladies were given a decent tip as a total of 1700 baht went to the party of smiling pushers and prodders. 'See you tomorrow,' they were told as the beach workers went off to split the spoils and seek out their next victims.

'Well, maybe,' Sheila One waved a limp hand after them, others were beyond movement. The lazy afternoon gave way to a certain amount of dozing and posing along the waters edge. Cazza in her tissue-top bikini and hat with its 'Dinki Di' message on the front proved to be attention-grabbing to say the least. Tourists and Thais alike chatted to her, calling her Dinky or Di as they took in her major assets. Some actually asked if she could spare a tissue as they felt a sneeze coming on.

The bay was filled with speedboats towing hang-gliders beneath bright parachutes. They were high enough for the flyer to gain a spectacular view of far-away islands yet low enough to allow them to recognise and wave to friends below.

'Fancy a go girls?' Sheila One asked the others as they strolled beneath what was an obviously popular frequent flyer activity.

'Sure, why not?' all responded with certain daring. Their walk took them to the take-off point and negotiations commenced with the accountant of the beach-flying school. The flying was dearer than the massage but after much discussion and feigned shock, horror and disinterest the Aussie-Singapore Squadronettes settled on a figure for formation flying and duly prepared for take-off.

They returned to base to advise their male ground-crew that they were about to head *Up, up and away* high into the *Wide Blue Yonder* and would be passing above them very soon.

'You're kidding,' was the reaction from Simon.

'No we are not. We will be flying high in a few minutes time, so if you'd all like to sit here and wave as we zoom overhead then we shall think about waving back,' Sheila Three informed those in their flight-path.

'This we have to watch,' Tyrone announced with certain

admiration as the lady pilots selected their call signs…*Foxtrot Tango…Roger Wilko…Red Leader*…and *Hanky Pankie* – no prizes were given for guessing which one Cazza chose.

Sheila Two went first. After a few moments of being told what to do at take-off and when the boat turned around the bay, she was strapped into her flying harness and immersed in the water.

A harness, clips and ropes held her tight on the trapeze and a lifejacket kept her afloat. With a disinterested wave from ground-control – a sleepy fellow lazily waving a green flag as he paid more attention to a dripping ice-cream – the speedboat pulled away with the daring young lady in tow. Within seconds she was out of the water and rising high as the parachute picked up the prevailing wind. The airborne activity was cheered with great excitement by those at sand level. Two twirls of the bay, much yelling and waving from the beach as the flyer passed overhead, followed by a rather splashy landing and she returned to earth declaring it all 'Bloody marvellous. Great. Too right!'

She quietly marked the moon as her next target.

The three other girls then took to the skies. Cazza had the greatest number of volunteers offering to help her into the harness, all of which she appreciated – and all of which they appreciated.

The subsequent flyers loved it just as much as Sheila Two and all four were declared recipients of the Wings of Phuket award by their much-impressed and grounded male non-squadron members.

The 'ladybirds' were subsequently advised that the accolade was one which allowed them to get the first round of drinks in at the Sundown Session after they returned to the Paradiz Delight Hotel later.

Miss Thailand was now on duty and to some nudge-nudge wink-wink encouragement Tyrone was dispatched to get the room keys and to chat up the lovely in doing so. 'Hello Pui,' he smiled.

'Oh you know my name,' she exclaimed, obviously surprised.

'Yes, I asked,' he grinned like an idiot 'can I have our keys please?'

'Sure,' she smiled asking 'so may I know your name and where are you from?'

'It's Tyrone and yesterday we came from Singapore but quite a few days before that we all came from Australia.'

'Yes – I see your kangaroos,' she confirmed as he wondered how she knew he had roos on his bathers as they were now fully covered by a pair of green and gold shorts. Though perhaps not.

'Oh, that's nice,'

'Yes, I think so too.'

He wondered what exactly she meant by that and turned to his waiting colleagues. The keys were passed out and saying he'd be up to shower shortly he continued to chat to Pui 'What time do you finish work?'

'Ten.'

'Would you perhaps like to go for supper and maybe have a drink with me?' he rolled the dice…they both came up on zero.

'No,' she smiled, his world crashed 'thank you but I have a rule not to go out with any guests. They are just here for a good time and I am not like that.'

'Neither am I,' he shot back. She looked at him questioningly 'Well, not really. Sometimes. Well, maybe. Now and then. You know…' he confessed.

'You see,' she laughed 'are you sure?'

'Sure. Ridgie-didge and shake me wombats tail.'

'Sorry, can you speak English?'

'Oh, that was English, sort of. Look, I promise to behave if you will have supper with me. Or just a drink, or a cup of tea or a glass of water….Please…pretty please,' he pleaded as his arms reached out across the desk, palms upwards. She laughed.

'Oh, OK then. If you promise to behave, I will take a chance.'

'I do. Honestly…I'll be here at ten…but will you?'

'Yes, but you'd better behave otherwise I'll be gone.'

'OK. I will. Thanks. Great,' and with that he leapt up three flights of stairs in a single bound. He was feeling no soreness from the sun they had soaked up all afternoon, ready for whatever the night would bring.

After refreshing showers and a glowing regrouping downstairs Sundowners were taken next to the pool in the leafy rear garden of the hotel – first round on the lady pilots. A bunch of German tourists lay nearby on half a dozen loungers they had commandeered at first light of day…and were now plotting as to how to keep them for the next.

The Aussie team sat well away from the scheming Europeans and relaxed over ice-cold Singha beers for the ground crew and exotically bedecked tropical cocktails for the flighty ladies. The girls wore hibiscus blooms of a variety of colours in their hair while the lads were facially bright with a red that would have outshone any traffic light.

'Can't be bad, I reckon,' Bruce proclaimed to the gathering, sitting back happily.

'Not bad at all, Blue,' Sheila Three endorsed the thought.

'OK tour-leader, what's the programme for the next 24 hours?' Simon asked Tyrone on behalf of the party.

'Good question,' he responded taking on his role again with certain relish 'we have a choice of various types of dinner.'

He referred to a small tourism magazine on the table 'There's a Special Thai Seafood Dinner on offer at The Muay-Thai Seafood Centre.'

'I thought that was Thai boxing,' Sheila Two questioned, red hair merging with her red face rather fetchingly.

'It is, perhaps you have to wrestle with the fish before eating it,' Bruce suggested.

His audience gave him the fishy beating he had played for.

Tyrone continued 'Or there's the Lopburi Lobster Lovers Lounge – with a special tonight on crabs,' his eyes opened wide at the thought.

'Pepper or chilli?'

'Please yourself, they're all on special it seems,' he let the shelled options bite 'then there's the Aussie Cozzie Thai Barbie and Karaoke Korner, which sounds multiculturally great to me!' The decision was unanimous in favour of the last contestant. Following a few more poolside tinnies and cocktails, plus an occasional squirt of mosquito spray around the ankles by the ever-helpful staff, they surrendered their chairs to the lurking Germans and headed off in a convoy of three tuk-tuks.

Shouting merrily to each other as the spluttering turn-on-a-tanner dodgem-car look-alikes raced along the beach road anticipation was high as to what lay ahead. The tuk-tuk driver sat up front, a noisy motorbike engine coughing and belching beneath him while behind as many people as possible squeezed onto a plastic seat. Both sides were open to the elements so by the time they arrived at the Aussie Cozzie Thai Barbie etc... each of them sported a horror-movie hairdo.

The girls produced brushes from bags to repair the damage while the lads shared Tyrone's comb – the luminous green and gold one. Finally presentable once again, they moved towards the entrance from where the tones of 'I Still Call Australia Home' beckoned.

'Are you sure we want to do this?' Sheila Two asked Simon somewhat hesitantly.

'Too late to back out now I think, we're here.'

'S'roight. Better to just lie back and think of the Outback,' Red Leader thought about the options, teeth flashing.

'Goodday blue,' a beaming Thai greeted them at the shiny bamboo door entrance 'Yewz gonna have a great time. Foster's on special.'

'Are you Aussie?' Cazza asked, confused at his Oz accent yet Asian looks.

'Ridgie-didge darl,' he confirmed 'from Melbun.' speaking in the vernacular.

'Amazing,'

'Ditto,' Sheila Three came in fast behind the opinion.

They made their entrance and found themselves in a large open-air part of a most sizeable restaurant.

The waiters all wore Aussie bushman's hats – complete with corks hanging from their brim – and the decor of the place was in green and gold. Simon wondered if he should have brought his own cork-covered hat. Tyrone was totally taken.

'Great mate,' he announced following the waiter to a 'table for seven please, cobber,' which turned out to be close by a pond of lotus plants and giant goldfish.

The drinks all had Australian names. The ladies settled on a Perth Passion-rouser (Cazza), Barrier-Reef Bomber (Sheila Three), Canberra Cannonball (Sheila One) and Moonie-Ponds Moon-shine (Sheila Two). The first three came with orchid adornments, the last with a gladdie. The lads stuck to the more mundane, and perhaps less lethal, Aussie beer.

The place was well patronised by mainly farangs - they had cottoned on to the local word for foreigners by now - with quite a few tables of Japanese tourists continually shouting 'mushi mushi' at passing waiters. Holidaying Aussies though made up the vast majority of those present.

Their waiter's name-tag showed him to be a Bruce, obviously it wasn't his real name but he told them they had all been given Aussie names when they took the job as part of the overall Oz flavouring of the place.

'Got any Sheilas?' Bruce asked.

'Yes, many – four or five I think,' he advised adding 'and six more Bruces.'

'Yewz gotta be joking!' Bruce was shocked 'Then how about the deal that when you have guests with the same name as a waiter they get a free beer?' The Thai lad gave him a puzzled look ''Strue mate,' he confirmed 'says so on the board outside. So as I'm a Bruce I will claim my free tinnie now, please.'

All was said with a straight face and a flashing wink.

'And we'll have three Ayres-Rock Aphrodisiacs to go along with that little lot thanks,' Sheila Three announced in support of his name claim. She waved her passport at him and pointed to her given name before pointing at her two namesakes and advising 'Same name...'.

'Moment please,' he requested and left in certain confusion. They awaited the reaction from Drinks Control wondering what would happen next. It wasn't long in coming as a Thai fellow of around forty something came over to their table as a classic Olivia Newton-John number came over the speakers.

'Is there a problem with the drinks?'

'Yeah, we ain't got any,' Tyrone was rather pointed.

'And,' Bruce took up the tale 'old Bruce Gough Whitlam there (referring to their waiter with the name of a past Aussie prime minister) says that you've got all these Sheilas and Bruces working here and weez just happen to have the same names. So we told him we would like to claim our free drinks – as it says we can on the board outside.' He finished the explanation off with a straight face and another quick wink.

The Thai laughed 'How many Sheilas are there?'

'Three,' the chorus sang out as the trio stuck their hands and passports up.

'And Bruce's?'

'Just the one but I'm worth four Daryls.'

'Great, first drinks coming your way compliments of Dame Edna,' he left with a chuckle and a shake of the head.

'Do you think he's really an Edna?' Cazza wondered.

'Must be, there's a lot of them about,' Simon felt. In two minutes the drinks appeared and the evening was under way.

The food format was such that they each selected their choice of steak from a long table of various cuts displayed on ice under glass. This was then grilled before them as per their wish for raw, medium or well-done.

Whilst the semi-incineration was taking place they collected Thai salads, jacket potatoes, bread rolls and anything else they might fancy from the well-stacked table, returning to the barbecue area in time to collect the burnt offerings. The steaks were quite delicious as they had a touch of Thai spices on top. As they were woofing it all down in great delight the karaoke contest started.

Diners were invited to take part and asked to preferably sing an Aussie song. All seven declined the free entry but joined in the cheers as a Vietnamese Viagra salesman got up and sang *Love Is In the Air* before passing out free samples to the gents on the front four tables.

A hard act to follow, noted Cazza. Stiff opposition, agreed Bruce.

Two singers from the Japanese table then got up to belt out a fast moving *Waltzing Matilda-san* with certain style and a great deal of bowing. The group of ten or so obviously Aussies at the table next to the teachers were having a great time singing along and cheering everyone on.

Smiles had been exchanged a few times during the evening and after one particularly cheery singalong that had them all swaying the lady nearest to Sheila Three leant over and introduced herself and party in friendly Aussie style.

'G'day,' she smiled 'I'm Betty Bopp and this is my sister Lola,' she pointed to a beaming lady of similar middle age to herself sitting alongside. The parties exchanged official greetings 'and over there is my youngest daughter…Shazza.' She waved at the teenage girl who sat opposite, munching a burnt sausage, with a droopy hibiscus dangling from behind her left ear 'all of which makes us – B Bopp, Our Lola and She's my Baby'.

She sang the opening line from the Gene Vincent rock and roll classic rather slowly, pointing around the table as she identified the people featured in her family version of the song. A stunned Bruce looked at Sheila Three and whispered 'What is she going on about?'

'Don't you get it? *Bee bop a lula, she's my baby….*' Sheila Three sang to him

'Bee bop a lula, I don't mean maybe….' Sheila Two continued teeth fully forward. The rest of the two tables joined in the song, swaying along with the beat before cracking up laughing as they got to the deep 'My baby now, my baby now, my baby now.'

'Very good,' Cazza smiled at Betty.

'Yes, well it breaks the ice, usually. Once people cotton on,' Betty felt, grinning at them over a glass of white Thai wine.

'Yewz three famous ladies gonna sing that up there then are you?' asked Tyrone.

'Can't darls it's gotta be sung by a man.'

'Get yer husband to do it then,' Simon suggested.

''Fraid not darls, he's pickled is our Bazza. Havin' a great time he is. As usual,' she smiled happily.

'All of which means that we've got Cazza, Shazza and Bazza appearing here tonight folks,' Sheila Two totted up the three members of the uniquely Aussie 'Azza' Club who were present.

'Where's yewz all from?' Betty asked.

'Singapore,' Sheila One took the question.

'Don't look like it from here,' Sister Lola chipped in.

'Well no, you are right, we're all teachers there. We are actually from Cairns, Brizzie, Tassie, Sydney times three and Perth,' Simon went around the table pointing out their origins.

'Well weez from Adelaide, and are here for ten days. Love it. Come every year we do. Same hotel, same time of year,' Betty responded with their travel patterns.

'Good for yewz,' Bruce agreed as two rather wobbly Aussies from a faraway table started their own rendition of *Click Go The Shears Boys.*

'Weez can't just sit 'ere and let those two drongos win the contest,' Bruce announced as a loud '*Click, click, click,*' came over the microphone, supported by exaggerated hand gestures from the two crooners.

'Come on girls get up there and do something great' he urged the females amongst them with audience appeal.

'OK. come on then Sheil…' a rather well-oiled Sheila One egged on her namesake 'Let's give 'em a bit of good old Abba.'

'They're not Australian, theyz from the North Pole or somewhere like that,' Tyrone felt their choice didn't qualify and checked his watch carefully as it edged slowly towards ten.

'I know, but their music was all through 'Muriel's Wedding' which was one of the greatest ever Aussie films, so it qualifies.' A statement of fact carried the argument.

And as the shearers made their way back to their table the two Sheilas got up, spoke to the sound controller, went on stage to rapturous applause and a moment later were belting out *Mama Mia* like seasoned professionals – movements and all. They brought the house down and followed the opening number with a rousing *Dancing Queen* which had half the diners up and dancing along with them. Their fans wouldn't let them go so as an encore the rather slower *Fernando* blew the audience away.

They won first prize which was a Voucher offering 25% off the bill plus a huge bunch of purple orchids each. Instant fame was theirs, well at least amongst the patrons of the Aussie Cozzie Thai Barbie & Karaoke Korner for the night. Heady stuff indeed.

Tyrone slipped away around a quarter to ten and arrived at the Paradiz Hotel just before the agreed rendezvous hour. Pui was packing things away as he entered the Reception area, she saw him and waved signalling two minutes, at least that's what he thought she meant. He sat on one of the lounge chairs waiting for her to do whatever she had to. After a few minutes she came over, smiling. He stood and smiled back rather nervously.

'So you have a good time Mr. Tyrone?'

'Great. Miss Pui,' he informed her 'the others are still there having a few drinks.'

'And you, do you want to go back?'

'Oh no, a quieter place would be better I think. Shall we…?' he led the way out of the hotel and on to the main street 'So where would you like to go, are you hungry?'

'Anywhere and no, not really,' she answered.

'Well you're the Phuketian – if that's the correct word – so lead me on,' he said, adding 'as soon as you like,' under his breath.

'Actually I'm not from Phuket I am from Bangkok but I came here because the climate is better and there are not so many cars, pollution and people as in Bangkok,' she dodged a speeding tuk-tuk 'though still quite a lot,' she laughed, taking his arm for roadway protection. He felt rather faint at her gentle touch.

Taking the lead she steered him to 'The Surfer's Shack' a small coffee shop a short stroll along the beach. They took a table by the window with a view of the passing parade. Both silently thought this a wise move as it would provide something to talk about if they ran out of topics.

Pui ordered a milkshake and Tyrone a health drink. After some gentle persuasion she also settled on a piece of apple strude. He declined everything having lost his appetite for some reason or other.

It turned out that Pui was twenty-one, had worked in a big hotel in Bangkok for three years before deciding to head south a few months ago with a friend who also worked in the same five-star hotel. They both now did similar work in Phuket, but in different hotels. The two shared a flat ten minutes away from the Patong beach area and all in all preferred it to the chaos of Bangkok.

Not a word of this registered with Tyrone, as all he could take in was her exquisite face, especially the smile. Whatever perfume she was wearing was knocking him out with its light tropical bouquet. He wondered how long it would be before he fainted and fell into her strudel, squirting whipped cream all over the table.

Her English was excellent though both had certain difficulty with the others accent. This was the cause of certain mirth when some things were rather misunderstood, all of which added to the relaxed atmosphere. Before he knew it the wall clock behind the counter showed half past eleven and Pui said she had to go. His face showed disappointment but he accepted that she'd been working all day, unlike him, and was probably tired.

'Well thanks for coming, can I get you a tuk-tuk?' he asked gallantly. She laughed and agreed. There were actually dozens driving by and within seconds of leaving the restaurant she was heading home. He walked back to the hotel wondering where the hour and a half had gone.

When the six songsters arrived back in Paradiz Tyrone was sitting in an armchair in Reception.

'G'day Blue,' Sheila One greeted him 'how's the late date?' They moved in to surround him and receive his detailed report.

'Great,' he answered. Silence. They looked at each other wondering if there was anything else to be said.

'That's all, just *Great*?' Cazza probed.

'That's all,' the starry-eyed one rose and turned to go to bed.

'No, no, no, no. Not so easy,' Bruce stopped him 'weez all having one for the road, so come on,' steering him toward the hotel bar which beckoned brightly. The girls had added orchids and gladioli to their hair and were feeling very tropical as Simon put the order in.

'Don't forget that weez going to Phi Phi Island tomorrow,' Tyrone reminded them, taking up his tour-leader mantle again, despite his daze. 'The bus will pick us up at half past nine and the ferry leaves at ten. So be ready, otherwise you'll miss it.' The love-struck Tasmaniac had spoken and was passed a cold Singha beer for his efforts.

All seven were down for breakfast by half past eight. Slightly the worse for wear they went over the events of the previous night with a certain amount of gusto and giggling. By half past nine they were in the foyer awaiting the minibus – Pui was again on late shift which prevented Tyrone from jumping ship. By ten they were climbing onto a small ferry packed with tourists from all six continents, taking their places on rather hard wooden benches.

'OK Cazza, when the whistle blows I want you to row as hard as you can,' Bruce ordered.

Miss Cairns, who was sitting at the side of the vessel, nodded in agreement before mentioning 'I've lost my paddle though.'

'Then use your hands,' Sheila Three quickly suggested.

The name of the island was pronounced 'Pee Pee' and they arrived just over an hour later. There were actually two islands next to each other and the ferry headed, not surprisingly, to the larger, finally mooring in a bay surrounded by cliffs which they had seen on numerous postcards around Phuket.

They were free until lunch at one o'clock so wandered lazily around the beach considering the offerings of the many stalls and barrows along the dusty track. Simon bought a small plastic bubble snow-scene of the island for Siew Moi which was totally inappropriate but he rather liked it, especially the way the snow fell over the mountain peaks when he shook it.

Sheila Two bargained for a large jar of Thai chilli as she had taken to using it in cooking since arriving in Asia and as it was so cheap she couldn't resist. The time passed pleasantly as they gradually made their way to the luncheon venue – the Phi Phi Paradiz & Delight Hotel.

'There's a lot of them about,' Sheila One commented.

'What?' Tyrone asked.

'These Paradize hotels.'

'Maybe they just like to keep telling you that this is paradise,' Cazza mused.

'Quite right,' Sheila Three agreed as they entered the hotel and passed over their lunch vouchers. The offering was a Thai buffet during which none of them drank any alcohol, sticking to the soft-drinks-only-during-daylight agreement.

They all fell asleep on the beach after the meal and awoke around five, just in time to make their way lazily to the ferry for the six fifteen departure. Their 'Day Trip' was over by half past seven when the vessel chugged into its landing pier back on Phuket and were back in the hotel by eight.

Seven showers and some twenty seven minutes later the party gathered in the downstairs bar for drinks and discussions as to plans for the evening. Tyrone had caught up with Pui and arranged another ten o'clock rendezvous but first dinner for the group had to be considered. The Phuket Visitors Guide was again referred to and a Seafood Centre at the southern end of the bay was chosen as the target. The team duly headed off in another convoy of three spluttering tuk-tuks, waving to fellow visitors rather regally as they zoomed happily along the beach road.

The food was fine, the drinks great as usual – especially the prices - and they made the most of the evening. After Tyrone left early to meet up with his lady-love, the others relaxed under the spell of the island life which they all agreed produced a rather perfect state of mind.

The next day they hired a minibus. Tyrone took the wheel with Pui sitting next to him as she had the day off and willingly took on the role of official local guide.

First target was the island's centre where they planned to try a herbal sauna. All were thankful that Pui was with them as she spoke to Thai petrol-station people about directions and once they arrived at the sauna checked the price as well as procedures.

The party were soon wrapped in eight fluffy towels, sitting in a rapidly warming wooden box with earthy scents wafting up and over them from peat and herbs smouldering beneath the cabin.

Those who couldn't stand too much heat went outside and dipped into shuddering-inducing tubs of cold water before returning to the steam. All in all they were in and out of the hot spot for an hour or so.

By the end of the experience they each felt clean and well scrubbed as the attendants had all but skinned their backs with rough brushes after their final watery dip. 'Gets the rubbish out of the pores,' Bruce announced from behind a very red face, this time from steam not sun or beer.

'Feels great,' the three Sheilas agreed as Cazza asked Pui how you said that in Thai. She was told but couldn't get her tongue round the words so finally echoed the opinion in English. Lunch was taken at a Thai restaurant off a winding hilly road which Pui directed them to and the afternoon was spent at a small beach on the north east coast of the island. Tyrone and Pui lay next to each other, gazing silently into eyes with looks that spoke volumes.

'Reckon he won't come back with us?' Bruce asked Sheila Two.

'Got to, he's left his pole vault in Singapore.'

They took the coast road back to Patong, greatly impressed with the unspoilt scenery, getting back to the hotel just after six in time for mandatory showers and sundowners. Pui used the facilities in one of the girls' rooms and was obviously comfortable and at ease in their company. This was perhaps due partly to the fact that she was used to meeting farangs in the hotel and could understand them…well, some times.

There were just six at dinner, Tyrone and Pui having gone off on their own. They took the meal in a candlelit setting, poolside at the hotel, and were careful to avoid another bunch of Germans hiding behind towels and bushes marking out well-located chairs for the morrow.

By midnight they realised that their Phuket adventure was almost over, all voted it great – ten out of ten – which called for yet another round of farewell drinks. Tyrone drifted back in about half past twelve, starry-eyed and happy. He joined them for the last of the last rounds and advised that their airport transfer would leave the hotel at 10.30 in the morning for the start of the journey back to Singapore. All of them slept well that night, having dreams of a variety of themes and flavours.

Pui was on duty as they gathered in the lobby the next morning and came over to say her farewells. Yet again she looked beautiful and elegant in her stunning Thai silk uniform. As the minibus arrived she and Tyrone moved to a far corner of the area for their own special words.

Physically they were back home in Singapore by late afternoon, mentally they were all still in Phuket. Rather reluctantly they began to turn their thoughts to the next day – the first day of school in the Year of the Sheep.

Chapter 6

Lambs To The Slaughter

Simon called Siew Moi on the Monday evening after their return and they arranged to meet for coffee at the Bun In The Oven near her bookshop the following afternoon after he finished school.

Tyrone sent flowers to Pui in Phuket with a romantic note and seemed somewhat absent minded about most things. He actually forgot his foldaway pole on Tuesday morning which meant the planned afternoon high-flying gymnastics had to be replaced by boring old running-on-the-spot for the twenty-two kids grounded.

Just after five on the same day Siew Moi came through the door of the busy Bun In The Oven and gazed around until she spotted Simon in the far left corner sitting behind a palm. She waved and smiled as she made her way over, dodging chairs and people as she headed towards the palm tree. He stood, took light hold of her shoulders and kissed her on the left cheek, she happily returned the greeting.

'Well, long time no see,' he stated the obvious.

'Yes indeed, you look very well. How was Phuket?' she sat down and picked up a menu without looking at it.

'Oh great, we -I mean you -' he corrected himself quickly 'should go some time. We had such fun, everyone loved it.'

'Well done. You must tell me all the gory details when we have more time,' she smiled knowingly.

'And you? How was the New Year celebration?'

'Fine, much the same as usual. Family, family, family and friends

- in that order. The first three days we spend with the immediate family and relatives, on the fourth we visit friends,' the traditional timetable came forth.

'Oh, well I wouldn't have seen much of you then even if I hadn't gone to Phuket.'

'That's right. So while you were lazing away on the beach every day I was slaving away over a hot wok at home.'

'No rest for the wicked,' he commented and received a pointed tap from her menu in return 'and did you get many 'red packets'?' he referred to the traditional passing over of the small envelopes, wondering if she was now quite well off.

'Well a few but they all came with a price.'

'A price?'

'Yes, as usual all the aunties wanted to know when I was getting married, which drives me mad. It's the same every year, that's all they can think about,' she shared her frustration.

'But you're only twenty-two, aren't you?'

'I know,' she laughed 'but to them I'm ancient as they all got married in China years ago. Some of them were as young as sixteen. To them I'm an old maid,' she really was feeling her years.

'God. Sixteen!' he thought about it 'Never mind, I brought you this from snowy Phuket,' he changed the subject and produced the small snow scene in its plastic bubble.

Siew Moi laughed 'Thank you, kind sir, it's just what I wanted. I shall keep it on my desk at work,' she shook it and watched the snow fall on the mountains, fascinated 'Such a rarity, snow in Phuket. And you were there! Global cooling they call it I think.'

'Just good timing,' he laughed 'it's good to see you.'

'Good to see you too,' she shared the opinion 'I want to ask you something,'

'Carry on,'

'You'd better not say yes until you hear what it is though,' she warned him.

'Go on then,' he looked rather concerned.

'Would you care to come to the dinner at my parents home to mark the end of the Chinese New Year, which is on the fifteenth day of the celebrations? It's very traditional and I thought you may be interested in experiencing such an event…' she trailed off 'but then again if you'd rather not…'

'I'd love to,' taking her hand across the table 'that would be great. Thanks for thinking of me, I am indeed honoured. So when is it exactly?'

'A week tomorrow, you'd better make a note. I should warn you though, it won't be like the usual dinners you go to,' she thought about it and her eyes took on a distant look 'No sweet and sour pork, promise.'

'Which will be a nice change and should cut the confusion. Thank you very much…lah,' he added for emphasis 'in the meantime if you are free on Saturday night, how about we go to a film and then have supper?' She readily agreed and they decided to leave the film choice until later in the week.

The three Sheilas had been invited to a Musical Evening at the Russian Embassy on the Friday evening. Why they and no one else in the household got the nod was anyone's guess but then three out of seven wasn't bad really.

'Someone got our names off the School Registry Board it seems, and as my surname is Kowalski, a very Eastern European name, they obviously think I have a Russian background,' Sheila Three explained to Bruce on the bus 'And as there were three Sheilas they probably weren't sure if we were actually just one with three different names – for general disguise and spy purposes – or there were actually three people sharing one name, so sent three Invitations to cover all possibilities,' she finished detailing the musical plot.

'And so here we are, all set to meet Olga from the Volga and her mates on their musical instruments in a few days time,' Sheila

Two had her two roubles worth.

'Good for yewz,' Tyrone commented 'you'll soon find out what else the Ruskies get up to during those cold winters other than sitting at home singing about Mother Russia and drinking vodka and tonic.'

All three agreed to wear some form of red as it would be rather appropriate. The invitation had said 7pm …for drinks…followed by the Recital starting at eight. The Head Music teacher, Miss Finn, was also attending as were Matilda and Dot Com. What they had first thought to be an exclusive invitation from The Czar was fast becoming an open offer to half the school it seemed.

Sheila Two spent a few days wondering how to play Russian Roulette properly. She had always loved dice games and was looking forward to having the chance to have a spin on the wheel in the appropriate setting. Maybe even win a little spending money.

The Embassy was set back from a main road in the outer city centre and was beautifully lit by spotlights carefully placed in trees and bushes. The three of them arrived at seven ten and regally made their way up the wide entrance steps at the top of which a uniformed soldier saluted and welcomed them in perfect English.

They showed him their Invitations and were ushered into a grand multi-chandeliered hall to the right of the entrance where the Ambassador and his wife were lined up together with other welcoming dignitaries.

They shook hands and introduced themselves as they went down the line. Their hosts bowed with great dignity and presented warm Russian welcomes. At the end of the line Sheila One turned and whispered 'If anyone can remember just one of those names you win a free Sputnik for breakfast.'

All failed and sorrowfully accepted that toast and muesli would have to do, as usual. They moved slowly into the centre of the most elegant room.

'Lofly ladies,' a deep baritone voice from behind Sheila Two addressed the girls. They turned, 'I am The Baron Boris Mosco-Spartak, from Mother Russia.'

A beaming fellow of some three score and ten summers introduced himself, bowed, clicked his heels and kissed each hand in turn before continuing 'And this is my friend Count Horacio della Fountain-Penna, from Italy,' he ushered forward a gentleman of similar decades who also kissed each hand.

The Baron continued 'And here is our dear friend Sir Morris Minor from England,' the third gentleman was of the same age vintage and did the rounds of the female knuckles with certain style. He then asked in a very British accent what they would care to drink. All three settled on wine – red and Russian of course – and the six-some duly set about getting to know each other over tall crystal glasses.

Boris, Horace and Morris were full-time diplomats. They obviously knew each other well from the diplomatic cocktail circuit, having donated their livers to the cause of international relations over three lengthy lifetimes. The fact that they were all more than twice the ages of the three Sheilas didn't matter as bright sparkling eyes began to flash between the six of them.

The three Aussies had been around the surfboards a few times though and knew which side of the barbeque their bread rolls were buttered on. They played their three ageing admirers quite beautifully.

'Tell me cara mia,' the Italian Count consulted Sheila Two 'how do you get to be so beautiful? Does it have something to do with all that Australian sun?'

'More likely the gallons of Australian Nivea Cream to keep the sun at bay,' Sheila Two informed Count Horace, wondering at the same time if he was related to the Count of Monte Cristo by any chance and they had the same first name. She had loved the film and it would perhaps be some common ground for them to talk about later, if needed.

'Would you care to see my Samovar some time?' Baron Boris asked Sheila Three conspiratorially.

'Well I'm not quite sure how to use one correctly,' she told him innocently 'do you pull it?'

'Actually no, you suck it,' the Russian count revealed.

'Well, that's just what I'm here for,' she gushed, eyes closing in anticipation 'I'm quite partial to that kind of thing actually, on the right occasion of course.' her eyelashes fluttered.

'It's well hidden at the moment.'

'Like all good things,' she nudged him in the ribs and got stuck into more Russian wine. For a moment she wondered why they only had red.

Sir Morris questioned Sheila One 'Did your ancestors come from Blighty?' He was referring to Britain by its naval term and perhaps by implication to the fact that many original settlers in Australia were convicts from Britain.

'Of course. Two murderers, three rapists, four bread-stealers and six penny-pinchers. All deported,' she smiled quite demurely before continuing 'Actually, it's a wonder I've managed to keep my hands off some of the rather attractive silver in here,' she gazed around the room before quietly adding 'and some of the rather attractive men.'

'Quite,' the Knight of the Realm agreed wondering if she was related in any way to Ned Kelly and how she'd look with a metal bucket over her head. Plastic was simply unimaginable. Maybe he could find out later.

'My seat's in Dorset,' he advised.

'Is it? Which explains why you have no furniture in Singapore and have to stand up all the time you're at home?' Sheila One questioned ancient British history.

'No, no,' he burbled rather 'what I mean is my family estate, or *seat,* is there. I am here.'

'I can see that. So are you asking if you can sit on my knee?'

Sheila summed it all up with a knowing wink. The Knight was getting somewhat confused but another glass of red should settle things nicely he felt, looking round for a tranquillising tray.

The girls' wanderings took them to the outside garden where a large Russian flag, under spotlights, was standing proud in the middle of an expansive manicured lawn littered with people taking cocktails and caviar.

'I love the colour red,' Sheila Three told Boris.

'I am so glad,' he smiled 'it means you have much passion in your veins.'

'Is that the name of the wine?' she asked, sipping more of her tasty tipple.

He chuckled before adding 'Perhaps I can also show you my genuine Cossack hat later, if you like.'

'That could be nice. Where is it?'

'Under my bed,' he leered at her.

'What size?'

'Six and seven eighths,' he drew breath at the thought.

'A perfect fit,' she announced, flashing her eyes across the wine glass knowingly.

'Well that is the general opinion,' he smiled smugly to himself before adding 'maybe I can take my hat off to you some time later then?'

'Oooooooohhhhhh yes please, that's just what I need,' the mouth opened knowingly as her tongue flicked over bared teeth.

He opened his mouth wide in a mirrored response and his upper denture flopped onto a quivering tongue to wobble rather imaginatively and seductively before her. A somewhat original and personalised Cossack dancing tongue movement Sheila felt.

'My family's in spaghetti,' the Count della Fountain-Penna told Sheila Two.

'That's nice. Mine's in New South Wales,' she returned the location menu.

He smiled, obviously missing much of what she said because of her strong Aussie accent 'Isn't that rather messy?' she asked, filling in the silence with the first thought that came to mind.

'Only when you open the cans,' a faraway look taking over his fast flushing face.

Perhaps he's back in Padua thinking about wrestling in all that sauce Sheila Two wondered. 'I love Italian food,' she told him.

'Good, maybe I can prepare something special for just the two of us to get stuck into some time?'

'Yes but what about the food?'

'Cheeky,' he laughed heartily as he pinched her on the bum causing a loud 'Whooo…' to shoot across the lawn and ruffle the folds of the rather droopy flag close by. The warm tropical night air was very still, even if certain guests were not.

'Ladies and gentlemen, may I have your attention please?' A young Russian attaché spoke into the microphone positioned outside the open French doors. 'On behalf of His Excellency, The Ambassador, may I welcome our guests this evening to a special presentation of the best of classical Russian music.' He paused, the guests applauded politely 'Tonight we have six of the finest young musicians from the Kirov Conservatoire to play for us. Their unique and beautiful presentation, featuring music from various parts of Mother Russia, will last for approximately an hour and twenty minutes. May I then ask you to make your way to the Ballroom, which is on the opposite side of the hall where welcoming cocktails were served, and the performance will commence shortly.'

It took a good ten to fifteen minutes before everyone was settled. The three Sheilas parked with their diplomatic attachments alongside, filling the six ends seats on the left side of Row 18, almost half way back from the orchid-covered stage – the beautiful floral arrangements all being red.

The six-some had 'charged' their glasses before sitting down, the considerate Count had smoothly lifted a bottle of wine from a passing tray for top-up purposes during the performance. The lights dimmed and the musicians entered to polite applause, the performance started.

Reading from the left, facing the stage, the seating of the six read Sheila One - Sir Morris, Sheila Three - Baron Boris, Sheila Two and Count Horace. During the fourth rendition all three gentlemen started twitching fingers in tune with the music. Their movements resulted in a certain amount of prodding of the ladies on their left. In response the three Sheilas began to slowly edge away from the incoming attacks as imperceptibly as possible.

The movements on Row 18 were more subtle than those on stage, though equally emphatic and drawn out. By the time the final movement commenced on stage the movements of the six on Row 18 had resulted in each of them showing an overall list to the left of some forty-five degrees.

The people in Row 19 and the rows immediately behind wondered what it was that was so worth looking at on stage which was causing those in front to do so at such an angle. A good number of them also began to tilt left, trying to spot exactly what is was that they were missing. Within minutes most of the people in the half a dozen or so rows behind the sextet were also listing over at rather strange angles.

As the music built to its finalé the diplomatic gentlemen realised that both time and sheet-music were fast running out. They thus redoubled their attacks as far as the specific touching, grabbing and groping of their would-be paramours were concerned, abandoning all caution to the woodwind.

The reactions of the three Sheilas were to angle over

ever-increasingly, quite perilously it proved as with the crashing ending of the last chords Sheila One fell off her chair as both the music and the groping Sir Morris reached their climax. The remaining four also over-balanced but were saved from too much damage by the two prostrate bodies on the left cushioning their fall.

Fortunately the enthusiastic applause killed the noise and commotion caused by the mass keel-over on Row 18. As the audience stood to express their appreciation so too did the three Sheilas return to the perpendicular and rush to the Ladies as quickly as possible. The girls slammed and locked the loo door behind them, gasping and breathing deeply.

'God, what a bloody carry on,' Sheila Two exclaimed through barred teeth. All three leant against the wall, catching their breath.

'And just what were you doing on the bloody floor?' Sheila Three asked of Sheila One.

'What do you think! Escaping from *The Claw* that's bloody what.'

'Well you looked bloody funny rolling around down there with him spluttering all over you from above and still trying to grab you,' Sheila Three was laughing so much she was almost choking.

'Bloody amazing if you ask me,' Two felt.

'What, the music or the three old codgers?' One queried.

'Both. I think,' they began to breathe easier 'you do realize that they will be waiting for us outside once we unbolt the door, don't you?' Two informed the others who groaned and threw their heads back against the wall at the thought 'Do you really fancy more of the same treatment?'

'Oh no…' two heads shook vehemently in response.

'Maybe we can escape. These places always have secret tunnels in them don't they?' Sheila One suggested, she being the most avid James Bond fan amongst the trio.

'Yeah but surely not from the bloody dunny, you dill,' Three wondered if escaping from the Conveniences could be conven ient. She had used the Aussie slang for toilet in case their conversation was being heard via a microphone hidden in a red toilet-roll holder.

'OK then it's out the window we go,' Sheila One decided, pointing upwards. The three of them began to climb, firstly onto the closed toilet seat of the nearest loo, then onto the cistern and finally up and away through the open window above.

Their escape went well until the last escapee, Sheila Three, fell backwards out of the window, having caught her hem on the metal hammer and sickle motif on the window-frame, and landed on the other two then lying against the base of a travellers palm. Commotion, confusion and cackling accompanied the crash landing.

'What are you doing in there?' The question came their way through a border of red canna lillies. Fortunately it was not from a bunch of red border guards, which was their first thought, but rather from Head of School, Matilda. She and Dot Com had left the auditorium and were passing when they heard the din going on in the bushes and stopped to investigate.

'Oh, Miss Wilson,' Sheila Two stepped forward, shaking soil off her being and smoothing down her dress. She had a red – of course - flower in her red hair and was trying valiantly to put on a brave face 'we were looking for a kitten we heard meowing in here, that's all.' The alibi was presented. Her teeth shot forward in grinning delight at the fact that she was looking at Matilda and not down the muzzle of a Kalashnikov rifle.

'With all the noise in there we thought you were perhaps wrestling a Russian bear,' Dot Com felt.

'Actually that was a little earlier, and a British bulldog, and an Italian stallion,' Sheila One informed them of their international interest as she too emerged, dragging the remaining Sheila out behind her.

They escaped from the compound escorted by the two academic leaders, either of which they felt could offer them diplomatic immunity of a sort were they to be challenged by any Siberian soldiers at the gate. Once clear they ran to the main road faster than any entrant in the Sydney Olympics, flagged down a taxi going anywhere and made good the final part of their escape.

The first need on getting home was a cold bottle of wine – white this time, they insisted. The second was a refreshing shower before the tale was then told to eagerly awaiting fellow house-occupants. Over the next couple of hours or so, while the contents of quite a number of bottles went down easily amongst narrators and audience, so too did their story grow in content and drama.

'So when are you going to see his Samovar then?' Bruce asked as the clock struck one.

'Never!' Sheila Three exclaimed, adding 'Or his bloody Siberian goldmine.'

The other two Sheilas looked at her in questioning surprise 'What Siberian goldmine?' the question came in duplicate.

'Oh didn't I tell you that part?' she smiled knowingly, nodded, and took another sip of the Chiraz.

On the fifteenth day of the first moon of the Year of the Sheep Simon met Siew Moi after work. 'Now I must warn you that this won't be like your usual Christmas dinner with the family in Perth,' she told him.

'You mean, no turkey or pulling of crackers?'

'No way,' she took on a thoughtful look as they headed for the MRT train entrance at Orchard Station, one of the busiest on the network.

Swept along with the crowds they finally squeezed into a train heading north and stood close together in the air-conditioned carriage, all seats being taken.

Three stops later they pushed their way out of the carriage at Toa Payoh station and made their way to the adjacent bus station. Siew Moi had obviously done this hundreds of times and showed the way to the queue for Bus 237.

When it arrived the various streets it served were shown on a sign by the entrance. They joined other office workers returning home after a day's work and sat back to take in the sights of the tall blocks of flats passing by. A few minutes later they alighted in Lorong 6 – *Lorong* means Lane in Malay, Simon was informed — and made their way to a nearby Housing Development Board block.

'Here we go,' she whispered to herself with a slight hint of apprehension as they entered the lift. Alighting at the ninth floor they walked down a corridor towards flat number 09-1256, from which a certain amount of noise was already coming their way.

She smiled up at him nervously when they arrived. They each removed their shoes, leaving them amongst the already considerable pile of footwear outside the door, and entered.

'Ma, Pa,' Siew Moi greeted her mother and father who answered, presumably in Hakka, he thought. The talk was totally in Chinese as Simon was introduced all round and shook hands with numerous people in the brightly lit home. The overall number of adults and kids must have been around 25 he reckoned as he smiled back at everyone. A television set blasted away by the far window as five or so children of varying ages lay on the dark red carpet in front of it, piling food into welcoming mouths. The intake did nothing to reduce their outgoing noise levels in any way, he noticed. Siew Moi asked him to sit in an armchair near the television, close to a Chinese fellow he reckoned to be about thirty.

'Hi, I'm Jason, Siew Moi's brother,' the smiling man stood and reached out to shake hands 'two of these noisy fellers are mine, the rest are from other sources.' He shared his offspring count.

'How old are they?' Simon did the social thing and was told seven and four, and that the two boys sitting closest to the screen were called Nicky and Dickie 'And your wife's name is Vicki?' he was playing it for laughs.

'No,' came the straight faced answer 'Alice actually.'

'Right,' he wished he'd never thought of it and that he could have a beer. A plastic-covered cardboard packet of drink was thrust under his nose by a little girl 'Thank you,' he smiled as she fled and checked the label ,'Green Tea, just what I need,' he grinned at Jason.

Siew Moi had vanished after placing him in his armchair parking lot but returned a short while later, hair back and in a change of clothing that made her look much more relaxed. He wished he felt the same. She smiled at him from the centre of activity, the dinner table. He noticed that she joined in the general cacophony by chatting to many people as she moved between the kitchen and lounge area. The majority of the guests seemed to be in the kitchen he estimated, wondering what time the last train left.

'Simon, these are my sisters Siew Choo and Ruby,' she was back, standing next to his chrysanthemum-patterned chair with two girls who bore a close resemblance to her.

He stood and said Hello. They both giggled and said they didn't speak much English before zooming off back towards the kitchen as soon as decently possible.

'Like dat lah,' she announced, shrugged her shoulders and followed them. Checking on the hamburgers he wondered.

He sat down again and tried to appear completely enraptured with the Chinese quiz show now filling the screen though he seemed to be the only person watching.

Nicky and Dickie had moved into a nearby room to play computer games, a fact he realised from the loud *ping* and *zapp* sounds floating his way.

Activity around the dining table grew in numerical and equipment intensity as seating, eating and utensil instructions, all in Chinese, were passed between elders, young adults and children.

They were having a steamboat he noticed between sips of green tea, which wasn't green at all but a pale yellow – a fact which puzzled him for a few seconds - as numerous plates of uncooked food were laid on the table by willing hands. Small plastic stools were placed alongside other more sizeable seats and after bowls of steamed rice were placed before each place he was beckoned to join the group at the first sitting, there being too many people to accommodate everyone at once.

He sat in between Siew Moi and Jason which gave him access to the English language on both sides, something he wouldn't have had in any other arrangement he realised. Plastic plates, bowls, spoons and chopsticks lay in front of each seat and a smiling Siew Moi encouraged him to get stuck in with a 'Go on then, no need to be shy.'

He picked up his chopsticks, looked over at her mother and said the only Chinese words he knew 'Xie Xie,' (pronounced *shay shay*) which meant *Thank you*. She smiled back revealing a rather fetching mouthful of red prawns.

He had his own wire scoop into which was piled the food choice of the moment before plunging it into the now-bubbling water in the centre of the table. There it joined many other scoops and if one wasn't careful the chosen food could easily drift away.

After a couple of minutes in the boiling stock it was deemed cooked and then retrieved to be eaten along with the rice. Easy, he thought, and at least there are no slimy fish heads to put me off. His comfort was soon crushed as a plate of leering watery eyes amongst shiny scaly heads slid onto the table in front of him.

Tableside conversation built up in volume as people fought to outdo the telly. No one was watching yet there was no movement by the residents or relatives to either lower the sound or even turn it off and save electricity. He could understand nothing of what was going on around him so concentrated on the floating food. The only familiar words spoken with certain consistency were 'Ah choo' and he wondered how come so many of them had colds.

'So you're a teacher is it?' Jason asked between intakes of chicken.

'Yes indeed,' Simon grinned, grateful to hear his mother tongue again, adding 'English, and you?'

'I sell insurance.'

Simon cut him off at the pass and sought to kill any signing up prospects immediately 'That's interesting, the school covers all of us completely for the time we are here, which is handy,' lock it in, he thought, end of story. No policy problems this evening for me.

'Who handles it at the school?' Not quite, can't get away so easily perhaps.

'I'm not really sure, probably best to write to the Head and ask,' how he wished it was Easter.

'I can save them a lot of money.'

'That's great but I can't really help that much as I don't do maths. I'm not very good with figures.' Trying to quickly think of a change of subject he asked 'Do you go surfing much?' before remembering that there were no surfing beaches in Singapore. The response though was quite surprising.

'Oh yes, every night after work.'

Knowing how most Singaporeans worked late he wondered how it was done 'How can you see? Isn't it dark?'

'No, I put the lights on.'

'At the beach?'

'Where got beach? No at home in the spare room where we surf the net,' the explanation came in with a rush onto embarrassed dry sand.

'Oh, I see…' he felt stupid and turned his attention to a prawn surfing past. Siew Moi had been listening and smiled at him in encouragement. Speech, he realised, was perhaps not the best option tonight as clear reception would have been difficult under the prevailing winds anyway.

They ate, and ate, and ate as people left and joined the table as stomachs filled. Those departing signified satisfaction with numerous burps and belches of various volume. He was told that such releases were indications of appreciation and contentment with the meal. He smiled at the thought; he had a lot to learn.

By nine the meal was over and he was invited to return to his chair, with some more green-yellow-tea, while the army of family and friends cleared the table. He sat back before the screaming telly as cast-off prawn heads, bones, chopsticks, tablecloths, seats and the cherished steamboat itself were taken into the kitchen by the small army of helpers.

A Chinese period costume drama was now on the screen. He watched in amazement as the cast took it in turns to fly through the sky, robes flowing and swords flashing as goodie fought baddie – all without wings. Why they just didn't slug it out on the ground like most other people who can't stand each other would do he couldn't work out. At the same time though it did add an extra dimension to the more regular way of things and would be very economical on shoe leather, he realised.

'How was it?' Siew Moi was sitting on the floor next to the chair.

'Great,' he smiled 'loved it.'

'Liar,' she looked quizzically at him.

'No, honest. It was fine, I loved the prawns.'

'Yes but you're not supposed to eat them with the shells still on, you know,' she pointed out quietly.

He looked at her with open eyes 'Really?' she nodded 'Oh what a prat I am. I bet they all think I'm a real peasant. Why didn't you tell me?'

'Well you seemed to be enjoying them actually, so why spoil a good thing,' she summed up the table topic.

'Actually they were rather nice and crunchy, I must say,' he thought back to the meal.

'Well there you are then, no harm done. But don't do it again.'

'No…first the Sweet & Sour, now the Prawns…what next?' he felt like an idiot.

By ten o'clock he was shaking hands and saying *Goodbye* and

Xie Xie to everyone he met on his journey from the Concorde take-off noise level telly to the front door – about 300 of them he later estimated.

They all smiled at him and spoke in a flurry of what he took to be Hakka – which he later found out is referred to in simplified form as K. No doubt they were saying 'So you're the dill who eats his prawns with their shells on, eh?' He responded with a knowing smile. Siew Moi walked with him as far as the bus-stop.

'I don't know if I should mention this but this date on the Chinese calendar is the equivalent to your Valentine's Day,' he looked at her with interest as she continued 'it's when the young boys and the girls go out looking for a wife or husband – not that you should feel I am trying to corner you by mentioning this,' she laughed.

'Wow, so now I know why I got that sexy Valentine's Card this morning,' he came back at her with a straight face. She looked surprised until he gave the game away by laughing.

'You!' she admonished 'Was it awful?' she asked, turning the attention to the meal.

'No, no, not at all, why should it be? It was fine, great, wonderful, magnificent. Loved it, terrific, many thanks,' he gushed, overplaying the enthusiasm somewhat before finishing off with 'Different.'

'Except for…?' she left the blanks for him to fill in.

'Except for nothing actually,' he smiled, nodding to confirm the statement.

'Come on, it's me…you can speak…I won't throw a fish-head at you,' she reminded him of his table-side Achilles heel.

'Well, don't get upset but can I ask if it's always so loud in your place?'

'Was it?' she wondered, then went on 'That's not loud, that's typically Chinese…we like to be surrounded by sound.'

'The answer to Question One then is – Yes, too noisy to die by. And…if they all keep sneezing like that why don't they use tissues to stop the germs going all over the food? If you don't mind me asking,' the Second Question was put delicately.

She looked at him, completely lost … 'Sneezing?'

'Yes. You know, you must have heard it. They all kept going *Ah Choo*…and yet not one of them pulled out a tissue.'

She stopped walking and her mouth dropped open 'That's simply because they were talking about my sister Ah Choo. They were not sneezing!' she started laughing.

'But her name is Siew Choo I thought you said, not Ah Choo.'

'Yes it is but the Chinese drop the first name and replace it with an Ah when being familiar. So she becomes Ah Choo amongst friends and family…just as I become Ah Moi,' the name game rules were changing.

'Now I wondered what that was all about as I heard it a great deal too.'

'That was me,' she was killing herself laughing.

'So there isn't a 'flu epidemic on the ninth floor of your block then?' He sought medical confirmation and clarification.

'Certainly not, in fact they all seem to be quite healthy to me,' the head nurse's opinion came forth.

'Well they were certainly in 'fine voice' one could say,' he summed up the evening as the feeder-bus pulled up.

Standing at the entrance, he expressed his thanks as effusively as he could. 'Listen, thanks for inviting me, that really was great, honestly, truly, I mean it completely, not a word of a lie, loved every minute!'

'You'd better stop otherwise the bus will go without you,' she waved to the driver to hang on for a second before kissing him goodbye on the cheek. 'Happy New Year of the Sheep.'

'May I never get your goat,' he added with a smile.

Chapter 7

All Down To Fete

It was the first week of May when Notices appeared around the Staff Room announcing that the School Fete would be held on Saturday June 7th in the school grounds. In charge of the event would be Deputy Head, Ms. Comardy, who would liaise with staff regarding activities and involvement.

Each teacher then received a circular asking for ideas and suggestions for stall themes for the Feteful Day. A plan of the area, with the layout of stalls, accompanied the circular. Staff were asked to 'Let your imagination fly' and take it from there. Submissions were requested by Friday May 9th – with a Fete Meeting slated for the following week.

Cazza announced that she would be running a Second Hand Books Stall, adding that even though she didn't have a specific class of her own she already had more volunteer assistants than would be needed. No one wondered why.

Tyrone elected to organise a Long-Jump Competition for Parents at $2 an entry, with proceeds to the Athletics Department. Bruce confirmed he would be going for a geography theme, the exact details of which would be revealed soon.

The three Sheilas decided to get away from their day-to-day connections and run a Bring & Buy Stall which sounded great until Bruce asked what would happen if no one brought anything. Simon settled on a Poetry Writing Competition & Sale … with framed selected entries available at $5 a copy. He was helping himself to coffee in the Staff Room one morning later in the week when a warm 'Hellllllloooooo....' came the way of the coffee beans.

'Oh hello Chauncy,' he responded without turning as he didn't want to spill the contents of the rather full cup. He slowly moved over to grab some milk and at the same time allow Chauncy to help himself to the hot brew. 'So how are things?' he asked the artist.

'Oh fine, dear bois. You know, taking it easy somewhat at the moment, but don't tell that to Madam White Snake upstairs,' he gasped conspiratorially.

'I wouldn't. So what are you planning for the School Fete?'

'Well, do you know,' the right hand went to the right hip – the left being occupied in holding his mug of coffee 'I thought I might have a Potter's Bar stand.'

'Isn't that somewhere in London?'

'Exactly. Well done, ten bonus points, you should be doing Geography instead of English,' he laughed at the thought. They moved to sit at a nearby table and Chauncy produced a packet of biscuits out of a bright red canvas shoulder bag.

'Go on have one, they are no good for you in any shape or form – which is what I like about them. I think all this biscuit business is just a devilish plot to make us all dependent on sugar, which I never take in coffee anyway, only on biscuits,' he cooed.

'OK, thanks,' Simon joined the conspiracy theory and helped himself 'so what happens at your Potter's Bar then?' he asked the sugary artistic one.

'Well in simple terms all visitors are invited to get sloshed on Australian and Kiwi wine, or good old Pommie ale, which seems like a splendid idea to me. All can sample said watery wonders in mugs made for the occasion by my students, which they can buy later – the mugs, not the students, that is. And I just happen to be the Head Barman and General Factotum Socialite in the midst of all this activity. How do you like it so far?'

Simon smiled, tipping his head slightly to one side in interest and as an indication to continue. Chauncy was now off and running, picking up speed he went on….

'I can't be bothered with all the usual mundane offerings of cake corners, book fairs, poetry displays….'

'That's me,' Simon interrupted. Chauncy's hand shot up to cover his mouth.

'Cancel that. I LOVE poetry,'…he went down on his knees, nose resting on the edge of the table 'Oh whatever made me say that. Silly C! Silly, silly me. So, seeing as it's going to be roasting hot – what else in Singapore, I ask you! – I feel that the mums and dad's will all need nice drinkipoos by the time they get round to me. After which they can buy the mugs they have supped from for a mere $5. These fine examples of exotic pottery can then be taken home in memory of a wondrous afternoon and kept on the sideboard for evermore,' he grinned with delight at the potty thought 'what do you think?'

'Who pays for the wine and the ale in the first place?'

'Oh aren't you the basic, down to earth, boring one? I bet you belong to the Greens Party and eat lots of yoghurt to improve your culture level. Actually that's a very good question, quite sensible in fact. I have a chum or two in a certain winebar and they are going to donate copious amounts of grog and general what-have-you…so it's all taken care of. Fixed. And every mug we sell is pure profit – thanks to the pure genius behind it all – which happens to be little old MOI!'

He grinned in total rapture once more before adding 'So let's roll out the wine barrel and have a good time!' twirling around the table in delight at his creative concept. Bruce entered the room as he was on his final spin.

'Byron!' he cried in welcome.

'Chaucer!'

Clever, thought Simon.

'Look, how are you?' it was obviously his 'Be Friendly to Bruce' week Simon thought as Chauncy gushed at the new arrival.

'Fine thanks, can I join you?' the Brisbane bomber was also being pleasant for a change. Maybe.

Chauncy gasped and his right hand flew to his chest in shock. He was wearing an emerald green smock as he had a tryst in an Irish pub planned for later in the evening and was dressing for the occasion.

The fact that he was also wearing green and white shamrock underwear was apparent to no one, a situation which might change later…with just a little bit of leprechaun luck. 'Of course,' he twittered 'look have a Nice biscuit, they are sooooo nice.' He thrust the packet towards Bruce and in doing so the first six biscuits shot out of their wrapper and landed in his lap. Chauncy dived after them. The Queenslander pushed his chair backwards to escape the attention, trying not to panic.

'Look, it's OK, really, don't worry. I love them actually. Just….just…leave me alone, I'm fine. Please…' he smiled, flapping Chauncy away.

Chauncy stopped in mid-scoop. 'You are? Yes of course you are,' he retreated back to his seat, crossed his legs in a knowing way and grinned at them both, chin on fist, elbow on knee. 'So what are you planning for the School Fete, Bollinger?'

'Bruce.'

'Whatever.'

'I'm having a *Win a Weekend on a Desert Island with The One You Fancy Most Competition*,' he announced with a straight face. Chauncy choked on his coffee.

'Are you? What a jolly good idea. How does one enter?'

'Well first you need to get an empty beer bottle.'

'Anchor or Tiger?' Chauncy sought to clarify which Singaporean brew, ever the one for detail.

'Foster's,' it was a down-under response.

'Of course! Right, carry on,' he nodded, slapped his knee and edged forward.

'Wait,' he stopped Bruce from continuing 'Large or small?'

'Large.'

'Of course. Always,' he nodded and signalled for him to continue.

'Then you need to write your name and the name of the wished-for companion on the official Entry Form. Roll it up and place it in the bottle. We provide special Desert Island Dream bottle-top stoppers, otherwise they'd all sink.' Chauncy was taking it all in, making mental notes.

'And then?'

'Well then you come down to my stall, which consists of a dreamy tropical island surrounded by water, and you cast your bottle, or bottles, into the briny.'

'And?' Chauncy was now having trouble breathing.

'At the end of the afternoon the bottle that is washed up closest to the single palm tree on the island as the final tide goes out is declared the winner.'

'Brilliant,' the aquatic artist gasped, smacking his thigh in admiration and rocking backwards 'but how do you guarantee the wished-for person will go with the winner?'

'Ah well, let me just say that we will make it well worth their while. So much so that I am sure they will be unable to resist the offer,' he smiled knowingly, adding 'money talks.'

Chauncy gasped 'Of course it does, quite right, quite right,' his attempt to remain calm lasted but a few seconds 'how much is the entry Brett?'

'Bruce.'

'Whatever.'

'Five dollars a bottle.'

'Right,' Chauncy stood up, shook the biscuit crumbs off his smock and turned.

'Where are you going?'

'To the bottle-shop for half a dozen large Foster's – where else!'

and he was gone in a rush of flapping dark green. They both laughed.

'You shouldn't set him up.'

'I wasn't, that really is the theme of my stall, so you'd better watch out otherwise you could be packing your cozzie if he wins. First choice island partner – for sure.'

Simon's face took on a rather concerned look.

Simon and Siew Moi had been seeing each other two or three times a week for what now seemed like ages. While their relationship had reached a certain stage it was true to say it hadn't really stepped into the deep waters of either physical or personal commitment. Having discovered a great Chinese outdoor restaurant not far from the Katong house Simon decided to try to move matters forward somewhat during a roadside dinner.

They met after school on the Thursday evening in question and after a pleasant coffee in the nearest Bun In The Oven made their way to Katong on the good old Number 14 bus. Half the other tenants were at home, the others were out doing their own thing. Simon poured Siew Moi a glass of Isotonic drink and went upstairs to change while she chatted with Cazza.

'So how is the library going?'

'Fine, quite busy actually. Madam Tan says she's never seen so many kids taking and returning books as there are this year. Didn't used to be like this in other years it seems.'

'I wonder why,' Siew Moi kept a straight face.

'Actually I just love the feel, smell and overall atmosphere of being surrounded by books.'

'I know exactly what you mean. There's nothing quite like opening the pages of a new book and allowing the aroma to waft over you. All rather intimate,' the Singapore bookseller agreed.

'Sounds a bit like Kings Cross,' Cazza mused.

'How?'

'Well you know, appealing aroma and intimate. Just about sums him up, especially after he's had a shower.' Cazza's eyes clouded. 'So how is he?'

'Fine. He changed his car a few weeks ago for a blue two-door BMW. Which meant the green hair had to be changed to match the new trim so now he's blue on top.'

'Has he had you round for dinner at home yet?' Siew Moi delivered the line rather carefully as she was fishing for a reaction to compare to Simon's.

'Oh God yes,' Cazza gasped 'all the noise, though the screaming kids were actually out-screamed by the television. So loud! I couldn't believe it.'

Siew Moi laughed, the opinions tallied it seemed.

'And I have no idea what anyone said to me as first of all I couldn't hear them and secondly it was all in Teochew,' she sighed.

'Anyway I've told him I'm not going again, so there. Aren't I awful?' her eyes begged for a denial response to the statement.

'Not really. I've told Simon, noise is a part of the Chinese way of life – and death – here. If you ever go to a Chinese funeral you'd think it was the Singapore Symphony Orchestra out for a ride, such is the noise level and the variety of musical instruments used.'

'Enough to wake the dead.'

'Well not quite, maybe just a crashing pots and pans stir-fry departure to see them on their way.'

Simon came down the stairs in shorts and floppy t-shirt, bare footed. 'Miss anything?' he asked of the chatting bookends.

'No,' Cazza confirmed 'just a few tales of traditional China.'

He looked puzzled as he helped himself to a sip from Siew Moi's glass and mentioned that they should get going soon.

'Care to join us for an outdoor dinner at the Sin Hoi Sai down the road?' he politely asked Cazza. The librarian declined, diplomatically claiming fatigue.

The two of them hopped off the bus at a stop along East Coast

Road opposite a large church and walked back some twenty yards to the rows of round tables that stood on the pavement. They had long-since sussed out the fact that the ones by the edge of the road were the best on offer as they caught the evening breeze as well as provided excellent viewing options for watching the world go by, be it on foot, by bus or car.

They were lucky to get a small two-seater next to the kerb and settled down in anticipation of the delights to come. They were becoming quite attached to 'Drain View', as they had dubbed it, and the friendly lady owner, Khim, was soon standing in front of them smiling as she awaited their order. Her brother Joe loomed up alongside and asked about their drinks. Simon went for a beer, Siew Moi a barley water.

Ah Khim took down their food choices which were for spicy stingray, chicken in blackbean sauce, kang-kong vegetables and steamed rice. Simon poured the fast-arriving beer over ice and the chitchat was easy and quite general. Having planned and rehearsed his presentation many times that week he waited until the first dish had arrived and both parties were getting stuck into the chicken before he served up his own offerings.

'Have you ever been to Malacca?'

'Ages ago, why?'

He glanced at a white Mercedes trying to nudge a stray cat out of the way and park alongside their drain before delivering his second serve to the Royal Box end. 'Well I was reading about it and it sounds very nice, seemingly all olde-worlde and quaint and full of original, unspoilt areas,' he hoped he wouldn't be called for a foot-fault.

'So they say,' her return was non-committal, without much interest. He took another sip of the ice-cold beer and served again, a slower one this time to the backhand court.

'It's just that I was wondering if you'd fancy going for the week-end. You know, a change from Singapore, nice drive and a visit to

177

Malaysia – where I've never been.'

It was a kicker which she watched with great care. She thought about the response.

'What do you mean '*Nice drive,*' you haven't even got a car so how do you plan to get there?' she kept the ball in play with a little slice.

He had anticipated the deep response and was ready 'Actually I can borrow Chauncy's car,' her eyes opened wide as his game plan was slowly revealed. Simon continued, going wide for the tramlines this time 'He has an old banger it seems and he offered me use of it at any time, and if you don't mind the colour…' the eyes opened questioningly as she threw up a deep return lob, somewhat under pressure 'it's er pink.'

He coughed and kept up the pace, this one a half volley 'I thought it might be a nice chance for us to have a weekend away together,' There, it was said and done.

He'd served for the game and all he waited for now was the call from the umpire's chair as to whether or not it had been a double fault.

'Sounds great,' the confirmation that he'd clipped the outside line and that success was his echoed around the open-air arena. He raised his eyes to meet hers.

'When shall we go?' she asked, obviously recognising the potential for a well matched event. Both players had a lot to offer and would undoubtedly provide high quality play if the conditions were right.

'Well how about the weekend after the School Fete?' he breathed deeply.

'Which is?'

'Er…it's on… Saturday, June 7th. So are you free the following weekend?'

She thought for a moment before answering 'As a bird.'

The invitation was accepted without hesitancy. He wondered

how he'd manage to finish the tasty stingray as his stomach was all tied up in knots. The answer seemed to lie in another Anchor beer which the ever-attentive Joe quickly saw to. Advantage Simon.

There were still two more sets to play though.

The staff meeting after the School Fete Notice went up had forty odd teachers in attendance. Dot Com went through the suggestions for stall themes. As the inner quadrangle had a large lawn in its centre there was ample room for all disciplines to establish their presence. There was also enough space for the likes of Tyrone's Long Jump Competition plus a Sandcastle Sculpture Area to the left of the landing zone.

Bruce explained the Desert Island plan to his colleagues and it was agreed that he could have some buckets of sand from the long jump pit to help with island construction. As for the water around the island he arranged to borrow a number of water troughs from the Chemistry Department which, with a little construction work, would collectively make a perfect moat.

Progress reports were requested by Dot Com on a weekly basis and a Steering Committee was elected. The process was quite democratic with Matilda having already chosen six people to oversee key elements of the event. Dot Com read out the names as given by her leader and there were no arguments.

On the way out Simon bumped into Chauncy and invited him for coffee. Once in the nearest Bun In The Oven and settled with two frothy lattes the objective was to carefully steer the discussion round to the pink automobile. Chauncy was, as usual, all ears in Simon's presence and gave him an update on his Potter's Bar theme – 'Perfect, just perfect, and loads of wine and beer arranged. All I have to do is paint a Sistene Chapel look-alike ceiling in a certain bar and the duty is fully paid,' he beamed.

'Is it that simple?'

'For me – yes. For anyone else – no. I happen to have the exact design of the masterpiece and can dash it off in a weekend. Hopefully without any paint dripping into the wine awaiting me down below.'

'So Chauncy,' Simon brought the discussion to a head.

'Yes, dear bois? What is it that you are absolutely wetting yourself about asking me? I can tell you know, you give yourself away so easily!!! Except to me that is – or maybe not! Is that why you are so nervous, has the moment arrived, at last???' He gasped in mock shock 'No – don't speak! Don't say it! No need to question me – I WILL go to the desert island with you — at any time you so wish. Just tell me where the ferry leaves from and I shall be there ready for cast-off,' he grinned knowingly.

'Well actually it's not that,' Simon threw the wet blanket over the thoughts. Chauncy crumpled across the table, dramatically dejected.

'Do you remember the other week when you said I could possibly borrow your car for a couple of days some time – if I asked nicely?'

'Yeeeeeessss…' the responder rose to the perpendicular slowly. He was now sipping his latte with certain delight and wriggling in his seat at the conspiratorial plot evolving.

'Well I was wondering if it could possibly be available over the 14th and 15th of next month????'

'Not a problem,' Chauncy declared immediately 'for that is when I shall be flat out looking up at the ceiling and seeing as they are providing the transport and paint I need do nothing but get to the wine bar and be creative and brilliant – as is my wont.

And after I return to earth once more they will feed and water me for the rest of the days in question…so I will not be needing the usage of good old Hector.'

'Hector?'

'Yes dear bois. Hector is the name of the car,' he paused before adding 'beautiful boy that he is.'

'But I thought your car was pink.'

'It is. That's his favourite colour. There's a lot of it about you know,' Chauncy was back amongst the poster paints 'You see, the name came about when I got him a few years ago. There was so much wrong with him and no one really wanted to house him – hadn't had a grease and oil change for yonks, big end broken, you know the kind of problem I'm sure.' Deadpan face.

He looked wickedly at Simon 'But I said '*Oh what the heck*' and took him anyway…hence the resultant name… Hector.'

'Right,' Simon gulped down some more latte to help absorb the details of the naming ceremony.

'Planning a little trip O.S. are we then?' Chauncy asked knowingly, lips pursed together.

'Well…' Simon started to answer before pausing and asking 'what's O.S.?'

'Overseas! What else!' Chauncy slapped his thigh and tugged down the current Cape of Many Colours he was wearing. By the look of it the drape had started life as a bedroom quilt which over time had been turned into a patched kaleidoscope coat.

'Oh I see. Well yes, sort of,' Chauncy looked at him, waiting for the confession 'well …er…yes…actually.'

'It's OK, you can tell Uncle Chauncy,' he paused and then continued 'how far are you planning to go? Geographically speaking that is.'

'Malacca.'

'Oh that's OK. Hector's been there THOUsands of times, practically knows the way there by himself without anyone telling him where to turn,' he laughed 'and I take it there will be a…companion travelling?'

'Er yes, actually, there will.'

'With whom you will perhaps be looking out for some nice books – in between other things?'

'Well, maybe,' the questioning look was back 'er, yes.'

'Fine. Just let me know what time you want to collect Hector on the Saturday morning and all will be in readiness,' he smiled benignly.

'Thanks Chauncy, you're great. That is so kind of you and I honestly will look after Hector, and fill him up with petrol and polish him before I hand him back,' Simon prattled on somewhat.

'Hush!' Chauncy had spoken 'None of this twittering. Just do the right thing – as I KNOW you will – and all will be well. Mmmmmmmmmmmm….' Simon was so grateful to his eccentric chum he insisted he have another coffee.

Of all of the occupants of the house Bruce was by far and away the most Internet savvy. The others were interested enough to know how to read and send e-mail and were satisfied with that. Bruce though seemed to be in 'advanced' Internet mode most of the time.

After some drawn-out negotiations in Sim Lim Centre, the specialist computer zone, during the second term he had upgraded to the very latest in supersonic computers. The follow-up to which was that he would spend even more hours than previous on the new machine, clicking happily away upstairs on most nights of the week.

Once dinner was over his evening activity would invariably take him skywards to work on the delights and attractions of the Internet. Many hours later he would appear in the lounge for a closing late-night drink and chat with whoever was still up, usually around eleven.

'What yewz doing on that machine all the time?' Sheila Two asked one evening when the adverts were proving more appealing than the programmes on the telly.

'Surfing,' came the athletic response.

'Where's yer board?' Cazza took up the questioning. She herself having just come in after an evening ride around town with the Blue-Boy in his blue BMW.

'Don't need it, I do body surfing.'

'Selling yer body again eh?' Sheila One pondered the prospect.

'Special price,' he confirmed 'two chicken rice takeaway dinners and a couple of cans of Tiger beer,' he grinned at the thought, what a bargain.

'Yer know that 92% of people surfing the net are looking at porn sites?' Sheila Three asked him.

'Yeah, I've heard that.'

'And yewz?' Three moved forward.

'Please lah,' he resorted to the local expression 'how can? I am a good boy,' he feigned shock.

'Good at what?' Cazza giggled.

'That's for me to know and for yewz to wonder about,' he collected two cans of Anchor beer from the kitchen fridge and passed one to the listening Tyrone on his return. 'Do they have e-mail in the Paradiz Hotel in Phuket, Ty?' he asked, diverting attention somewhat.

'Sure do,' Tyrone confirmed 'and me and Pui are sending hot messages through the ether to each other all the time.'

'So romantic,' Sheila Three cooed.

'Half yer luck,' Sheila One thought out loud.

Sheila Two was speechless but grinned all the same as it seemed a nice thing to do.

'Well I've just got to finish off something on the screen so I'll see yewz later,' Bruce wandered back upstairs, frothy beer nightcap in hand. He had left the computer on while he went downstairs as he was expecting an incoming e-mail. On settling down again he moved the 'mouse' slightly and waited for life to return to the black screen.

A few seconds later both contact and vision were restored and the message he'd been waiting for was there, glowing brightly.

'OK Big Boy,
I will meet you on Saturday the 14th off the 11am ferry.

I will be wearing a red blouse and white skirt. I will carry a sign that reads 'Big Boy' as you suggest. How about you, how will I recognize your body?'

Love to my very Big Boy.

Yati.'

He was tempted to respond
'I will be wearing nothing but a smile – so I'll be easy to spot,' but instead typed....

'I am five ten, fair hair, no beard. Will be wearing a blue t-shirt, grey shorts and white jogging shoes.
I will be carrying a black bag over my right shoulder with a gift-box of Nobby's Nuts *under the other arm.*

Big Boy.'

He was referring to the popular brand of salted nuts which many Australians loved to eat…but perhaps not many Indonesians. A fact he hadn't considered when he thought about taking her a tasty gift. The plan though seemed to be developing nicely.

The truth of the matter was that his nocturnal Internet activities over the previous weeks had led to a romance with a girl on the nearby Indonesian island of Batam.

Their Internet exchange and budding affection had built rather rapidly as each had 'revealed' more and more about themselves over time. Things had progressed so much so that they were now at the 'rendezvous' arrangement stage. She had told him she was nineteen and worked as a pineapple chunk packer in a plantation factory during the day and in her spare time was undergoing astronaut training at night-school four evenings a week.

He in turn had told her he was from Australia, was a member

of the Queensland Royal Family and had a few hit records under his stage-name of 'The Singing Surfer'. He loved to surf when not recording and was easy to spot amongst the waves as he always wore a crown to indicate his royal heritage

The exchange had grown increasingly imaginative as well as passionate and both parties were now hot and bothered enough to arrange a meeting. The final parts were now falling into place for a Batam Island liaison just a few weeks hence.

He looked at the screen as the response came back.

'Hello Big Boy,

Why are you stealing nuts from your friend Nobby?
What's wrong with your own? Are they too salty to taste from all your time in the surf?
Yati

P.S.   How old is Nobby? Does he have an e-mail address?'

He decided to let her wonder about that one and turned the computer off for the night. He had already quietly checked on the ferry fare and times to Batam. There was a departure from the World Trade Centre at 1115 on the Saturday morning in question which would get him to Batam at 1100 local time – given the one hour back time difference and the 45 minute journey.

He had collected some brochures on the island from a travel agency near school as well as checked out a few hotels via their websites. He chose one and booked a double room - king size bed on request — vibrating another $10 — go on then, what the heck…in for a penny, in for ten dollars… - for the night of 14/15 June by passing his credit card details to the selected hostelry.

The plans were falling into place rather nicely he felt. They even went to the extent of him buying an Indonesian phrase book and learning certain words on the bus travelling to and from school, when alone of course. The clandestine communications would remain secret from his fellow academics he decided from the start. Well, for as long as possible as he knew that their inquisitive natures would find him out in the end. For now though he kept it all tightly zipped.

Tyrone announced that he would be going to Phuket on the weekend after the School Fete. As the flights left in the evening he would leave on the Friday night and return late on Sunday.

'Friday the thirteenth,' Sheila Three pointed out 'unlucky for some.'

'And lucky for a few others – perhaps.'

'Randy cat,' Sheila Two pronounced.

'Jealous.'

'You bet. Half yer luck.' Two agreed, teeth in gnashing mode.

'How's yer Thai?' Sheila One asked.

'My Thai what?'

'Smarty-pants!'

'Your bloody Thai language, Dill. Weez all seen the Phrase Book you've been pouring over for weeks. So are you any good at it now?'

'I'm very good at it actually, though not at speaking Thai. It's not really needed, we speak the language of love.'

Everyone groaned.

Life became quite busy for Simon, and for all of the household in fact, as plans for the upcoming Fete took over much of their spare time. He still managed to see Siew Moi as often as possible, usually between school closing at close to four and Fete Meetings starting at five. He told her about Chauncy agreeing to lend him the car and the subsequent arrangements surrounding Hector and got the impression that she readily accepted the fact that their planned weekend away would not be all sightseeing. Hopefully.

Siew Moi suggested they drive north via the Second Link connection between Singapore and Malaysia which would mean avoiding the bound-to-be-more-congested Causeway. If they went the way she mentioned, once over the border they could simply continue up the new highway which would bring them into Malacca a couple of hours later. He agreed without question. He didn't know anything about the roads or highways in Malaysia anyway and was relying on Siew Moi to be advisor-navigator and translator for the trip.

On the Thursday before the Fete there was a General Meeting immediately after school during which Dot Com and her Committee went over everything related to the event.

All staff were asked to be on site by 10am on Saturday. They would find their stalls set up and laid out as the Construction Committee would erect and furbish on the Friday evening. Each stall would be given a cashbox for which the teacher in charge would be fully responsible. The official opening time was 11am after which students, relatives and friends would be welcome.

A Collection Committee would visit each stall every two hours to pick-up monies collected. This would then be taken upstairs to The Hall where a Receiving Area would be in full operation – complete with its own safe. Mathematics Department staff would be handling this side of things – with abacus-bearing assistants on hand.

The Canteen would be serving a wide variety of food throughout the day…to complement dedicated food stalls offering the likes of sausage rolls…Aussie meat pies…Pommie fish and chips…Kiwifruit…cakes, scones and ice cream. The event would finish at 4pm. The Lucky Draw & Prizegiving of the Grand Raffle would take place at this time, followed by Thank-You Speeches by Matilda and special guests.

Lucky Draw tickets were already being sold with some 50 prizes of varying values up for grabs.

After closure stalls should be stripped of attachments as much as possible. A squad of workers would move in on Sunday and clear the area completely so that by Monday morning the overall image of the school would be as per usual. Dot Com thanked everyone associated with the event, both those in the front-line as well as the backroom staff. A few questions seeking clarification on certain points came from the floor after which the meeting closed. The final countdown had commenced.

On Saturday morning the occupants of the house travelled to the school on the 9.30 bus. They arrived on site just before ten, wished each other well and split up to take over their own stalls. Each was wearing casual clothing and in a patriotic rush Simon had even dug out his bushman's hat. This caused all sorts of well meaning comments around the house, especially about the corks. The fun theme of the day was set when he wore it on the bus, causing all sorts of looks from fellow travellers. He wondered what Chauncy would make of it and it wasn't long before he found out.

Simon's Poetry Stall was one lane away from the Potter's Bar and once the 'Potty One' spotted him while unloading a pile of mugs from a large cardboard box he made his way over, a knowing look in place.

'Well, Simon,' he took up a hands-on-hips stance and gushed 'don't you look the original Outback Drover?' He focused on the hat and, receiving no response, continued...

'By the way, do you know that your danglers are showing?'

'What, all of them?'

'Well I'd say it looks much like it from here,' Chauncy estimated 'though I don't know how many you started with.'

'The usual number.'

'Well that's what I'd have thought but why display them all today, shouldn't you be saving them for Malacca next weekend?'

'Not a problem,' Simon smiled 'they never wear out, are always working well and I like to get the air to them every now and then.'

'I'm so glad to hear that,' his interrogator spun and fled back to his stall as the sound of smashing pottery came his way.

Chauncy was wearing a droopy canary yellow smock the front of which showed a kangaroo and kiwi side by side, underneath it were the words Antipodean Academy Wonders. On the back he had painted maps of Australia and New Zealand in deep red and black - which he claimed to be Aboriginal and Maori earth tones. A green beret completed the ensemble and was meant to complement the almost-gold of the smock in depicting the Australian colours. Tyrone eat your heart out.

There were three students helping him set up the stall, the front and back of which was now covered in posters from numerous Australian and New Zealand wineries. The centre of the table was filled with both bottles and flagons of wine in front of which were signs suggesting

'Chug A Mug - $4 a Tipple.' and 'Take home the Mug - $5.'

Mugs of every colour imaginable were lined up to the left and right of the wine display.

The father of one of the children assisting Chauncy wandered over and read the signs. 'Five dollars to take home a mug,' he spoke out loud.

'Correct,' Chauncy gushed 'all proceeds to help the school. And although we don't officially open until eleven you can have a tipple or choose a mug now if you really like.'

'Who's the mug I get to take home, you?'

'Not today thank you,' the Potter bristled 'I am not for sale, and even if I were you could not afford me.'

He turned his back on the parent and ignored him completely. At the same time he wondered how he'd get through the day if this was an example of the kind of remarks he'd be getting – only by having a few swift slurps along the way, he decided.

Tyrone was in his most glorious Aussie colours. Green running shoes, gold socks, shiny green shorts with a clinging golden vest above. A floppy green hat with a kangaroo badge completed the presentation. He was checking the runway markers on his long-jump and raking the sand when the three Sheilas came along.

'Enough room for them to get a good speed up?'

'No worries mate.'

'What are the prizes?'

'First prize is a SANDwich – get it?' he paused for effect before continuing 'Second prize is a book on building SANDcastles and third is a Bucket and Spade filled with SAND. Perfect don't you think?'

'Wow. Riveting. Very creative,' Sheila One thought out loud.

'Wanna enter?'

'No thanks,' they chorused 'hate the feel of sand between the toes anyway.' Sheila Two informed him with one of her nonetheless encouraging molar displays.

'Got anything worth having on your stall?'

'Well we have a wide variety of tropical jams as contributed by many mums of our little darling students,' Sheila Three explained. 'Actually they have been very creative as we now have jars of Rambutan, Banana, Chiku, Papaya, Mango, Jackfruit and – wait for it – Durian, all on offer!' Sheila Two listed the flavours available at their Jam Session Stall.

'Amazing,' he agreed 'though I don't fancy the Durian and it's pongy smell so don't open it near here …spare me!' He was not a fan of the pungent fruit which one either loved or hated, there being no in between.

'There is also a rather nicely decorated Guzunder if you need one,' Sheila One mentioned, seeking her first sale badly.

'What's a Guzunder?'

'You know, it's an adult potty that goes under the bed. You use it if you need to 'go' during the night and there isn't a loo handy,'

Three explained.

'No thanks, sounds revolting. Been used before I take it?'

'Of course.'

'Oh no, it's not for me. I'll stick to pole vaulting into the outside dunny and all will be well. Unless I miss the landing of course.'

Cazza's bookstall looked as much like a library as it could under the circumstances. She had rows of books laid out across the table. Signs indicating 'Romance' : 'Adventure' : 'Travel' : 'Careers' : 'Outer Space' and 'Computers' stood along the top informing potential buyers what lay before them. She looked almost matronly as she wore her once-much-discussed long batik skirt – still opening on the left when the wind was coming from the right direction — and a conservative plain white blouse with a neck-hugging ruffled collar and three quarter length sleeves.

Though each stand had been allocated 3 student helpers for the day Cazza already had eight assisting her in laying out the stall, placing the signs and marking prices.

She got on well with all of them and even Madam Tan, her erstwhile assistant-cum-Singaporean-'mother', had taken to her totally. She enjoyed chatting and gossiping to her when in the library, though in somewhat hushed tones of course.

Her assistants were all boys – what a SURPRISE – around the twelve to fifteen age bracket. She did wonder why there were so many but as long as she smiled at them every so often they seemed quite happy to stand around and smile back at her.

The Librarian had brought along a huge bag of soft-centre sweets for her assistants to consume during the course of the day.

She saw it as a little gesture of her appreciation for their help and handed them out at the hourly shift change. It wasn't long before word got out that Ms. Latham was allowing students to suck her soft-centres when helping on her stall. The news led to even greater numbers of volunteers appearing and Dot Com had to finally bring in crowd control measures to keep the student masses at bay.

Bruce took up residence on his Desert Island wearing what he felt was appropriate clothing of a grass skirt and pompoms around ankles, wrists and head. Pacific Island tattoos covered his bare top, legs and arms, the patterns of which had been carefully copied by Sheila Three, following a picture of a Tahitian chief, by using a black marker-pen. The suggestion of getting Chauncy to decorate had been rejected rather emphatically. It was all very tropical and South Sea Islandish Matilda commented to Dot Com as they wandered past. The stall sign read 'Win A Desert Island Dream Weekend With The Companion Of Your Choice'. Head of School had been rather concerned about the legal commitment of the wording but had been assured that things would be worked out to the satisfaction of everyone involved so let it pass.

Shortly after opening time Chauncy appeared at the Island with half-a-dozen empty beer-bottles. His eyes opened wide as he caught sight of the bare-chested Bruce standing between flares and palms.

'Very Fijian,' he commented as he off-loaded his bottles 'I must say you've captured the mood perfectly Bradley.'

'Bruce,'

'Whatever,' he praised the overall display effusively and moved quickly into coral-reef mode 'now what do I have to do exactly to enter?'

'OK Chomley, listen carefully,' the islander read out the rules, 'Give us $5 per bottle entry fee. Write the name of the person you'd like to go on a *Naughty Nookie Desert Island Weekend* with on the entry forms. Then add your name on the bottom bit …and Bob's your uncle, Sally's your aunt and very soon you'll be as happy as a tit in a trance.'

Bruce passed over six entry forms and winked knowingly 'Bung the paper in the bottle, seal it with our Official Stopper and cast it into the briny when you're ready,' He pointed to the moat which surrounded the island and its solitary palm which was already beginning to look rather droopy as the heat of the day built up.

'But your 'ocean' looks rather limited for space, one would think, given that you could have dozens of entries by the end of the day. I'm just wondering how you would cope with them all in the water.'

'Good point cocker,' Bruce agreed 'just to keep things flowing, as it were, we will have the tide going out every hour on the hour, which will allow us to clear out the losing entries. The bottle nearest the palm tree each time the tide goes 'out' will make it to the final Float-Off…which will take place at four o'clock.'

'Brilliant! Though how will you do all that?'

'We pull the plug from under the tubs and the water washes out onto the ground below. Simple,' the inner secrets of south sea island life were revealed.

'Won't you get wet?'

Bruce lifted up a leg from beneath his grass skirt and 'clunked' a bare foot onto the stall. 'No problem, no shoes – I am the Barefoot Island Chief today,' he grinned at Chauncy 'like it so far?'

'Wonderful. So what I'll do is give you $30 now so I'm fully paid up. Now let me see how to play this….' he thought about numbers for a moment 'I shall enter one bottle for the first four tidal movements then two in the last. That way I can have an even spread over the five qualifying tides.'

'OK mate,' Bruce was getting friendly 'winners of the heats will be kept to one side pending entry in the final. Good luck to you.'

'And to you too,' Chauncy gushed 'and may the best bottle win.'

Simon's Poetry Stand did steady business throughout the day. He had given his entrants various themes on which to submit their poems. Subjects included 'Life' : 'School' : 'My Pet' : 'Weather': 'Parents' : 'Home' and 'Computers'. There was also a 'Special Interest' category which basically opened the competition up to any form of submission.

He had also brought in a few dozen poetry books from Siew Moi's bookshop on a 'Sale or Return' basis to support overall efforts. The agreed commission was 15% and during the day he and his helpers (though not as many as at the other book centre where one Cazza Latham was still knocking them in the aisles with her soft centres) sold some sixty odd books of varying authors and titles.

A dozen or so prizewinning poems were displayed around the stall, alongside others worthy of merit. The presentation attracted numerous parents checking to see if their offspring were indeed as gifted with the written word as they had thought, hoped or dreamed about. Some were, some weren't.

By two o'clock Chauncy's stall was proving to be the most riotous as he had visiting parents sampling drinks and buying mugs in great numbers. The attention and interest level coming his way was almost as acute as that at Cazza's stall. In her case though it was mainly from a younger clientele, far below the official drinking age.

Bruce's Desert Island was also grabbing plenty of attention. Entrants were captivated by the dancing Bruce who had got himself into a hula-hula mood thanks mainly to Chauncy trying to bribe him into favouring his entries with regular samples of Potter's Bar wine.

The crowd, and the heat, was at its height in the middle of the afternoon by which stage Chauncy was feeling no pain. He had now taken up residence in a canvas 'film director' chair and was busily setting the world to right with his many visitors. At the same time he was setting up a few portrait commissions amongst those who liked the idea of an oil painting of themselves against a tropical backdrop.

Cazza, meanwhile, had been joined by Kings Cross who had frightened away her legion of helpers with a single look and a shake of his blue hair. He began to help himself to the soft centres by placing the end of one in his mouth and forcing the other end into Cazza's, the culmination of which was one big sloppy smackeroo.

The smooching was terminated by the arrival of Dot Com who gave out a loud 'IF you please!' as she came round to collect the takings and caught the pair in mid kiss. K.C. broke the suction clamp and blew her a kiss which didn't go down well with either Cazza or Dot Com, who blushed somewhat and hurried off to check the social behaviour on other stalls. Cazza hit him over the head with a handy hardback.

Chauncy arrived at the Desert Island just before four for the last tidal movement.

He was told that two of his entries were in the final float-off and that his chances were considered promising by watery watchers. The once upright palm-tree had now turned into a droopy, wilted leaf. The assisting island staff were showing signs of similar status.

There were five bottles in the final tidal surge for the grand prize, each of them a heat winner. Chauncy carefully checked out the opposition drifting by as the time for the last tidal tug came closer, he realised that if he closed one eye it gave him a better sighting of things.

Bruce was almost out of it as he swayed to the hula beat coming from a portable cassette player at the back of the stall, now showing obvious signs of 'island fever'. The three Sheilas and Simon had also managed to make their way over to witness the final flush.

Simon was still wearing his bushman's hat as well as a rather worried look at the thought of Chauncy possibly winning the 'drain off'. Sheila Two hove up alongside and asked 'Got your island cozzie ready darls?'

'I haven't entered,'

'I know you haven't but I was thinking about you being the prize more so than the winning entry. Old Chauncy there has got you down for a starry starry night underneath the swaying palms old mate. Cozzie or no cozzie – preferably the latter I would think.'

Simon smiled weakly and wondered what he would do if Chauncy actually won and had indeed written his name down as the desired accompanying body.

Bruce struck his portable gong to gain attention, stood on a rather wobbly stool and announced that the final 'tidal wave' would start in sixty seconds. The crowd cheered as he confirmed that the winner of the wonderful weekend prize would shortly be revealed. Loud hoots encouraged him as he did a little hula before falling off the stool and signalling to a spotty boy standing by the biggest trough to pull the plug.

The boy did as bid and slowly the water level receded leaving a couple of bottles lying on the island's sand, one of which was a Chuancy entry. The rest of them went down the drain.

'We have two sandy finalists,' Bruce declared looking at the last empties of the day 'I would ask our adjudicator Deputy Head Ms. Dot Com to judge which of the two is closest to our *beautiful* palm tree – which looks a bit daggy now but it was so beautiful earlier on, like seven hours ago.'

The crowd cheered and applauded Dot Com as she approached the island. After careful consideration and tape-measured assistance the lady selected a small Heineken bottle as the winner. Chauncy groaned inside and knocked back another glass of chilled Riesling.

Dot Com passed the winning bottle to Bruce who duly unscrewed the top and retrieved the inner entry form. The crowd hushed.

'The winner, as you can see,' he held the bottle high 'is this Heineken entrant so let me reveal the name of the person who the lucky winner has nominated as their companion for a dirty weekend...' he corrected himself 'Sorry, a romantic weekend on the desert island of our choice. Not theirs,' he clarified the last part of the deal with a leery grin.

He unravelled the paper and his eyes opened wide as he read 'The chosen accompanying companion of the prize winner is

…Mr. Chauncy…from the Art Department of the Academy.'

All eyes turned to Chauncy who went into shock. He gasped at the mention of his name as the chosen body. The crowd cheered and clapped as he slowly sat down, unable to take it all in for the moment.

'Are you sure you didn't enter?' Sheila Two checked with Simon who shook his head emphatically 'Looks like you have a rival then.'

'Let's hope…' Simon wished.

Chauncy was now gasping to catch his breath 'Who, who, who entered the bottle?' he asked between gulps.

'Dunno,' Bruce declared 'there's no entry name here.' He looked around at the crowd 'Will the person who entered this Heineken bottle come forward please?' he asked of the masses before him. There was no movement from anywhere as people looked at each other questioningly.

He waited for a few moments before announcing 'OK then it looks like we either have a reluctant winner, though I can't see why,' he leered at Chauncy and swayed his hips and grass skirt to keep the mood of the moment going 'or they have gone home …so we'll have to wait until next week to find out who claims Mr. Chauncy as their prize.'

And in so saying he closed the stall for the day claiming he needed a drink rather badly.

Chauncy was dumbstruck.

'There ya go then Chauncy. Wanted, but not in much of a hurry eh?' Sheila Three put the prospect to him.

'Quite. How odd,' he summed it all up 'oh well, let's see what next week brings. And if it doesn't bring the winning entrant maybe I, as the accompanying nominee, will be allowed to reverse the process and take the prize as well as select the companion,' his eyes misted over at the thought.

The day was declared a rousing success by Matilda at the 5 o'clock Fete Summary. Initial figures had the overall income up some 24% on the previous year and all staff were heartily congratulated on their creative and committed efforts which had made this year's Fete so successful. Sincere thanks were also expressed by Dot Com and everyone was invited to partake of closing drinks and snacks in the canteen.

As for Chauncy and his romantic interlude, well he decided to leave it all to fate and wait and see what happened next.

Chapter 8

Travellers Tales

The following week brought excited anticipation towards the coming weekend away for the three boys. There was much ribbing of both Simon and Tyrone by the four girls on a daily basis. It wasn't until Thursday though that Bruce's secret plans were revealed thanks to Sheila Three finding a Batam Ferry timetable in the kitchen with the 11.15am Saturday departure circled.

After a certain amount of questioning while strapped in a chair, sitting under a naked light in a darkened room with a slowly dripping can of beer above his head Bruce finally confessed his Indonesian plans.

He managed to keep the initial revelation to just his ferry departure and arrival times. It was only after the tightening of the rope behind his back, and neck, that certain contacts on the island came to light.

The fact that the male members of the household were leaving on a 'Naughty Nooky Weekend' left the girls feeling somewhat undesired and unwanted. Except for Cazza of course who still had her 'Blue Boy' very much on hand. The girls decided that they would have a special day out for themselves over the weekend — on the Sunday — as their own treat.

'So there, we shall also be out enjoying ourselves,' they told the travelling male trio, which made them feel slightly better.

Simon saw Chauncy for coffee on the Friday afternoon before 'D (for departure) Day' while details of the whereabouts of his flat and directions as to how to get there were exchanged. It was agreed that Simon would come round between half eight and nine the next morning to collect Hector.

Tyrone had been a dithering wreck for most of the week and come Friday the 13th was diagnosed by fellow residents as being in urgent need of tranquillisers.

'Course ya know what the date is don't ya mate?' Sheila Two mentioned 'Maybe yewz should have just have stayed in bed all day like the old saying suggests.'

Sheila One took up the opening 'Maybe not darls, he'll be staying in bed all weekend anyway.'

'With a bit of luck,' came the supporting comment. Their dry humour could be quite wicked, as well as pointed, when they felt like it.

Tyrone kept telling himself to think of pole-vaulting rather than the Patong Paradize and managed to get through the day in one piece before heading off to the airport around five. Cheers, smutty advice and encouragement saw him off in a taxi, as did all other occupants of the house.

On Saturday morning Bruce and Simon travelled on the same bus, the former heading for the ferry terminal at the World Trade Centre, the latter for Chauncy's flat not that far away from the port.

The Number 10 bus did them proud and after half an hour or so of sitting upstairs Simon stood up to leave, wishing Bruce 'Salamat Jalan' as he did so.

Bruce looked at him rather mystified and shouted after him as he moved down the upper deck 'What's that mean?'

'Enjoy the trip.'

'Thanks mate, you too,' the good wishes were reciprocated.

Bruce got to the World Trade Centre extremely early and although there were ferries leaving for Batam every twenty minutes he curbed his urgency and sat down. He told himself to be patient and wait for the 1115 departure otherwise the whole rendezvous could be stuffed up, which was the last thing he wanted.

He went for coffee and cake at the terminal Bun In the Oven opposite the ferry check-in desks and read the sports pages of *The Straits Times* four times as the hands on the large clock hanging from the roof moved slowly forward.

He finally checked in for his chosen departure an hour earlier than necessary – just to make sure it wasn't full. After what seemed like another age of just sitting watching people come and go, and having read the football, golf, tennis and cricket scores a dozen more times, he finally boarded the ferry. After almost an hour of gentle bobbing along on a busy waterway route, with many other ferries passing by heading in the opposite direction, his watery chariot finally nosed its way into the jetty on Batam island.

'*Welcome To Batam*' a rather tatty sign at the end of the short wooden landing stage read. He alighted, and walked rather slowly towards the terminal behind a few dozen or so fellow travellers. Immigration was quick and after a deep breath he walked outside to take stock of the waiting crowd and look for the welcoming colours.

There were far more people around than he had expected and he began to wonder where the QE2 had berthed. Initially he couldn't spot anyone in a red top and white skirt, though it was a difficult task given the size of the crowd. He slowly walked through the bunches of noisy welcomers, trying not to make it too obvious that he was carefully looking at the clothing of the ladies, fearing that he may be challenged because of his scrutiny of the innocents.

Suddenly he heard a distant cry of 'Big Boy,' and looking in the direction of its likely origins spotted not one but two smiling girls waving enthusiastically at him from across the dusty road. The 'two for the price of one' presentation took him by surprise and he wondered why he was getting a double welcome. He waved back and slowly made his way across the busy road towards them.

'Yati?' he asked, looking from one to the other questioningly.

'Me,' the girl on the left giggled, dipping her knees in a slow curtsy, no doubt in recognition of his regal heritage. She was wearing a blue blouse and black skirt.

'What happened to the white and red?' he asked as the other girl also curtsied. The question obviously flew over their heads as it went unanswered.

'Welcome to Batam, Big Boy,' Yati presented the official greeting, still giggling and curtsying once more. She had probably been practicing for weeks.

'Thank you,' he responded with a weak smile 'and you are?' he asked turning to the companion.

'Watti, your majesty,' she also dipped a knee.

Oh God, they think I'm the bloody Prince of Australia, he realised and felt he had better get his position in line to the throne correct in case asked later.

'Is my friend,' Yati explained.

'Well, I more or less thought so.'

'You hab nice flight, Your Kingness?' Yati asked, another knee-bend following. The concern about his travel experience was touching to say the least.

'Yes, fine, a little bumpy on the landing but OK.'

'Where you want go to bed?' she was getting down to the point rather quickly.

'Well I don't know really, I've never been here before. Where do you want to go?' he was keeping the fact that he had made a hotel reservation under wraps for the time being.

'Yes,' Watti answered for the two.

Right, he thought, quickly moving to Plan B - treat it all as an experience. A smiling young man then joined the expanding welcoming committee.

'Aba kabar?' The newcomer asked of the royal Aussie as he thrust out a hand and bowed. Bruce suddenly realised that he understood the question, which enquired how he was.

'Fine thanks. Bagus,' he answered, feeling rather smug enough to answer in Indonesian with the word for 'good'. Then he realised that he wasn't really fine at all or very good either if the truth were known. All three of his new-found friends smiled at his linguistic abilities.

'OK we go to hotel,' the young man announced 'which one you book?'

'Just a minute, who exactly are you?' Bruce wanted clarification as to who was who in the royal welcoming retinue, wondering how many more would soon take their places in the official line-up.

'I her father,' the lad smiled, pointing at Yati.

'Oh Christ,' he called for heavenly help 'how can you be, you look younger than her.'

'Yes, he our brother,' Watti interjected, dipping the left knee again and confirming the relative claim.

'And you?' he asked of Yati.

'She is my mother and he also my brother,' she smiled at the family members surrounding her.

'But he just said he was your father.'

'He in village now. Cannot come to meet you just now, will see you later for a drink - mate.'

She again smiled as both girls seemed to think they had fully explained the family tree and made everything crystal clear in terms of the bus-load of relatives which would turn up some time later. It was all getting a bit too much for the Royal Surfer .

'Now wait a minute, just what is going on Watti?' he asked of the girl who seemed to speak the most English 'Who exactly are you, who is he, and why are you both here when I am supposed to be meeting Yati – alone?' The question was put to the court of appeal as he pleaded for an explanation.

'You see Mr. Big Boy, Your Princeness,' she dipped a knee in respect. The use of his supposedly-secret internet call-sign plus the added mention of his royal position caused mounting concern. Though a passing couple who heard it looked at him with certain respect and gave him a smile which caused him to respond with his own rather regal wave.

Watti continued 'Yati not so good on e-mail, so I help her with Indonesian-English dictionary, together with our friend who not here just yet. She come soon,' she smiled at the revelation that there would soon be yet another in the official party.

Oh dear God, another one, soon to be seen, he thought, feeling rather dizzy from it all.

She went on 'Our friend help with Yati messages to you, in return for free cans of pineapple chunks,' she winked at him knowingly 'anyway where you put Nobby – I come to see him, and his nuts. Is nice no? How many he bring?'

Now he realised why there were two of them.

'Nobby is a nut, and so am I, I think. It's confusing for me as to who's who around here. So where is the third person, our mystery writer, then?'

'She join us later for lunch, is working just now.'

'Then who exactly is this fellow?' he pointed to the male.

'He our uncle-aunt.'

Bruce looked at her non-plussed 'I mean brother, and he take us to hotel. Is OK?'

'Well I don't want to stand here all day so we may as well go somewhere, but no it's not OK with me.' His displeasure was displayed, whether or not it was understood was another thing.

He passed the young man his hotel confirmation slip as he'd received via the Internet and wondered what the sane people in the world were doing this day.

'Is OK - good,' the lad declared after checking the details and they trooped off to a clapped-out car nearby. In an attempt to find out how much English she actually knew Bruce sat next to Yati and tried some of his previously rehearsed 'Chatty Yati' lines on her.

When questions as to where she originally came from and how long she'd worked in Batam produced answers relating to the weather and the price of a can of pineapple chunks he decided to close the interrogation.

Some 20 minutes later the car pulled up at the Batam Paradiz Hotel & Towers. It was probably the best one star hotel on the street by the look of it, Bruce decided, as all four of them entered the dark and rather dismal lobby.

His three companions ushered him towards the Reception Desk announcing the arrival of 'Mr. Big Boy' from Australia to the staff member who stirred rather slowly without showing much interest in the name and without any curtsy.

'How long you stay?'

'Well, as per the confirmation here,' he pointed at the printout 'One night – perhaps,' adding 'maybe,' and leaving the final answer open.

'No booking but is OK, we no full,' came the response which he received with surprise as he had the confirmation there.

'OK you room 629, have a nice time – Mr. Big Boy,' she smiled before adding 'I pinish at four.'

'Do you. Well go straight home, take your mum some nice fish and chips for her dinner and don't talk to any strangers on the way.' His minders ushered him into the lift and all four rose skywards like one of Yati's night-school rockets, some perhaps more ready for take off than others.

Room 629 was at the far end on the top floor and as the young man opened the door all three Batam residents rushed excitedly into the room. They were giggling happily with an adrenaline rush, racing around the room, switching the lights, television and radio on as they went. Then they started throwing themselves onto the large king-size bed like amateur bungee jumpers, rolling around the covers in unbound delight after landing head first.

Bruce stood in the doorway in total shock, a glazed look on his face. He was simply unable to enter the room, realising this wasn't what he had worked on for so many weeks.

'Is nice Big Boy, no?' Watti asked from beneath the bulging duvet.

'Come siddown,' a grinning Yati invited him from the centre of the cover. She was patting a part of the bed which sunk rather alarmingly, presumably from over use in that particular area.

The young fellow rolled off the right hand side, landing on the well-worn carpet, leaving enough room for a little one ...though perhaps not enough for a 'Big Boy.' He then rushed into the bathroom and seconds later running water and singing could be heard as he was seemingly trying the shower.

Bruce didn't move.

Finally clearing his thoughts he decided this couldn't continue, enough was enough. 'No,' he spoke quietly.

The giggling on the green and gold quilt stopped – maybe I should get one for Tyrone as a gift on the way out he thought, ever the considerate housemate even in the most worrying of situations – as did the singing from the bathroom. How the waterlogged lad had heard him, given the din he was making, was surprising, but things beyond the bathroom door were now also quiet.

'This is not right,' Bruce stated the case for clearer Internet communication.

They looked at him.

He went on slowly 'I came here to meet Yati – not Yati, Pattie, Tattie and half her family including father, grandfather, brother, mother, cat and canary...whichever the two of you may actually be. Plus other friends and passers-by who you say will be joining us before and after lunch. This is not what I expected - or wanted.' They looked slightly saddened but kept weakening smiles in place. 'Yati, you claimed to speak fluent English yet it is obvious that you could not have written any of those e-mails I received,' she continued to smile though the glow was leaving the grin somewhat.

'Yes, Your Majestic Kingdom Come,' she agreed and followed

the statement with another curtsy into the covers.

He responded automatically with the regal wave.

The lad came out of the bathroom drying his hair on a damp towel and stood listening.

'I have come all this way for what was supposed to be a quiet weekend with an Internet friend,' which was not really the case he thought to himself but carried on nevertheless 'not to spend two days with Yati and the village people.'

The responding silence bounced back at him and he realised that it was the first time all three of them had been quiet at the same time since he'd arrived.

'So, I think it's best if you all just go and let's say *Goodbye* here and now, before the situation gets any worse. Thank you very much for meeting me at the ferry, nice to see you and I wish you all the best for the future. Farewell.'

The message had been delivered by the Royal Male, his face stamped with frustration.

The three of them came together and slowly made their way towards the door, the final throw of the dice he had expected rolled his way.

'You want massage?' Yati asked, half smiling.

'No thanks.'

'You want sponsor me visit Australia, stay in your palace?' she was going for the royal approval stamp.

'No thanks.'

'You want lunch?' Watti wondered.

'No thanks.'

'Ten dollars,' the still unnamed fellow asked as he dropped his wet towel at Bruce's feet.

'For what – the massage or the lunch?'

'Ferry transfer.'

Bruce's face dropped but he felt it small payment for ending the experience. Opening his wallet he passed over a ten Singapore dollar note.

'U.S.' the young man continued the negotiations.

'No way. Now OUT!' he told him emphatically and pointed to the door.

He was greatly relieved to bolt it after all three had left. Though it was just after noon local time he let out a sigh of relief, flopped back on the bed and reached for a cold beer from the minibar. It was after three o'clock in Brizzie anyway.

He had once told himself he would never, ever, use hotel minibars as the prices were always ridiculously high. However, the current situation called for urgent calming actions and the beer in Batam was cheaper than in Singapore anyway.

He had fallen asleep after a couple of quick drinks and it was the ringing of the 'phone that woke him some time later. As he turned over to pick up the receiver he noticed the time on the bedside console was just after four.

'Hello,' he sleepily answered.

'Mr. Big Boy?'

'Yes,' he acknowledged his Internet call-sign automatically now.

'I am Eppi on Reception, I am free now so would you like me to visit you?'

'No thanks I'm going out.'

He dropped the 'phone back on its cradle and flopped back on the bed wondering exactly what he had got himself into. He promised himself never to use the term 'Big Boy' again — ever, ever, ever — and to be very careful as to what he got up to on the Internet in future. He also decided to abdicate from the Queensland royal family forthwith.

Yet again he felt the need for another calming ale and reached for the minibar once more, telling himself that he'd fast turn into an alcoholic if he stayed on this island much longer. He propped himself up against a couple of pillows, supped the calming liquid, checked the entrance door to make sure it was still latched, barred and bolted, that the barbed-wire fence was in place, and turned on the telly.

He settled back to watch the same news stories on both CNN and BBC World, the newsreaders accents being the only difference between the two, and wondered if it might ever be safe to venture outside again.

Chapter 9

Foreign Exchange

After Simon jumped off the Number 10 bus he followed Chauncy's map and instructions and in a couple of minutes was standing in front of an old four storey colonial building along a quiet road. He checked the number, 42, opened the gate and walked past the expansive lawn to the front entrance. A staircase took him to the second floor and his goal, Unit D.

He lifted the heavy brass knocker and dropped it to announce his arrival to those within. Within seconds the door was flung open by a Chauncy bedecked totally in black, the material of which seemed to have come from a dustbin-liner. His hair was hidden under a black scarf and he was barefooted.

'Dear Bois,' he exclaimed laughing excitedly as usual 'you found it! Well done – ten bonus points. Come in at once, if not sooner, and we shall take coffee on the verandah. Mmmmmmmm…'

He stepped back theatrically and ushered Simon into a spacious lounge to the right of which was a long balcony overlooking the large lawn. He pointed to the furniture on the balcony and suggested 'Do sit, make yourself at home and take the morning air while I fix the coffee.'

Simon wandered over though remained standing to absorb the view of the lush lawn as well as the airy feeling of the place. Two Persian cats watched his approach from their obviously comfortable position on one of the chairs, he wondered which was Originality and which Inspiration.

Chauncy reappeared 'I know, isn't it SUper!' he gushed as he fiddled and faffed about with the two steaming mugs of coffee. He plonked the drinks on the glass top of a small wicker table in the middle of the balcony and gestured for Simon to take a seat.

'Do sit, make yourself at home. Don't worry about the man-eating tigers, they've been fed this morning. One had the gardener, the other the milkman.' He made faces at the two Persians, who completely ignored him, and sat on the settee. Simon took the remaining chair.

'Now then, I know you want to get on your way – can't think why…mmmmmm,' he winked and nodded knowingly at the cats 'anyway you don't have to linger here, and I of course have to be flat on my back somewhere down the back of Boat Quay. very soon Imagine! And it's not even dark… Mmmmmmm….' the thought consumed him.

'So, we shall plan to leave here around nine, my pick-up is coming about then anyway, so let's just sit back and relax and have nice chats for a little while.' Their easy discussion meandered into various areas and Simon finally brought the subject round to the Desert Island prize.

'Thought you'd never ask,' Chauncy declared 'well as far as I'm concerned I am the prize…it's just that your friend Bertie…'

'Bruce.'

'Whatever.'

'Says that the entry form claiming me as the prize – can you imagine, I am SO sought after,' he squirmed with delight 'did not carry the name of the entrant. So, until that person comes forward I cannot be 'claimed' as it were. It's rather little like spending the rest of your life in a Left Luggage locker waiting to see who turns up with the key.'

He looked somewhat sad at the situation 'Don't suppose you have any idea who it could be?' he asked both pointedly and hope-fully. Chauncy sipped his coffee while his eyes looked for a hint of tropical desire from his visitor. Simon gazed blankly back at him from behind his white *Sadlers Wells Thermal Tutu Tour - Antarctica 1996* mug. He smiled inside but answered with a straight face.

'Not the foggiest, I didn't even enter, though I know many who did. So now I take it you are designing OWNER WANTED posters to place around school featuring a picture of a small, sandy, Heineken beer bottle?'

'Exactly,' Chauncy slapped his knees in agreement, causing the two cats to leap in the air in shock and shuffle off towards the kitchen.

There was a honk from the downstairs driveway. Simon looked at his watch as Chauncy shot up, hung over the balcony railing and waved to the driver 'Hiiiiiiii......just coming,' he gasped in delight as they prepared to leave.

'OK dear bois, here are the keys. Hector knows you are taking him out – I told him – so no need for formal introductions. And off we all go then...Mmmmmmmmm. Just leave him where you found him on your return and, if I'm not here, slip the keys in the letterbox downstairs and all will be well.'

Having closed all doors and windows they made their way downstairs to where a young Chinese fellow was waiting. He wore a collarless red shirt, baggy white shorts and blue plastic sandals. 'Hiiiiiiiii... Eesaw,' Chauncy gushed 'meet my friend Simon.' He introduced them dramatically, grinning excitedly and advising 'Eesaw is from the bar I am painting and is my designated – and dedicated – assistant for the weekend,' he laughed rather hysterically.

'OK, all ready? Let's go then,' and each went their own way across the gravel drive. Chauncy waved farewell to Simon, mouthing 'Good luck,' and winking knowingly as both cars eased their way into the morning traffic.

Simon took things slowly along the busy roads as Singapore drivers seemed hell bent on beating each other, and him, to corners, crossroads, turnings and traffic lights.

He arrived at the selected rendezvous point some twenty minutes later miraculously still in one piece. The arrangement to meet

Siew Moi at this location was because it was the easiest point to get to from Chauncy's flat which didn't involve expressways and roundabouts.

Simon was praying to the God Of All Drivers Of Unfamiliar Cars that she'd be standing where she said she'd be and that he wouldn't have to take another spin around the block. She was there and he thanked the God of Open Roads & Green Traffic Lights as he pulled into a 'No Parking' spot. She hopped into the old car with a warm smile and small overnight bag.

The chat was easy as she guided him along busy roads to the Ayer Rajah Expressway, a major road which would take them directly to the Second Link. A smooth half an hour later and they were in Malaysia – the weekend had really begun.

Hector purred along and showed no signs of any overheating, fatigue or burnout. Simon nursed him gently with no excessive demands or suggestions, just a few words of encouragement.

'It was very nice of Chauncy to lend us his car,' Siew Moi felt.

'Indeed,' he agreed 'though his main concern currently is to find out who chose him as their Desert Island Dream Man…and then backed out of the arrangement,' she had heard all about the episode in full detail shortly after it happened.

'Any ideas?'

'None. All very strange if you ask me.'

'Very,' she concurred.

They drove into the main street of Malacca just before one o'clock and slowly made their way to the Famous Melaka Dream Hotel. Simon had seen some blurb about the hotel on the Internet and as it was quite inexpensive and claimed to have a car park he'd chosen it for their little weekend tryst. They parked at the rear and entered via the car park door. There were a few people in the small lobby and Siew Moi sat on one of the rattan chairs while Simon went to Reception and registered.

He walked towards her a few minutes later and signalled for

her to follow him to the lift. The hotel only had 30 rooms and they were on the fifth floor in room 525. Turning left out of the clunking, lurching, old lift they found their room three doors down on the right. On entering it turned out to be very small – the brochure Siew Moi had picked up downstairs described the rooms as 'cozy' … hotel-speak for tiny.

It had a direct view of the main road and if one stood on a ladder, opened the window, hung out and grasped the gutter then turned to the right a strained sighting of the river could be made, endorsing the 'river glimpses' claim of the brochure. Just.

Simon was rather nervous about things and having dropped his overnight bag by the double bed asked 'Would you like to go for lunch or…em…well… ' the question trailed away as she came to him.

'I'd rather have room service actually, starting with you.'

He was both surprised and relieved at the direct invitation as he had been imagining how to play this moment since she had agreed to the trip. Siew Moi reached out to unbutton his casual shirt after which matters moved forward rather quickly as a hurried flurry of hands assisted the other remove unnecessary garments.

'Close the curtains,' she whispered and as he turned to do so she disappeared into the bathroom.

The room was dark when she returned and it was then his turn to use the facilities, checking that the entrance door was locked as he did so. When he returned she was under the cool white sheet waiting for him. He moved round to the far side of the bed, lifted the sheet and slipped slowly in to join her.

Their urgency and passion was total as each explored the other's body to the full, abandoning hesitancy, seeking perfect physical communication. No words were spoken, none were needed, as they touched and explored the other completely and without any hindrance.

The sheet was soon abandoned as the duo writhed around the

bed in various positions. Mouths, lips, tongues, teeth and fingers sought out sensitive spots and maximum responses, their commitment complete. He took her with a force that was at the same time both gentle and strong as she encouraged him with hands and legs intertwined around his pounding body. She arched beneath him, thrusting herself back at him as his urgency increased until they both reached their final fulfilment together. She clung to him and gasped his name as his body froze at the very moment of total expression.

When it was over they lay back, spent. There was silence, each with their own thoughts, each with their own feelings, each now within a new world. They fell asleep soon afterwards and when Simon awoke it was almost five. He could hear the shower running as he lazily stirred from what had been a very deep sleep.

She came out of the bathroom with a fluffy towel wrapped around her body, drying her hair with a smaller one.

'Nice sleep?'

'Yes, fine. You?'

'Great, just what I needed. Now are you getting up so we can explore the town and maybe have an early dinner – as I'm starving – or what? We missed lunch you know.' She was focusing on food as most Singaporeans do.

'I can't think why,' he commented with a deadpan face as he slid out of bed and made his way to the bathroom to shower and freshen up. As he passed her she slapped him on the backside and laughed.

'Careful,' he advised 'you don't know where that's been.'

'Actually I do.' She corrected him and moved off towards her overnight bag to seek out fresh clothes, flicking the retreating derriere with the end of the towel as she went.

Malacca is an old town with ornate Portuguese and Dutch period buildings from centuries past much in evidence. Numerous antique shops dotted the landscape and the duo meandered in and out of many checking out the offerings.

'Just looking,' they advised pleasant and not-too-pushy staff. Their wanderings finally brought them to a small Chinese restaurant not far from the river and though it was not quite seven o'clock they went in, enquiring if the 'Pink Lotus' was yet open. Assured that it was they took a small table by the window and watched the world of Malacca stroll by in the fading light of day.

Siew Moi did the ordering as Simon noticed there was no sweet and sour in the list of choices. He had a beer with the meal as he felt the need, though he was by now a lot more relaxed than when they had first arrived in town.

It was closing in on nine and starting to rain when they got back to the Famous Melaka Dream Hotel and Room 525. Each was ready for the other again and within seconds they were back in bed carrying on from where they left off just a few hours previous. Their lovemaking was much less urgent this time as they explored areas, angles and actions that had been missed during the rather hurried afternoon activities. They were both more comfortable and imaginative with each other and culminated matters twice before falling asleep as the corridor clock struck eleven.

Having watched four editions of CNN and BBC News and sampled a similar number of local Bintang beers, Bruce felt himself sufficiently charged to step outside again and discover the town for himself.

He showered then broke down the Batam Wall and hit the streets just after eight. The road outside the hotel was packed with motorbikes and old cars making their way slowly, noisily and dustily to who knew where. A number of touts smoking sweet-smelling cigarettes and wearing mock leather jackets – in this climate! – approached and offered a wide variety of services.

'You want ferry transfer? You want go nice bar? You want shopping tour? You want suit? You want box of peanuts? You want prawn

crackers? You want massage? You want pretty girl? You want pretty boy?' He declined all with a pleasant smile and dismissive wave before setting off on his exploration tour.

After half an hour of wandering he felt the need for a drink building up. The thought of a cold ale wouldn't be a bad idea at all, he told himself. The narrow street he was then on had a number of brightly-lit restaurants and bars any of which he considered as being worthy of his patronage.

One bar finally took his eye, the 'Jalan Bagus – Minum Bagus Bar.' Seeing as how he could translate the name *(Good Walk – Good Drink)* he felt a certain affinity with the place and decided to sample the inner offerings.

It was very dark inside and what light there was came mainly from strings of coloured lights around the bar and a few small spotlights hidden in the ceiling. Loud music filled the air, as did the now-familiar sweet smelling cigarette smoke.

He made his way to the bar through groups of animated and smoky Indonesians and asked for a beer. Settling onto a stool he took his time in getting adjusted to the dim light and taking in what the place had to offer.

A slim girl with long black hair cascading down her back moved in beside him, almost without him noticing.

'Hello, where you from?'

'Singapore,' he returned the smile.

'Cannot be, you not Chinese,' she questioned his answer.

'No I'm not, but I live in Singapore though I am Australian actually,' he ended her nationality torment.

'My friend live in Australia. Her name Miranda, you know her?'

'No, I don't think so, though I may have met one or two of her relatives at the ferry earlier today.'

'What your name?'

'Bruce, and you?'

'Tutti,'

'As in Tutti-Fruiti?' she nodded 'What a great name.'

'What you doing now?'

'Talking to you,'

'I mean what work you do?' she was now under the Careers heading.

'Oh, I teach,' he clarified 'and you?'

'I singer,'

'Oh really, a pop star eh? Are you going to sing here?'

'Sure, in ten minute, I sing every night.'

'Don't think I know that one, how high did it get on the charts?'

'Yes,' she told him.

'Very good. What do you sing?'

'Songs,'

'Right,' he took another sip of his beer.

'You have special request?' she asked her audience of one.

'Well not really, anything will do.'

'OK you buy me drink, I sing for you.'

'I thought you'd be signing for everyone here, not just me,' he claimed before giving in and asking what she'd like to drink.

'Vodka Cooler,' the answer came back faster than a Cossack dancers scissors kick. He ordered his singing companion one and another beer for himself. What she was served looked more like a grapefruit juice to him but he didn't say anything, concentrating instead on his Bintang beer.

True to her word and some ten minutes later she made her way towards the stage. Following a rousing introduction by a rather flashy compere, whose sequined jacket dazzled all before him, Tutti burst into the spotlight and was soon belting out a number of songs.

The music and vocal backing came from what he presumed was a karaoke set somewhere in a far corner, controlled by Mr. Flashy Jacket.

The songs were varied, her vocal range extensive and rather impressive he thought, especially on the low notes. Towards the end of the set she dedicated the next song to her friend *'Bernard, from Singapore but really Australia.'*

Shades of Chauncy he thought, wondering why his name was so difficult to remember by people in these parts. On the other hand maybe it was just immediately forgettable.

She waved excessively to him sitting at the bar beyond a sea of smoky tables packed with loud revellers. He waved back as everyone turned round to look at him. He wanted to die as she then blew him kisses and went into *'Nothing's Gonna Stop Us Now'*.

From doing what, he wondered.

Tyrone had finally arrived at the hotel rather late in the evening though Patong was still throbbing with life, as usual. Pui was sitting on a small chair in the Reception area of the Thai Magic Hotel as he walked in carrying a green and gold overnight bag.

They were both much relieved that the rendezvous had worked out exactly as planned. There had been no flight delays, no transfer problems, no mix-up with the hotel arrangement and so here they were. He kissed her on both cheeks and she returned the gesture.

'I have checked us in already using your name but they want to see your passport before they hand over the room key.' she told her Australian visitor. He tugged it out of the side pocket of the bag and passed it to her. She hurried off to the Reception Desk and had what was obviously a friendly chat with the girl on duty. A few minutes later and she was back 'All OK, she is my friend so we get upgraded room.'

'Honeymoon suite?' he asked with a straight face.

'No! Don't be so terrible. You!' she slapped his arm and feigned a look of shock as they made their way to the lift 'You so awful!' she laughed at his suggestion.

'You so wonderful,' he countered, slipping his arm around her smooth shoulders.

The hotel was at the northern end of Patong Beach and as they entered their room the full sweep of the bay with its curved strip of bright lights stretched before them through large open French-windows.

'Just look at that,' Tyrone gasped, dropping his bag by the wardrobe and moving onto the balcony to take it all in. Neither of them thought about turning the lights on.

Pui followed and put her arms around his waist 'Is beautiful?' she asked.

'Perfect,' he concurred 'you did well. I have missed you so,' he told the beautiful creature beside him.

'Me too.'

They came together in a deep and passionate kiss as hands and mouths expressed feelings and longings that had built up over the last three months which could never be put into words.

'Wait,' she told him.

'You will feel better after shower. You have had a long journey so better freshen up, only takes a few minutes.'

She was right of course and he rather reluctantly agreed. He asked 'You?' as he started removing his rather grubby clothing.

'I just had shower before I come to hotel, so am OK,' she smiled, adding 'I think.'

'Oh you are,' he confirmed 'quite OK,' as he ditched another of his yellow and green ensembles onto the cool tiled floor. When he returned, still drying his hair, she was already in bed. The only light coming into the room was from the outdoor display which was plenty enough and added a most romantic touch. A light breeze filled the room, gently stirring the white lace curtains at the side of the open windows.

A delicate orchid had been placed on each pillow to add a special Thai touch to their welcome, one was now tucked in Pui's hair. The shafts of light that fell across her face as she lay against the white pillow highlighted certain areas. Tyrone just stood there, totally captivated by the sheer beauty before him.

'What's wrong?' she queried, wondering why he was standing so still and making no movement to join her.

'Nothing. I just want to lock this moment away for all time.'

Her speaking had broken the spell and he dropped his towel before sliding under the crisp and welcoming sheet. Three months build up for both of them meant they were eager and absorbed with the immediate intention of releasing harnessed feelings. He was on top of her in seconds and within a few expressive moments their passion was fulfilled amidst whispered words.

She lay in his arms, her hair draped across the left side of his chest 'Do you want to go out for a drink?' she was wondering if he wanted to join the outside activity.

'No, I'm quite happy here,' he summed up the situation 'in fact I don't think we'll go out at all for the next two days.' She laughed happily and gently caressed his athletic body.

They were soon joined once more, this time the urgency was not so acute and the lovemaking easier and gentler – and perhaps even more enjoyable as they took things at a slower pace. As he finally drifted off to sleep Tyrone began to wonder where this would all lead.

By tennish Bruce was feeling great while for her part Tutti-Fruiti was feeling much of his body from the stool next to his. Her ministrations were most enjoyable in fact as she paid attention to legs, arms, shoulders and neck as she smiled and cooed to him. I could sit here all night soaking this up he told himself.

Talk between them had become less stilted as the evening wore on and he gathered a better understanding of what she had been trying to say, at least he thought he did. She told him her nick-name was *Sugar Plum Fairy* and asked what his was.

Somewhat slightly the worse for wear after quite a few more Bintang beers he told her he was known as *Big Boy*, adding that he was exactly that in certain parts. The wide-eyed reaction to which had been one of obvious interest as well as certain imagination and intent. 'Oh, nice,' she declared, suitably impressed.

Shortly afterwards Tutti suggested they move on to his hotel for a nightcap after her last set of numbers – which had him wondering for a moment if she was going off to play bingo for a while. It was at this point that he realised he didn't have a clue as to where he was or how to get back to the hotel anyway so could do with some help.

They left the bar just after eleven thirty, over the course of the evening they had become quite friendly and laughed easily at each others jokes. All in all things seemed to be turning out better than they had looked earlier on, he told himself.

'Do you have a minibar?' she asked as they entered and gazed into the crowded bar just off the hotel lobby.

'Yes,' he confirmed 'let's see what it has to offer.' They headed off towards his room. The small lamp on the bedside table was lit and the air-conditioning was on which made the place most welcoming.

Tutti immediately parked herself on the side of the bed and switched on the in-house music while Bruce opened a Vodka Cruiser and Bintang beer from the minibar.

He sat next to her, passed over the drink and they saluted each other as smiles were exchanged. Bottles were then placed on the side table which allowed hands to reach out and search the other body, clothes then began to be removed in an increasingly frantic manner.

'Wait,' she stopped him, saying she wanted to show him some of her special Oriental touches. She smiled alluringly and asked that he lay back on the bed so that she could disrobe him in her own way. He thought this a perfectly good idea and lay back with eyes closed as soft Balinese gamelan music filled the room from the in-house music console. Can't be so bad he told himself, things certainly seemed to be turning out for the better, after a bad start.

Her hands moved about him with obvious expertise, speedily

removing item after item. In a matter of moments he was completely naked. Her tongue then began to slowly lick him from top to toe. She moved downwards from his neck and all around his writhing body in an exploratory search of pastures previously unfamiliar. Bruce groaned in absolute delight.

After a few moments he opened his eyes and gestured that it was his turn to return the complement. She signalled *No,* whispering that she would take her own clothes off and that for now he should just close his eyes again and lie there until she told him to open them. He did as bid, lay back and allowed his imagination to run riot as he listened to the rustling of garments being tugged from this most alluring and exotic person.

For Yati read Tutti he thought as he felt her move back onto the bed, position over him and finally whisper 'OK Big Boy, take a good look,' He slowly opened his eyes and the first sight was of her passionate face leaning over him, burning fire in the eyes.

As he pushed himself upwards onto his elbows she swayed backwards onto her calves allowing his eyes to pass down the dark shimmering body. While they were meant to stop initially just below the collarbone there was no reason to do so in this case. So they continued downwards to finally focus on a bobbing thrusting brown weapon standing proud before him as Tutti swayed from side to side and offered him her full upright glory. Tutti was indeed a fruiti.

Bruce gasped in shock as he took in the sight of her – now his – thrusting pole which, he noticed, twitched rather cleverly in time to the Balinese music like a conductors baton. He gulped as his own previously upright stance began to subside, completely speechless.

'You like, Big Boy? Now we two Big Boys together eh?' Tutti asked huskily, slowly moving over him in full frontal attack mode.

'No, no, no,' he stammered, trying to think and sit up at the same time 'You've read me all wrong, I thought you were a girl.'

'That's OK, close your eyes and think same again if you like, is OK,' Tutti suggested 'then we have nice time,' and in so saying she threw herself on top of him.

The writhing around that followed was passionate on the one hand and traumatic on the other – depending on who one was listening to.

The assailant tried all he-she could to score a direct hit on his-her target while the victim tried all he could to escape the thrusts and grasps of his once desired, now unwanted admirer.

Tutti proved to be a great deal stronger than she'd looked and certainly gave as good as he-she got – or didn't get. The grabbing, stabbing and slapping became quite frantic, accompanied by screams and cries from the wrestling participants. So much so that the people in the next room hammered on the wall and yelled '*Quiet in there – or we'll call the police.*' Bruce prayed they would.

While one of the battling duo was yelling 'I want you Big Boy,' for all he-she was worth the other was responding 'But I don't want you!' with as much emphasis as his current shortage of breath allowed. After a particularly vigorous movement Bruce fell off the bed and continued rolling as Tutti dived after him, barely missing his-her target. As Tutti tried to re-group Bruce was at last able to stand and in so doing stuck his hand out, much like a policeman stopping traffic.

'Look, I am not like that. OK? So stop!' he gasped.

'Is OK, I told you. I am like that, so let's have some fun Mr. Big Boy, I also a nice Big Boy eh?' his admirer came towards him again, hips thrust forward.

'No. STOP!' Bruce ordered, voice rising, naked body crouching in a self-protective pose 'That's it. Enough. No more. You go home, I go back to Australia.'

'No ferries, too late, all gone,' he-she advised 'we may as well stay here and have some fun,' Tutti came at him again.

'No we may as well not. Stop! Now!' he realised he was yelling and tried to compose himself.

He took a deep breath and tried to look serious, though to be taken as such when standing naked in front of a predatory naked man probably diminished the desired effect he admitted to himself.

'Put your clothes back on and let's say *Goodbye*,' he requested – realising he kept using this word to most visitors to this room.

Tutti stopped the advance, pouted, gave a final baton wiggle in a last attempt to get a positive response before seeking final clarification 'You sure?'

'Yes. Get dressed.' He was upstanding again, well 98% of his body was. Only Tutti of the two of them remained erect in all parts.

'OK,' he-she shrugged, resigned finally to her fate it seemed, and started to dress.

Bruce breathed a sigh of relief and stood there trying to look serious. He was still naked but not moving to pick up any clothing as he wanted to make sure the full re-robing of his guest was fully carried out first.

She finally announced that all was back in place and with a swish of her hair, a pout of the full lips and a deep breath whispered demurely 'OK, it was nice. Thank you,' and swayed towards the door.

Bruce opened it to allow her departure, keeping his body behind the wood and out of view of anyone passing. She paused, looked at him through flashing black mascara eyes, grabbed him *downstairs* and sighed 'Now I know why they call you Big Boy,' and was gone with a departing wink. Out into the night to who knows where.

He closed the door, locked, latched, bolted and stuck a chair behind it, laid out the barbed wire fence again and returned rather unsteadily to the bed and a much-needed calming beer. Never again, he told himself for the second time this day, will he play on the Internet – you can never tell just who you're likely to meet, especially when using the call sign Big Boy.

The stay-at-home ladies quartet were rather peeved and somewhat jealous of their male companions weekend trysts. All except Cazza, that was, as she had the 'Blue Boy' lined up for a hot night of clubbing and dancing on the Saturday.

The hottest thing the three Sheilas had in mind was the chilli-crab they got stuck into at the Sin Hoi Sai 'drain view' restaurant down the road which they had all fallen for completely by now. Mindful of the 'missing out' air of her three companions Cazza had taken up a long-standing offer from her librarian colleague Madam Tan to join her for breakfast over a weekend. It was agreed that this would take place at a hawker centre near where Madam Tan lived on the Sunday morning – and that there would be four lady teachers in the party.

So it was that at close to nine on Sunday morning four ladies piled into a taxi and asked that they be taken to a certain block along Avenue 1 in Ang Mo Kio, one of the city's lively hinterland estates. Some fifteen minutes later they alighted at Block 410 and made their way towards the meeting point via a busy 'wet market' where meat, fish and fowl of seemingly every description were on offer.

'Howz about we take our own fresh chuck along?' Sheila Three asked the others as she took a close-up look at a rather agitated chicken twitching away in a cage.

'No we can't, leave it alone,' Cazza advised 'Madam Tan knows what food to order,' Moving on through the flowers and vegetables market next door they eventually arrived outside a doctor's surgery midway along a row of busy shops.

Cazza consulted a piece of paper she'd been taking directions from, looked at the sign on the wall and declared 'Nawaz Clinic, Great. We are here girls, got it right. This is where Madam Tan said to meet her around quarter past.'

'Need anything checking while we're waiting?' Sheila One asked 'Could always get a quick once-over from the doctor inside, I'm sure he's very good.'

'I'm beyond hope, sorry,' Sheila Three responded.

'Me too,' Two concurred, a full set of teeth to the fore.

'Ditto, sorry, we're all too far gone,' Cazza filled out the final answer sheet. The black plastic seats in the surgery holding-area thus missed out on four potential occupants.

While waiting for Madam Tan to appear they wandered around, checking out the shops. One, opposite the doctors, was selling animals and birds of all shapes, sizes and colours.

'Who's a pretty boy?' Sheila Two grinned a rather bright cocka-too sitting on an open perch. The bird ignored her completely and continued to dig for bugs deep within its feathers. 'Please yourself,' she told it.

Sheila One meanwhile was looking closely at a cage housing three rabbits. Cazza wandered over and commented 'Nice, aren't they?'

'Hmmmmm…' the ponderous response came back 'Reading from left to right I've named them Simon, Bruce and Tyrone …for obvious reasons.'

'But Tyrone isn't wearing his green and gold,' Sheila Three saw.

'No but by the look on their faces they're probably all getting what we're not – in whatever colour combinations you'd care to consider.'

'Day off,' Cazza suggested.

'For some,' Sheila One looked blankly at her slim companion who was today wearing her Sunday-best high cork shoes, black minipants and a skimpy white top. A white frangipani flower, with a touch of yellow, behind the left ear finished off the rather trendy presentation. The other three felt somewhat more matronly in their otherwise 'sensible Sunday' outfits of jeans or floppy shorts and baggy t-shirts.

'Hello Carol. Hello Sheilas,' the voice came from behind them and announced the arrival of Madam Tan. All four returned the greeting. She had a little boy of about ten with her 'This is my son

227

Alphonsus,' she beamed as the child smiled at the four ladies rather shyly.

'Great name,' Sheila Three said 'how'd you get such a posh name Alf?' having reduced the boy to mundane name ranks in seconds.

'Dunno,' he informed his questioner as they followed Madam Tan's lead towards the food stalls. The party was soon seated on a mixture of red plastic chairs and stools around a large grey-topped table. A large number of stalls lined the inner area of the food centre though the group sat outside to take the morning air.

Madam Tan ordered a variety of food which was steadily delivered by a number of assistants from different stalls, all yelling at others in Chinese as they came and went. The party got stuck into the many offerings in hungry delight. After they had cleared most dishes Madam Tan went off once again on a *jalan jalan* - Malay-speak for *walkabout* — with Alf in tow, to order a few more 'final' dishes despite her visitors claims to be full.

While they were away Sheila Three leant across the table and whispered 'Cazza, there a fellow sitting outside the bird shop behind you who seems to be behaving rather strangely.'

The Queenslander paused in mid-bite of a piece of kaya bread - toasted bread covered in a mixture of eggs and coconut milk — and looked at her in questioning alarm. The two other Sheilas looked in the direction indicated before nodding, wide eyed, in agreement.

'Turn around and tell me what you think he's doing. Do it slowly as you don't want to frighten him or the thing he has in his hands,' Sheila Three grinned.

The outdoor librarian did as instructed. A man sat outside the bird shop with a cockerel standing on his knee. He held the bird's chest with one hand and stroked its shiny feathers with the other, smiling happily at the passing parade of admirers as he did so. Cazza watched in wonder before turning back to the girls.

'The man obviously enjoys taking his cock out in public and stroking it for everyone to admire,' The four of them howled, enjoying every minute of their morning experience.

'God, breakfast and birdseed, what next!' Sheila Three thought about the options.

'I wonder how many times a week he does that,' Sheila One mused.

'And for such an appreciative audience,' Two added, molars chomping away happily.

'Are there any blue bits around the lower parts of the feathers?' Cazza asked, as she turned her attention back to the kaya bread. Her three companions looked at her wide-eyed.

'You mean like as in…K.C….and blue hair?' Sheila Two asked slowly.

'Exactly.'

'Blue? Down under?' Sheila One questioned.

Cazza smiled 'Mmmm hmmmm,' as she bit into the bread.

'He dyed himself blue – there!' Sheila Three gasped.

'Sure. Why not – he had some dye left over once he'd done his beautiful head of hair so got to work in other parts with it. Waste not, want not, as the saying goes. I think that's very creative and futuristic actually, and you know how fashion conscious and trendy he is.' Cazza presented the case for the 'blue in most parts' boy.

'Started a fashion trend I take it then?' Sheila One summised.

'Quite, all his friends apparently now do the same,' they looked at her aghast.

'In different colours though, they're not all blue,' she clarified over another crispy crust before turning around and glancing again at the subject of discussion once again, 'Nice one,' Sheila Two looked at her questioningly.

'The shine,'

'Oh, I see,'

After an hour or so of eating, sipping thick tea and coffee from chunky cups and chatting away merrily they were all done. Madam

229

Tan had been the perfect hostess and Alf the well-behaved and enjoyable companion.

'That was great,' they each gushed as they left the table and Madam Tan led them towards a taxi rank. They each kissed Madam Tan on the cheek and Sheila Three passed Alf a large box of Macadamia Nuts. 'For your lunch' she winked, and they were off.

The late morning and afternoon were spent on the island of Sentosa which took ten minutes to get to by ferry from the World Trade Centre and provided a pleasant, if rather crowded, change from the east coast beaches.

As they returned to the 'big island' around five o'clock and made their way slowly up the wooden planks of the Arrivals jetty Sheila Two looked over at a ferry docking close by and suddenly screamed out 'Brucie!!!!' causing startled responses all round.

Sure enough, making his way along an adjacent Batam Ferries Arrivals walkway was Bruce – alias Mr. Big Boy.

Welcoming waves and screams were despatched across the five yards or so of international water dividing them and although Bruce seemed happy to see them there was a certain air of hesitancy about him in returning their rather jollificacious shouts, thumbs-up, whistles and bawdy banter. Back inside the World Trade Centre they waited for him to clear Immigration and greeted him like a triumphant round-the-world single-handed sailor when he finally came out of Customs.

He seemed somewhat hesitant and evasive in answering the questions they threw at him as they made their way to a nearby bus-stop and a homeward-bound Number 10. After about half an hour or so of vague answering Sheila Three cottoned on to the fact that he was holding back certain information and summed up the situation as they settled upstairs on their bus.

'OK possum, yewz obviously not keen on telling us very much about your dirty weekend, which is fine,' she preened herself. The other girls looked at her in disagreement but she continued 'So, if that's what yewz want then that's OK. Right darls?' She sought supporting agreement from the other three, who nodded on cue, rather reluctantly. She now turned round fully in her seat to look him directly in the eye.

'Let it be stated though Mr. Brucie,' - at least she wasn't calling him Mr. Big Boy, he thought with certain relief - 'here and now. We will hound you until we eventually get the FULL story, including all the gory bits, out of you…even if it means pouring an eighteen gallon keg of Foster's down your gullet in one go to do so!' Three assistant barmaids nodded in full agreement.

He knew they would probably get it all out of him one day but as far as he was concerned he was currently in recovery mode from his weekend experiences and still a trauma case. Time would heal the wounds, he hoped.

They had been back at the house for about half an hour when Tyrone arrived in a taxi. The expected raucous reception greeted him and by eight o'clock all six of them were seated around the floor exchanging tales of their weekend experiences and taking in a fast-food dinner with the appropriate supporting wine and beer. In the overall Question & Answer session the girls were the Q's and the two lads the rather reluctant A's. Bruce wasn't saying much other than he'd had a 'nice time' and even that was somewhat hesitantly.

Tyrone was obviously now totally smitten, a fact endorsed by the Advanced Thai Phrase Book he now carried, the Basic version having been cast aside.

Simon returned Hector to Chauncy in one piece, which by the look of him was obviously not the state of the owner. The Artist was lying immobile on the floor as the young Chinese fellow Eesaw answered his knock and let Simon into the flat.

'What's the matter?' Simon asked at the sight of the prone body.

Said body was lying on a mattress with a red sheet over him. There was a cushion under his head and an ice-pack on the lower back.

'Dear bois, I am undone,' Chauncy wailed moving his head slightly to look at him 'I have been on my back all weekend – which some people would think of as heaven I know – but I am now suffering painful seizures in the lower area and therefore need to lie still as much as possible,' he groaned in support of the diagnosis.

'The wonderous Eesaw here, mixer of fine paints, expert washer of brushes and talented wine advisor six nights a week, has the task of turning me over every half hour and then walking up and down my spine to help ease the stiffness,' he gasped at the thought. His personal medical massage man smiled contentedly.

'I can tell you though that it is no fun and I shall more than likely be like this for days,' Chauncy groaned at the thought 'my public will miss me I know, but that is how it is in the world of art. We can only display our best on certain days.'

Another traumatic gasp followed. An alarm clock rang and Eesaw announced 'Time to roll over Chauncy,' and removed the ice pack from the back.

'Do you want me to leave?' Simon asked, not wishing to see a grown man cry or maybe spoil anything that might be about to take place.

'No, no, dear bois. Stay do. I just hope you have a strong stomach when confronted by pain at its peak,' he announced as Eesaw sat down next to him and slowly rolled him to the other side of the mattress. The rollover seemed to go quite smoothly though the body was obviously rather taught. Chauncy groaned and gasped as his masseur carried out the task.

After a certain amount of pulling, pushing and rolling back to the original position Eesaw was ready to get to work. He slowly removed the red sheet to expose a Chauncy sans clothing except for his emerald green and white lucky leprechaun underpants.

Eesaw wiped the soles of his feet on a damp towel and stepped aboard the lower back. His 'subject' gasped at the weight now on him and went into advanced groan mode as the boy moved his feet over the problem area.

'Are you sure this is OK for your body?' a tense Simon asked, worried about the overall effect Eesaw's actions were having. A stifled response came back to him

'Oh' (gasp) 'yes' (gasp) 'my' (gasp) 'chiropractor' (gasp) 'said' (gasp) 'it' (gasp) 'was' (gasp) 'just '(gasp) 'what' (gasp) 'I' (gasp) 'needed,' (ugh) Simon wasn't altogether convinced at the claim but left it at that.

'How long does he do this for?'

'Five' (gasp) 'minutes' (gasp),

'Have you done this before?' Simon questioned Eesaw.

'No, but I lead the Irish Country Dancing in the pub on Friday nights so am well qualified.'

Suit yourself, Simon thought, wondering why the lad stuck to his rather unusual name and hadn't changed it to Patrick, or Mick, or Seamus or Mary seeing as he worked in an Irish pub.

'OK Chauncy I'd better go, thank you muchly for the kind use of Hector, his is now fully filled and shouldn't need any attention for a while.' Referring to the fact that he'd topped the petrol tank up.

'Welcome' (gasp) 'dear' (gasp) 'bois' (double gasp). 'Any time'…..'ooohhhhh.'

Eesaw was now dancing up and down the spine — rather daintily, it had to be said.

His knee movements could though have been a little higher if he wanted to gain true Irish authenticity, Simon felt. After all, he had seen a performance of Riverdance and felt a little more knee lift was needed.

As expected, the welcoming committee gave him a hard time when he finally got home somewhat after nine. He was though in good spirits and readily joined in the banter and in handling the cunning interrogation tactics the girls employed.

Like the lady residents he was interested to know how both Bruce and Tyrone had gone on. Though their responses were fairly noncommittal he got the impression that Bruce was rather disappointed with his weekend but Tyrone had obviously had a great time.

As for his own adventure well he summed it up to the team as 'Bagus' - meaning Good in both Malay and Indonesian.

The use of the word caused a shiver to run through Bruce's body which he could not suppress. Everyone noticed his reaction and wondered why it happened.

Puzzled glances were exchanged around the drinks though no one said anything. Time, and Bruce, would tell.

Well maybe, perhaps.

Chapter 10

Visitors

In the seven months or so that Simon had been in Singapore contact with the family back in Perth had been maintained on a regular basis. This mainly took the form of telephone calls supported by the odd postcard of what he considered exotic tropical locations around Singapore.

As had been threatened when he'd left in January a family visit was now on the cards. His dad called to confirm their plans one Sunday evening towards the end of August.

'OK Simon, just calling to tell yewz that all is arranged and weez comin' up on Thursday 18 September for 'five nights, six days,' as the brochure says. We'll be staying at the Kung Fu Dragon Hotel which I am told is a five star place by the Singapore River. Weez in a family room which the travel agent here says will be big enough for us all – so the whole gang will be bunking in together.'

Simon shuddered at the thought.

'Great,' he smiled back into the 'phone 'I'll meet you at the airport,' after which his father repeated the flight number and its arrival time four times. He then made him read the details back 'Just to make sure you got them correct,' convinced it was so he continued 'Weez on one of these package things so yewz don't have to worry about us during the day as we have a tour included…and yewz got to work anyway.'

'Good thinking, though I am off on Saturday and Sunday.'

'Yewz need us to bring anything?'

'No,' he declined the offer, knowing they would arrive with a tonne of goodies anyway 'Just bring yourselves and that will be great.'

'Roighty oh, we'll do exactly that. See yews then,' the line was cut. Simon started to wonder what he could do with them as well as what he could arrange that would be different from any of the usual tour programmes.

He'd been seeing Siew Moi a few nights a week since their Malacca Escapade and things between them seemed to be going well. From time to time, usually at the weekend, they would stay in a small hotel for the night, she declining his invitation to overnight at the house. The lady was enrolled to assist with suggestions.

They discussed the exercise over coffee in a Bun In The Oven a few days later and he invited ideas as to what he could do with the family that would be different.

By the following week he had a tentative outline.

Day 1 - *Meet at the airport - Thursday night.*
Day 2 - *'Drain View' dinner at Sin Hoi Sai - Friday night.*
Day 3 - *Singapore River cruise & Sentosa Island – Saturday.*
Day 4 - *Sunday afternoon-evening – grand barbeque at the house.*
Day 5 - *Monday – free (he'd requested a day off school).*
Day 6 - *Tuesday – return to Oz, evening departure.*

He reckoned that after three days away from Perth they'd be longing for a steak so the barbie was to be the highlight event of the visit. The 'home team' readily agreed to assist with arrangements as well as food and drinks and in compiling a guest list.

The red-letter Thursday evening finally came around and Simon made his way to the airport on the Number 36 bus, arriving around nine. He had decided not to take Siew Moi as he wanted to save her appearance until dinner the next night and let them settle in first.

Flight SQ226 arrived a little earlier than its 2115 scheduled time and some fifteen minutes later the family appeared in the Baggage Claim area. He chuckled quietly when he noticed that his father was wearing a bushman's hat, complete with corks. His mirth turned to a quiet groan when he noticed that the other four members of the family were also wearing the same model hat, avec corks. *Here come the Aussies…*he thought…though you'd never really guess.

The visitors grabbed three luggage trolleys and made their way to Belt 36 to await the arrival of their baggage. Simon stood back somewhat from the waiting crowd, many of which were pressed up against the glass waving to friends and relatives. Though his party could not as yet see him he could see them quite clearly.

His next of kin kept looking towards the crowd in between checking baggage coming along the belt. The hope was that theirs hadn't gone to some distant destination and that they'd be left with just their current clothing, and hats, for the next few days.

It was Kevin, his younger brother, who finally spotted him and with great excitement reported the positive sighting to other family members. Before he knew it five furry baby dingoes were extracted from hand baggage and excitedly waved at him in front of a backdrop of swaying corks.

He smiled and waved back in acknowledgement, praying that they would remove their hats before coming out, their baggage having now made an appearance. His silent request was not granted as three well-stacked trolleys were finally pointed at the Exit doors and the party moved forward. The hats were still in place with corks swaying nicely in formation.

Their beaming faces turned left out of the sliding doors, shuffled excitedly along the short railed area and finally gathered around their long-lost relative 'Excitement' indicators on 'High'.

His mother was the first to grab him in a grip that would have won any world wrestling title. Attempting to kiss him on the cheek she found that the bobbing corks kept blocking her efforts. The one big smackeroo that finally managed to land did so with a cork centre that left him with a strange looking red branding mark on the right cheek for the next few hours.

'Howz yew doing darls?' she asked of her eldest offspring, any answer to which was impossible as she was hugging the breath out of him. Other family members were also demanding his direct attention.

Twin sisters Oona and Kate grabbed areas left vacant by his swooping mother while his father and brother took up positions on the outer layer of the rugby scrum. All five sets of corks were jangling happily in front of five wide smiles.

A hundred questions were fired at him as he grinned back at his own famous, and favourite, five. After the initial excitement had died down his father produced a folder and announced that they were to be met by someone from Famous Ever Wonder Tours who would transfer them to their hotel by minibus.

Managing to take his attention away from his first-born for a moment he spotted a fellow standing nearby holding a sign that read 'Family Skeer'.

'That's us,' he declared and went over to the man to announce their arrival. He returned with the news that they would be leaving for the hotel in ten minutes or so and that it was OK for Simon to travel on the minibus with them.

'Ridgie didge. She's apples,' he declared happily, corks shaking rather nicely.

Two other families travelled on the same minibus and after dropping them first it was about half past ten before they finally settled into their Family Room at the Kung Fu Dragon Hotel. The room had a great view of the Singapore River from its balcony, which looked as though it would be most pleasant to sit on during the day and watch the watery world go by. Not bad, thought Simon, as he took it all in, not bad at all.

It was then downstairs for a nightcap and another hour or so of happy family chatting. 'How was the flight?' he asked the obvious and mundane.

'Beauty Newk,' his mother confirmed 'and we had this beautiful stewardess looking after us. Wasn't she lovely Percy?' she sought his fatherly confirmation.

'Yes darls,' he agreed, adding 'and she had this badge on with all these strange words I didn't understand so I asked her, after she'd kindly brought me yet another beer, if they were the languages she spoke,' he sipped on his present beer at the mention of the amber brew before adding 'And she said no, it was her name.'

They all fell about laughing.

'S'right. He did too, daft bugger,' his mother screamed, still in her bushman's hat and with her miniature dingo in the centre of the drinks table. She obviously wanted there to be no doubt about where she was from in anybody's mind.

'Anyway she took a real fancy to me,' his father continued 'well it was my hat actually - but oi told her that oi couldn't give it her as it was a family heirloom like – from Woolworths. I did though say that she could jangle my corks any time she felt like it over the next few days.'

Simon's mother hit him on the arm in mock shock, though she too was laughing.

'So you got a Singapore girlfriend?' Kevin asked pointedly.

'That's for you to find out, cheeky face.'

'We want to get some silk and other material for dresses Simon, do you know where we should go?' Oona asked.

He hesitated before answering 'No I don't but I know someone who will know and they'd be delighted to take you, I'm sure.'

'Oh yeah! I wonder who that can be,' Kevin commented cheekily and received a belt round the ear for his trouble from his mother as twenty spinning corks dive-bombed him in a follow-up attack.

Simon went over his programme arrangements for them and all agreed that they were fine. They had a morning tour in the package, which was the next day, after which there was considerable time available to do as they wished.

As much as he would have liked to stay and continue the chat they all had things to do the next morning and it was getting late. Confirming that he'd pick them up after school he left them and headed home.

The visitors were up early for their 'City Tour' which was enjoyed immensely, especially the Botanical Gardens with the numerous different types of orchids. They got back to the hotel around lunchtime and after helpings of burgers and chips – very Asian they felt – spent the afternoon by the pool. September in Australia is rather cool so being able to soak in some sun in such a nice setting was just what they needed. All five of them sat poolside in their bushman's hats which kept the hot tropical sun at bay when it got rather strong.

Simon had said he'd come to the hotel around five. He hadn't mentioned that he would be bringing Siew Moi with him or that she would be joining them for a 'Drain View' dinner later, which was to be the surprise. They were sitting in the hotel lobby – skins glowing from the sun and no cork hats in sight – when Simon and Siew Moi arrived. Amidst great glee, fussing and talking he introduced the young lady to the fivesome.

'Everyone, this is Siew Moi who works in a rather nice bookshop which I frequent – every now and then.'

'Call me Perce, darls,' his father told her smilingly as they shook hands.

'And this is my wife, Simon's mother, Gladys. Commonly known as Glad-Wrap,' he added with a cheeky grin.

'At her best as a see-through item that sticks to everything but can't keep the sound out,' Kevin commented and received a whack around the ear for his trouble.

The boy's mouth dropped when Simon introduced him, having never been so close to such a stunning Asian girl before.

The twins were delighted to meet Siew Moi and immediately engaged in clothing talk. Never a quiet moment, Simon thought as he ushered them out of the hotel to the taxi rank by the main entrance.

The plan was that they first go to the Katong house for sundowners on the verandah and to also meet the other tenants. They took two taxis, Simon in one with Kevin and his parents, Siew Moi in the other with the two girls. When they arrived the three Sheilas were in residence as well as Tyrone – in patriotic attire, as usual.

Following hearty introductions, many 'G'days' and a quick tour of the house the group settled on the verandah for thirst-quenching drinks.

Simon had shipped in supplies to cover the events planned for the next few days and a few Singapore Slings, ice-cold beers, diet soft-drinks, multi-flavoured crisps and nuts were soon spread out along verandah tables as the party sat back in wicker armchairs and couches. Once comfortable, guests and residents got stuck into sharing a few yarns plus a few tinnies and tropical cocktails as daylight faded.

Pockets of chattering Aussies plus one smiling Singaporean were enjoying a great chin-wag when Bruce, Cazza and K. C. came down the path.

'Coooeeee,' Cazza greeted them happily, clinging tightly to her Blue Boy.

'G'day folks,' Bruce covered the crowd in two words as they climbed the steps.

Simon did the introductions and as everyone settled down again his father turned to him and glanced at K.C.

'What did you says his name was?'

'Kings Cross.'

A puzzled look came back at him followed by a 'Yewz joking.'

'No.'

'As in London railway station?' Perce sought out the location.

'No, as in Sydney suburb. He studied there.'

'Didn't study bloody hair dying by the look of him,' his father chuckled, taking another swig of icy cold beer.

241

'He's a computer programmer from a filthy rich family.'

'Looks like a really nice lad to me,' Perce said nodding knowingly and took another swig of his Anchor beer. He caught the Singaporean's eye and signalled Cheers down the verandah, K.C. smiled back happily, raising his own tinnie in salute.

'Thought so from the first moment I saw him,' he claimed 'wonder if he's got a brother or two available for our Oona and Kate. Check out 'ow much they're worth will yer?'

Kevin couldn't keep his eyes off Cazza who had quickly changed and was now in revealing casual wear. The fact that he was sitting opposite to where she was draped at K.C.'s feet gave him a birds-eye view of her major assets, as well as other tropical delights.

Glad had agreed that Kevin could have a Sling seeing as he was on holiday but was watching him as closely as a kookaburra clinging to a gum tree. Any sign of straying out of line and she'd be knocking him on the head.

Oona and Kate were both doing Fashion Design courses back in Perth so it was fairly predictable that they would be discussing clothing with Siew Moi and the other girls. Arrangements were being put together for the three of them to go on a special tour of what Siew Moi considered the most trendy shops and boutiques in town.

Neither of his parents could get their tongues around Siew Moi's name very easily so she quickly became Sue to both of them which was OK with everyone concerned.

'So yewz teach geography eh?' Glad asked Bruce.

'S'roite.'

'Well could I enrol Kevin in your class for some lessons in finding his way home on a Friday and Saturday night? He's supposed to be in by ten…and always turns up gone eleven, claiming he got lost,' she added 'little swine,' before knocking back her Singapore Sling at the thought.

By eight the little soiree was ending and Simon gathered his team together for the second part of the evening's activities.

'Anyone fancy joining us?' he asked of the teaching staff, who declined gracefully, leaving him to cope with the event single handedly, well almost.

Expressive farewells and 'See yewz Sunday afternoon,' messages were exchanged between guests and residents as the party left. Moments later the seven were travelling down Mountbatten Road on a Number 12 bus heading towards the outdoor rendezvous where strange and mysterious food awaited. Well, to the visitors that was, others were quite familiar with the offerings.

Simon had called the owner, Ah Khim, earlier and made a reservation, roadside table by request. As they walked back from the bus stop to a large round table with a 'Reserved' sign on it the good lady herself appeared in the doorway of the restaurant and signalled that the one they were heading for was indeed theirs.

As they took their seats the ever-ready Joe arrived with two large bottles of cold beer, part of the great silent service Simon thought. These were opened and poured into mugs over ice while the ladies settled on a mixture of Chinese tea, barley water and lemon drinks. Kevin was given a coke – Glad having declared that he had drunk enough Sling back at the house to float the Raffles Hotel.

Plastic-covered menus were passed around by an attentive Ah Bee, Ah Khim's sister, and food options were discussed. Siew Moi, as usual, was acting as translator, advisor, describer, suggestor and recommendor.

'Not quite the same as Freo Markets is it Glad?' Perce pondered, sitting back comfortably on his red plastic chair and comparing the scene to a setting in Fremantle, near where they lived.

'Oh I dunno, those over there seem to be enjoying their pie and sauce,' she claimed, looking towards a group two rows in from the kerb. Perce followed the gaze to take in a table top crammed full of chilli-crabs and various other exotic food.

'Quite,' he said, taking another swig of the beer. He wondered if she was being funny, had supped too many Singapore Slings or needed to get new glasses before they went back to Oz.

'There's a cat looking at me,' Kevin advised the table, pointing to a tabby cat sitting by the road giving him the *poor starving me* treatment.

'Let's take it with us,' Oona suggested as the animal brushed up against Kevin's legs.

'No way. You don't know what it's got,' Glad gave the verdict 'for all we know it could belong to the owner and if you took it you'd soon have this lot chasing you down the street throwing chopsticks after you.'

A wide variety of food began to steadily arrive and was eased into the centre of the table for consumption. They were passed bowls of steamed rice and it was then up to each of them to choose from the dishes as to what they would eat.

'Well this is very nice Simon,' his dad commented, chewing on a hot scallop 'plenty of fresh air, well mixed with flavoured exhaust fumes from the cars and buses going by. Very nice indeed.' Perce smiled and took in the overall dining activity which covered about twenty yards or so of the wide pavement.

'Best food in Singapore,' Siew Moi stated 'at least as far as we're concerned.' This was the first time she had referred to Simon and herself as a unit, a statement which Glad did not fail to notice.

'What's this?' Kate pointed to a steaming plate of delight that had just arrived.

'Sweet and Sour Pork,' Siew Moi advised.

'How do you know which is which?' Oona asked.

Siew Moi looked across the table at Simon wide eyed.

'Runs in the family,' he answered before going back to concentrate on the chicken in black-bean sauce that lay in the middle of the table.

'It was quite cold when we left home,' Perce told Simon.

'Well it would be I suppose, that time of year eh? You can keep it for me, I'd rather be warm.'

'Yes but four seasons are a nice change, darl,' his mother felt.

'Maybe but if I want to feel cold I can always sit in the fridge for half an hour.'

'Or maybe half a day if you get stuck to the ice-cube compartment and can't get out,' the cheeky Kevin chipped in.

'How old are you now?' Simon turned to his younger brother.

'Fifteen.'

'Well if you have any plans for being sixteen I suggest you keep it zipped.' Siew Moi looked at him in surprise as she'd never heard him make smart remarks to anyone.

'Aw mum…' the baby of the family appealed for senior help.

'Just behave,' his father separated the combatants 'we are on our holidays – and weez *Going to have a Good Time,* as agreed before we left. Right?' They all nodded 'Good. 'Cos if you can't behave you'll get this kipper round your ear,' he threatened Kevin, pointing to a black fish covered in chilli topping.

'Actually that's a stingray,' Simon said.

'Even better, this kid could do with a good sting on a regular basis.'

Kevin was most put out at the barrage coming his way and went into an immediate sulk. 'Oh come on darls,' his mother reached over and cuddled him 'they're only joking,' she told him as she tried to kiss him on the nearest cheek.

The reaction was the same as any boy of his age 'Aw mum, stop it,' the wriggling one appealed to be left alone, slipping off his plastic chair to join the cat beneath the table.

'What's this?' Kate asked Siew Moi, pointing to a plate of vegetables.

'Kai Lan,' she was told and none-the-wiser picked some up with her chopsticks, tasted it and nodded in approval.

Perce began to choke on something spicy, coughing and

spluttering as he tried to clear it. Glad stood up and belted him firmly on the back which seemed to do the trick.

'Whatever that was it was hotter than Cottesloe Beach in the middle of February darls,' he claimed, sucking in wind to cool the throat and dabbing his eyes at the same time. 'God, that was a hot one Glad.' She smiled in vacuum-packed sympathy.

Perce duly recovered enough to sample another 'small beer' which was actually a large one but qualified as such in descriptive terms as Simon was sharing. Kevin came up from his position under the table and was allowed half a glass of beer for behaving himself. Well, for ten minutes anyway. Glad wasn't happy at the alcoholic gesture but Perce declared it OK for a number of reasons. Firstly, Kevin wasn't driving that night and secondly it would also help his jet-lag…when Glad pointed out there was no time change between Perth and Singapore Perce just smiled and winked at her.

By ten they had eaten 'Enough to feed everyone on Rottnest Island for a month,' Perce declared. Simon settled the bill and everyone said their thanks to the smiling hosts, crossed the road and sought out taxis for the journey back to the hotel.

As Siew Moi was going for a train and there was a station close to their hotel she again hopped into a taxi with the girls.

Simon travelled a certain way down Mountbatten Road with the remainder of the group before leaving them, confirming that he'd see them at the hotel around eleven the next morning.

'How'd it go?' Bruce asked as he walked back into the house.

'Fine, I think.' he said 'Families, you know what they're like, can't hold back on the comments for long. I think I need a beer,' he wandered into the kitchen seeking out a nightcap 'Not on the computer tonight then?' he asked as he returned and flopped down on the settee.

'Nar, lost interest lately.'

'In the computer or in who was at the other end?' Simon went for the bulls-eye.

'Why do you say that?'

'Just a thought.'

Bruce was obviously rather uncomfortable with the questions and slowly stood up, finishing off his beer 'Well I'm off to bed then. Goodnight,' he headed towards the stairs.

As he disappeared Simon called after him 'Goodnight Big Boy.' The sound of footsteps stopped for a moment before he continued his climb.

Saturday activity went as arranged though this time Simon was on his own, Siew Moi electing to next appear at the Sunday barbeque – the big event.

'OK folks, we are now going to travel on a bum-boat which will take us down the Singapore River,' he advised the crew when they met at the hotel.

'A what?' Kate asked.

'A bum-boat.'

'So called because yewz all have to sit on yer bum for the whole time you're on it – I take it?' Perce asked.

'Well I don't think so, but don't honestly know so you could be right.' Number one son didn't know the origins of the name.

'Failed, minus five points,' Kevin chipped it, then ducked smartly to avoid a belt from big brother.

'These are the boats that used to bring the cargo up the river from ships standing off the island years ago, these days they are used for short ferry rides. It doesn't go that far but you'll enjoy it. So, if you're all ready - let's go, follow me please…' and in so saying they wandered out of the hotel and over to the jetty at Clarke Quay from where the wide low-in-the-water boats departed. All five visitors carried their bushman's hats as the day was hot and the khaki cover would protect heads from the blistering sun, the corks from any mischievous mosquitos.

It was only a few dollars each for the short ride down the river to the cluster of tall buildings on the edge of the business district which lay beyond their landing stage. Simon paid and they climbed aboard together with a few other visitors – many of them in bushman's hats. The travellers all nodded and waved their corks at each other in recognition of the common denominator.

'G'day!' greetings were exchanged between sailors and friendly conversations struck up. The usual questions regarding city of origin, length of stay and name of hotel were passed about as those in port and starboard positions became instant mates, wondering if Captain Cook had perhaps passed this way on his sail to Oz.

'Cheap at half the price,' Glad commented on the small charge as she settled onto a welcoming plank of dark wood.

They were soon chugging under ornate iron bridges, past picturesque riverbank buildings and finally across a wide stretch of the river to their landing point at the southern end of Boat Quay.

'Very nice son,' Perce commented as they climbed the steps 'didn't feel all that sick.'

'Yewz were only on it for five minutes, how could you feel sick?' Glad asked.

'Yewz knows very well that I am not a good sailor, which is why we decided to fly here,' he deftly adjusted his admirals hat, this one the model with corks on it. 'I just don't like the water Glad,' he emphasised 'even feel sea sick when I have a bath, which is why I don't have one all that often.'

'Smelly belly,' she admonished him, missing the fact that he was setting her up. Perhaps.

They wandered past gleaming skyscrapers and down busy Change Alley towards Clifford Pier from where they took a Number 10 bus. After soaking in the sights from the top deck they alighted at the World Trade Centre and made their way to the Domestic Ferries area for the short ride to Sentosa Island. The ferries were frequent and in minutes they were strolling down the wide arrivals jetty on the holiday island.

After lunch in an open air café offering a wide range of Western and Chinese food the six-some took up residence under swaying palms on a sandy beach and settled in for the afternoon. Simon, Kevin and the girls swam in the lagoon while the more elderly duo remained on the sand dozing the day away.

Six bright red faces walked back into their hotel around six that evening and, after everyone had taken a shower, had a few sundowners on the balcony followed by dinner in the hotel coffee shop. Simon hadn't planned any big event as tomorrow's extravaganza loomed close.

After a day in the sun they were all rather tired and when the hotel residents settled down to watch telly back upstairs Simon left them to it. He had given them instructions as to how to get to the house the next afternoon, as they insisted they would make their own way there. They also had emergency house and mobile phone numbers in case they got lost, kidnapped, raped or robbed…or all of the above.

'Only things we have worth stealing are the hats,' Perce revealed 'mind you they are rather special and valuable.' He was thinking about their $9.99 price tags in their local Woolies supermarket.

Sunday's guests had been asked to arrive from 4 o'clock onwards which gave Simon and the 'home team' much of the day to set up the barbeque, salad table, bread baskets, ice and bar. The general sprucing up of the garden and house were also attended to.

Half a dozen eskis packed with drinks and ice were positioned under the long catering table which had rows of plastic beakers as well as stacks of paper plates and knives and forks on top.

The team had agreed to share the duties of the day with Tyrone volunteering to run the barbeque as he claimed to be expertly skilled in burning things. A taxi pulled up at quarter past four and in came the Skeer visitors, all in bushman's hats, corks swaying jauntily as they walked. Perce carried a carton of beer – Aussie, of course – and Kevin and the girls had a number of supermarket bags under their arms full of crisps, nuts, soft drinks and the like.

'Been stocking up 'ave yewz?' Bruce asked Perce as he welcomed the arrivals.

'Aw yer know, just a few bits and pieces to help,' the dismissive response was given with a smile. 'Kevin take these beers inside and ask where they want them to go please.' He passed the carton of 24 'warmies' to his second son whose immediate task was to turn them into 'coldies' as soon as possible.

Whoops of welcoming delight from the three Sheilas were shared amongst their first guests as Glad and the girls exchanged kisses with the residents on the balcony. Kevin declined the welcoming pecks though his father didn't mind at all.

'Well this is just wonderful,' Glad declared 'aren't yewz all just bloody marvellous,' she repeated the last two words to herself before adding 'going to all this trouble just for us.' Glad wrapped herself round each Sheila and kissed them all again.

Simon had been inside the house checking on the steak and sausage supplies when they arrived but came out in a white chef's hat to say hello once he heard the verandah chatter.

'Just look at you,' his mother exclaimed 'be cooking at Government House soon in that posh hat, eh?'

'Well I think your hats will keep the flys away better than this one will,' he said as she laid a giant smackeroo on his left cheek, having lifted the cork-screen first this time.

Glad was obviously in advanced kissing mode and had better be watched, he felt.

Tyrone was caring for the barbeque area to the left of the house. Having lit the coals a short time earlier he was now watching carefully as the heat built up from beneath his own green and gold chef's hat. Bruce opened an eski and produced four icy cans of beer for the fellers, bottles of Singapore Slings for the ladies and a coke for Kevin. His protestations fell on deaf ears though his father did say he could have a beer later – if he behaved.

'Cooooeeee….' the cry came from over the front gate announcing the arrival of Cazza and K.C.

'Oh just look darls, it's Cazza and Mr. Harbour Bridge,' Glad advised Perce, responding with her own 'Cooooeeee darls.'

'Kings Cross,' Oona prompted quietly.

'What? This is not the time to suggest a game of Monopoly, child,' her mother looked rather puzzled. 'Weez here to be sociable,' she declared, smiling at everyone and taking another swig of the cold pink Sling she had in her hand.

'G'day's' were exchanged between everyone as Cazza and K.C. made their way to the verandah.

K.C. now had bright orange hair which stuck up rather alarmingly from somewhat excessive use of sticky gel. Perce honed in on him.

'There was another feller here the other day who looked like you but had different colour hair,' he smiled before asking 'Do you have a brother, or two perhaps?'

Cazza passed K.C. a beer and sat at his feet. 'Yes I do but that was actually me. I was blue then but last night I turned orange.'

'Something you ate?' the Aussie enquired.

'No, something I mixed,' K.C. grinned and sipped his beer as Sheila Two wondered if he was 'orange in all parts' now.

'Oh I see because I hear you're all filthy rich and was wondering if your blue brother was available whether or not he'd perhaps fancy meeting our Oona or Kate.'

Perce maintained a straight face and continued 'You see we could do with some rich relatives, actually,' he took a swig of his Anchor beer before looking back at K.C. questioningly.

Glad paled visibly at his utterances before moving in to rescue the situation 'Take no notice of him Mr. Bridge. He's kidding you, our Oona and Kate are not desperate…I mean…' she stopped herself 'Oh God what am I saying? For a feller I mean, and neither of them likes blue as a colour all that much anyway,' she assured him, looking over at the twins as she did so. One was in pale blue, the other in navy blue and white check 'Oh gizzanother drink Simon,' the lady surrendered to the confusion and flopped back into an easy chair.

Kevin was given the task of being disc-jockey and handling the music. Everyone felt this would keep him occupied and away from gazing pointedly at Cazza's skimpy attire which today matched K.C's in that her short shorts were white and the minimalist top bright orange. Eight inch orange cork shoes added to the creative, casual allure.

The front gate opened again and Siew Moi came in. She was wearing an calf length red silk cheongsam with a white and grey mountain and clouds motif, a red hibiscus was behind the left ear. Simon almost choked at the sight, she had never looked so stunning. He moved down from the verandah and greeted her with a kiss on both cheeks. Smiling with pride he steered her over to the family and housemates who welcomed her warmly.

'Kevin turn that bloody music DOWN will yewz, I can't hear myself think!' his father requested as some song blasted out at the gathering 'Otherwise you will be getting no bloody tucker.' The threat of cutting off his food supply was quite a good move.

The decibels diminished as the gate opened again and a high-pitched approaching 'Hiiiiiiiiiiiii…..' came their way.

It was Chauncy, all in black…with companion, all in white…they looked like they had just stepped off a chess board. The black wide-brimmed hat flapped like a bat on take-off as he approached the house. His beaming face glowed above a billowing black cape, black pantaloons, black socks and shoes. He was in his element.

'Hiiiiii……… Hiiiiiiii……… Hiiiiii………everyone,' grin, grin, grin. He passed around his greetings as he made his way up the path, followed by a young man in a white collarless shirt and white multi-pocketed long shorts. He wore white running shoes to perhaps assist in a quick escape if needed.

Chauncy carried a large box of biscuits, his companion a few bottles of wine.

Perce watched the arrival in stunned wonder 'Strewth! Who the bloody hell is this?' he asked no one in particular.

'This is Simon's best friend from school,' Sheila Three advised 'he's the art master.'

'Looks like the bloody undertaker in all that black,' a deadly thought indeed.

Simon moved to welcome the artist who gushed with delight and excitement at being invited to the auspicious event.

'Dear bois, so nice, what a SUPER house you all have,' he said, taking it all in as he twirled on the top step, looking like he could burst into *Hello Dolly* at any minute.

'Look here's some biscuits just in case you get peckish later on, and here's some wine in case you get thirsty in the next five minutes,' he laughed rather hysterically as he turned to take the bottles off his companion.

'And this,' …pause…'is Alexander,'…pause…'The Great! Mmmmmm…' he gushed as Simon shook hands with the young man in white.

'Alexander is a graphic artist and he and I met recently at an exhibition of paintings by a truly BRILLIANT fellow from Xian. We got to talking about sunsets, then dashed off to dash one off together and here we are now…a couple of hours to go and we'll have another one to work on…in some depth I trust!' he declared before asking 'Won't we?' of Alexander who smiled meekly.

Simon did the introductions as Chauncy and Alexander were passed glasses of wine by Siew Moi. When Chauncy saw who it was serving the wine his left hand shot to his mouth

'Oh my God,' he declared 'Siew Moi you look STUNNing!' he kissed her on both cheeks before introducing Alexander and turning to Simon 'She gets more beautiful by the day.'

'Does Alexander get greater by the day too?' Simon wondered, the reaction to which was a gasped 'Of course! Though some days are greater than others.'

'This is my mum and dad,' Simon informed the duo as they reached the far end of the verandah line-up.

'So nice to meet you,' Chauncy gushed, shaking hands effusively 'are you having a good time?'

'Yes we are thanks,' his mother answered for them both.

'Oh I'm glad,'

'No you're not, I'm Glad,' Simon's mother clarified.

'Yes, well so am I,'

'I thought your name was Chauncy.' Glad was getting puzzled.

'It is,'

'Then why are you saying it's Glad, when I'm Glad and you're Chauncy. Can't be two of us here surely, or do you have a middle name?'

Chauncy turned to Simon, took a hefty swig of the dry white and asked 'What is going on, am I missing something? Do tell.'

By this stage Simon and his father were trying not to laugh too much but an explanation was due 'My mum's name is Gladys — or Glad - that's what.'

'Oh I see,' Chauncy cottoned on 'well I'm glad to know that Glad,' he grinned and hit the vino again. Gushes were back in place 'And this is my chum Alexander from Toa Payoh – who is just Great.'

'In what way is he great?' Perce asked.

'Every,' Chauncy responded as Alexander's eyes popped out and he wished he had been called James. Having commended him on his attributes he deftly guided him away from the group, with a 'See you later,' to the visiting parents as he left them to their drinks. The duo moved over to the barbeque area with Chauncy greeting everyone like long lost friends. Bruce was in charge of the drinks table and was opening a few cans of beer as they arrived.

'Babylon! Hiiiiiiiii......'

'Bruce,'

'Whatever. Look how are you? Meet Alexander...who is just Grrrrreat...mmmmmm....' He wondered if he was overdoing the line a little. Still, it broke the ice, so why not.

'Welcome Alex,' Bruce greeted the younger man 'yewz want a beer?'

'No thanks Bertie we have our wine,' Chauncy smiled.

'Bruce,'

'Whatever,' Chauncy grinned with frenetic excitement 'by the way, any developments on the Desert Island Prize as yet?'

'Zero mate, looks like yewz had it. Wouldn't pack yer cozzie just yet if I were you,' Bruce tried to look forlorn, but failed.

'Oh,' Chauncy looked sad 'shame,' a wistful look crossed his face before he added 'wouldn't need them anyway, I'm a *natural swimmer,* if you get what I mean,' and winked at the waiter.

The front gate opened again and in strolled Matilda and Dot Com. Tyrone went forward to say Hello as well as to relieve them of a couple of bottles of wine and a small carton of Heineken. Another round of introductions were shared between those present and those newly arrived.

The two ladies were delighted to have been invited and made themselves at home immediately. As they were more the age of Simon's parents they rather naturally gravitated their way.

'So yewz Simon's two bosses eh?' Glad clarified their status.

'S'roite,' Matilda confirmed 'though we don't keep him in after school very often.'

'Trust he's behavin'?' Perce asked.

'Oh yes I think so, most of the week anyway,' Dot Com thought about it.

'That's OK then, otherwise I'd have to sort him out for yewz,' he winked at her.

They were joined by two of the Sheilas at which point Perce couldn't avoid claiming 'And here's a couple of really good looking Sheilas if ever I saw any, that's for sure,' a played-for-laughs line if ever there was one.

Kevin also appeared as he'd had enough of changing the music and had put on a long tape to allow him to make his escape and see if he could find more appealing interests.

'And this is Glad's last born, Kevin,' Perce advised the two senior ladies.

'And Perce's,' Glad confirmed.

'Well, can't always be sure can you?' the father of the clan pondered 'You haven't seen our postman have you? Well if you had you'd get my drift…' he nodded knowingly 'just ask this kid what his favourite hobby is…and see what he says. Go on Kev, what is it?'

'Stamp collecting,' the boy answered on cue.

'There you are then, see why I've got me doubts,' Perce summed up the situation.

Glad thumped him in the ribs 'Stop it Perce, these folks don't know you and may think you're being serious, so just stop it.'

'Can I have a beer dad?' Kevin asked from beneath his curtain of corks.

'Oh OK, seeing as you're on your holidays and you're not driving us back tonight,' he paused to allow Matilda to glance at Dot Com in somewhat surprise at his oft-used comment.

'I'll get you a small one if you get me some stamps out of yer pocket for these postcards I've been carrying round all day.' Glad wasn't amused.

'Let me get the drinks,' Sheila Three insisted and shortly thereafter returned with a tray full of delight. 'Here you are Glad, wrap your mitts around that,' she suggested, passing over a Sling. She paused for the 'Glad' and 'Wrap' to strike home between the head and deputy head who both smiled knowingly, wondering when the puns would cease.

By the time it was completely dark the barbeque was in full charcoaled glory. Tyrone was glowing from both the fire and flames of the Hawaiian torches which bracketed the centrepiece.

'Come and get it!' he announced, ringing a bell, and fifteen or so people made their way over to the Gastronomic Delight zone. To a suitable chorus of *oohhs* and *aahhhs* they helped themselves to the freshly cooked food and supporting salads that stretched out before them.

'Can I join yewz?' Percy asked Chauncy and companion as he arrived at their table with his well-stocked plate.

'Surely,' Chauncy gushed 'come and sit down, nice to see you again. So are you having a super visit?'

'Beaut,' Perce advised 'bloody marvellous. Love it, just love it.'

'Oh I'm glad,' Chauncy was delighted at the news.

'No your not, Glad's my wife and you don't look much like her,' Perce took a chunk out of a soft roll.

'Quite,' Chauncy agreed, in no mood for any more glad tidings. Changing direction he asked 'So when you're not on holiday in Singapore, what do you do in Australia?'

'I've been in television for years.'

Chauncy's eyes lit up, suitably impressed.

'Oh that's wonderful, do you have your own television show?'

'No, I have my own television shop.'

'Right,' Chauncy paused to take another swig of wine, sad at missing the chance to speak to a man of the plasma screen, thoughts of his own art series down-under dashed. 'So how's business?'

'OK. These days everyone wants the big flat ones.'

'I can fully understand that,' Chancy had certain images coming to mind as his mouth twitched to one side 'I prefer that type myself actually, but what about the television sets?'

Perce get stuck into his t-bone and winked knowingly at Alexander. A few hundred calories later he turned again to the

Singaporean 'So what do you do young man?'

'I'm a graphic artist.'

'Get a special price on pencils do you?'

'Er, well yes, I suppose the company does, never really thought about it.'

'Don't forget to help yourself to a bag of charcoal from the barbie before you go.'

'Yes it's always good for a still life,' Chauncy agreed.

'That's what we call our Kevin when he's told to do something. Just sits still every time, just refuses to budge, little swine.'

'We've been playing golf today actually,' Chauncy told Perce who looked at him with certain surprise 'well you know me, I always like to play around.'

Perce wasn't sure if he was just feeding him lines or really was a sporting fellow.

'Hole in one?'

'Every time. We actually had two brothers to caddie for us called Tee – so had our very own personalised tea caddys. We called one Lipton, the other Darjeeling.'

Perce wondered if he could take much more of this and knocked back his beer to help matters along.

There was no escaping Chauncy though 'Yesterday we went to see one of the oldest Chinese temples here, fascinating. Have you been to any?'

'Not yet, looks interesting though and any help from 'on high' with things is always welcome.'

'Indeed, you should go, one sees loads of people in the temples waving joss-sticks towards the deities,usually asking for lucky numbers and to win large monetary prizes.'

'Does that include you?' Perce was following the Chauncy betting trail.

'Well, I'm not that bothered really. Not chasing a fortune as such, though a few dollars now and then would be nice. I put my requests to the God of Small Change, so we shall see if I perhaps win a little on the numbers later today,' he grinned excessively.

Glad, meanwhile, had sat next to Siew Moi. She gently began asking some of the many questions she had filed in her head over the last couple of days 'Lovely dress Sue,' she smiled as a burnt banger slipped down the throat 'beautiful colour, such good taste.'

Siew Moi wasn't sure if she was referring to the dress or the sausage. 'Thanks Mrs. Skeer,' she smiled at the complement, red and gold streaks of light from the barbeque shooting across her shiny black hair.

'Glad darls,' Simon's mother prompted, though Aussie instant familiarity did not sit easily with the rather reserved Singapore girl . 'So how long have you known Simon?' the first question was tabled.

'Oh about six or so months. He dropped into our bookshop one day, which is how we met,' she had also answered the second question which Glad also mentally ticked off the list.

'Come over to the house quite often do you?' she moved on, getting down to the juicier bits – of both food and questions.

'Oh you know, every now and then. We like to eat at the restaurant up the road, as you know, and the garden here is so wonderful to have in high-rise Singapore. It's just so nice to come over and be amongst trees and flowers for a while.'

Fairly noncommittal was the heading to that answer Glad had decided, though the girl obviously knows her way around the gum trees. The Aussie interrogator dug a little deeper 'So have you been anywhere nice with Simon, other than here and the restaurant?'

Siew Moi had realised what was going on and decided to play along 'Well we did go to Malacca,'

'Where's that?' Glad had never heard of the place.

'It's an old port in Malaysia, a couple of hours drive away.'

'And was it nice?' Glad wrapped her hands tightly round her cold Sling.

'Wonderful…' Siew Moi flashed her eyes at the memory.

The visiting mother knocked back a large intake of the pink drink and gulped 'And did everyone who went like it?' she was fishing for numbers.

'Oh yes, very much,' Siew Moi just smiled.

'So how many went?' Glad could resist asking though tried to sound casual.

'Two.'

Glad choked on a sesame seed bun but recovered in time to down another Sling.

Dot Com and Matilda arrived at their table with plates piled high 'May we?'

'Surely, come an' sit down,' Glad was glad of a little diversion which would give her time to sift through the answers received so far and prepare a Mother's Report for Perce to examine later.

Paper plates with meats, salads and buns were placed around their table top with a couple of small bottles of cold Heineken in supporting roles.

'This is great,' Matilda grinned, buttering a roll, 'so how's the holiday going?'

'Oh I love it, we've never been here before and isn't it just so wonderful how so many people can speak English?'

'It's the official language,' Dot Com informed her.

'Yes I believe so but most of the time they speak something which all sounds a bit like English with a topping of chilli,' Glad gave her Outback linguistic opinion.

Matilda looked at Siew Moi 'What do you make of that?' she asked while adding a dollop of chilli sauce to the side of her plate.

'Well, that's absolutely right,' the Singaporean agreed with Glad 'you will hear people in the streets speaking either Mandarin or Chinese dialects to each other, moreso than English.'

'If you speak to them in English though most will answer you,' Dot Com had her two-bobs worth.

'Yes, well that's what we thought. Though some time I think we miss what they are actually saying,' Glad felt.

'It's the expressions that have a different meaning to what you're used to,' Matilda told her 'like if someone says *I'm going to keep this,*' you would think they mean they are going to hang on to it, what they really mean is that they are going to put it away.'

'Go on,' Glad was amazed 'Any more?'

'Well, if someone says *Would you like to follow me?*' what they are actually asking is would you to go with them…not give them a five minute start and then follow.

Glad was picking up English for the tropical non-English fast, or trying to, as she had another tipple of the juice.

'And when you speak to someone and ask a question, they will often respond with *Ah Why?*' Siew Moi took the lecturer's position 'but they don't mean *Why?*' as you mean it…what they really mean is *What?*"

'Stop – I'm confused,' Glad had lost the plot 'better just stick to good old Aussie for now, doncha reckon?' Another Sling was due, she felt.

'Do you have a job Mrs. Skeer?' Dot Com wondered.

'Yes darls, well part-time that is. I am the tea-lady down at the Fremantle Philharmonic. Love it,' she smiled at the thought 'all that beautiful music.'

'Do you play any instrument?' Matilda came in on a down beat movement.

'No, though I do sneak a go on the drums when the musicians have left which is great. Perce thinks I should develop my musical talents, though without giving up the tea job, says he'll get me an electric kettledrum for Christmas so I can do both.'

Dot Com and Matilda almost choked on their beers.

Turning to Siew Moi after her steak had diminished somewhat Glad shared a desire 'Now listen Sue, one thing I want to do when I am here is have my fortune told by one of these Chinese mystics or whatever you call them.' She smiled at the local lass 'And seeing as you live here I was wondering if you knew anyone I could go to for an in-depth reading?'

Siew Moi thought about it before answering 'Well I do know a lady but she doesn't speak English, which is OK as I could come with you and translate. It would have to be tomorrow though as I am on day-off and working on Tuesday.'

'That would be OK darls,' Glad advised 'weez free...if you wouldn't mind, of course.'

'Sure, no problem. Let me see if I can get the number and call her,' and in so doing she pulled a mobile phone from her bag and punched in a number. She spoke in Chinese for a few moments before making another call, turning to Glad she asked 'She has a cancellation, is eleven tomorrow morning OK?'

'Sure darls, perfect,' Glad was tickled pink, like her drink.

Siew Moi continued to talk in Chinese then asked 'How many people?'

'Oh just me and Perce I think. The kids can stay by the pool until we get back.'

The arrangement was confirmed 'Fixed,' Siew Moi smiled.

'Thanks darls,' Glad was glad that all was in place, now all she had to do was persuade Percy to have a reading. Looking at him in animated conversation with Chauncy she decided to wait until a few tinnies later before putting the suggestion his way.

'I'll tell Simon we four are going as he's taking tomorrow off as well,' Siew Moi told her 'we will need to leave your hotel about ten, if that's OK.'

'Great,' the motherly confirmation came back.

Matilda and Dot Com took careful note of all this for future fortune telling of their own, if needed.

Bruce wandered over to Simon with tinnie in hand, having just finished off a mountain of food 'Great tucker, wasn't it?'

'Superb,'

'Are they having a good time?' he looked at the Family Skeer spread out across the lawn.

'Terrific, loving it, but then they always enjoy themselves.'

'Good travellers,' Bruce thought out loud before asking 'theyz not going anywhere else then, just Singapore?' He fed Simon the opening line he'd been waiting for.

'That's right, just here. Nowhere like Batam. But then you'd know there was nowhere quite like Batam, wouldn't you?'

'What do you mean?' Bruce was being cautious whilst trying to probe.

'Well, Mr. Big Boy, maybe you should be telling me, not me you.'

'Why are you calling me Big Boy?'

'I take it that you are the one and only Big Bad Brucie, alias Mr. Big Boy, as per the telephone call I took the other day, when I had the afternoon free and was the only one at home. The description given by the lady caller fitted you perfectly. Though I wouldn't know about the minute – or maybe not so minute – details of course, Big Boy.'

Bruce looked both pale and worried 'You took a call for Big Boy here?'

Simon nodded.

'From Batam?'

He nodded again.

'Did they say who they were?'

'Well I think she said her name was Trudy, or something like that.'

Bruce paled even more and sat down at the nearest table.

'Oh no…I can't believe it…her name is actually Tutti…but how did she get my telephone number?' His can of beer was shaking.

'Well I thought you must have given it to her as she said she'd been with you in Batam the other week, and had such a wonderful time.'

'She told you that?'

'Well she said you'd been in the bar she sings at, that she went back to your hotel - and that her friend in the hotel had passed her your 'phone number in Singapore. Sounds quite cozy actually….'

'Oh God, yes…I mean, no…it wasn't…not at all,' he was now looking quite ill 'I signed the hotel register of course and wrote my contact details – for half of Batam to share it seems.' He groaned before continuing 'What did she want?'

'Well other than saying Hello Big Boy, she called to tell you that she now has a singing engagement on a cruise ship which will be in port here in a couple of weeks time and that she would love to see you.' Simon thought Bruce was going to faint. Instead he simply remained speechless 'Well you must have impressed her, and she you too I presume?'

Bruce held his head in his hands. After a moment he slowly clawed his way up for air from fingered depths and looked at Simon.

'No. She didn't bloody impress me because Tutti turned out to be a Fruiti.'

Simon looked rather puzzled.

'She's a feller, she's not a girl at all.'

'Oh God,' Simon gasped 'a drag queen.'

'A singing drag queen, with the hots for me,' Bruce wailed. 'Mr. Big Boy,'

'Not in her – his – company, I can assure you. Oh God what am I going to do if she turns up in Singapore?'

'Well I suppose you could always run away to sea – though maybe not, she might be the on-board entertainment.'

Bruce looked at him open-mouthed as the horror sunk in 'Does anyone else know about all this?' he was anticipating a domestic catastrophe.

'No, none of them. I thought you'd like to surprise them when she got here, and perhaps bring her round for a singsong. Old Outback favourites by the barbie and that kind of thing…you know.'

'Oh God. Don't!'

'And you're seriously telling me you didn't realise that she was a he?'

'No, I didn't. Honestly. Remember, the bar was very dark and I had quite a few drinks during the evening.'

'And you didn't notice anything about the voice when you were talking to her?'

'Not at all, perhaps a bit husky…but...'

'Not even when she sang?'

'Well it seemed quite normal. Though looking back perhaps when she did *Old Man River* there was a hint and maybe I should have picked it up, but by then I was well oiled. All that cheap beer you know.'

'And you went all that way to see her…' Simon mused.

'Well no,' Bruce looked even more embarrassed 'I actually went to meet someone else.'

It was now Simon's turn to become semi-speechless though he managed to ask wide-eyed 'And what happened to that one?'

'Well that one turned out to be two - both real girls though, plus a bloke.'

'Orgy time.'

Bruce shook his head 'No, crackpot time. So I ditched them not long after I got there and then met this Tutti in a bar I just wandered into that evening.'

'My goodness Mr. Big Boy, you certainly are popular among the folks on Batam. And does this Tutti know that you know that she's a he?'

'Of course – I've seen the evidence.'

'You have? And you really don't fancy her - him?' Simon asked with a straight face.

'No, of course not, and I told her – him – so.'

'And yet he still fancies you and is obviously chasing you?'

'Yes, so it seems. Some folk just don't give up.'

'Amazing. The price of popularity.'

'All I can say is you really must certainly have something big going for you, Mr. Big Boy,' he was having a great time winding him up 'can I ask did she manage to check out the reason for your other name?'

Bruce paled 'Well actually yes, but only when I still thought he was a she. When I saw the truth standing before me my display changed rapidly,' he sighed at the pain of reliving the memory. 'It wasn't a game of two-up (referring to the Australian stick game) any more, in fact it quickly became a case of one up, one down.'

'And two to play for,' Simon finished off the equation.

'Except that one of the two didn't – and doesn't - want to play any more,' he wailed into his beer.

'Well I guess we'll just have to see what happens when your ship comes in.'

'Maybe I can be at the airport.'

Chapter 11

Tomorrow's News

The barbeque finished just before midnight by which time everyone was in great spirits. The one exception, if any, was Bruce, though once he had decided to drown out his sorrows and get stuck into the coldies in a serious manner he was soon feeling better.

Sleep though came slowly and when it did he dreamt of hairy ladies standing over him, tearing his clothes off and beating him with microphones in the shape of the male 'member'.

Though somewhat hung over Simon managed to get to the hotel around ten the next morning. Siew Moi arrived just after him, no doubt feeling much better than he did. He reported that he had just spoken to the family on the house-phone and that all would be down in a few moments. The chosen party could then start their journey to the fortune teller…and let the future begin here and now. The doors to one of the four lifts opened and out the visiting five emerged.

'G'day, G'day, G'day, G'day, G'day,' each unit greeted the other and for the next few minutes the happenings of the previous evening were rekindled, reassessed, recounted, remembered and reappraised. The only thing that would take a while to evolve as far as Perce and Simon were concerned was their personal recovery, though neither was admitting the fact.

'What a bloody bonzer night it was,' Perce declared as four supporting nodding heads indicated agreement. 'Though Kevin has a hangover, he says.'

He looked at the fifteen year old and shook his head in mock sorrow 'I've told his mother time and again not to let him drink and what notice does she take of me? None at all, and now look at him,' He sighed with emphatic regret as Glad hit him in the arm and Kevin just grinned.

'OK folks,' Glad took control.

'These three are going to the pool,' she indicated the twins and Kevin, already bedecked in swimming attire 'while we are going off to see if we will become rich and famous in the near future.'

All grinned.

'Roight Perce?'

'Roight darls. But yewz can forget the famous part, just go for the rich bit.'

Glad continued with the programme notes 'And the girls tell me they're going shopping with you this afternoon Sue, is that correct darls?' she was sorting out the day's events for everyone.

'Yes, absolutely. So after we've done the readings we can come back here and Oona, Kate and I plan to head off around two o'clock.'

'Perfect,' the twins echoed.

'Roight oh then, we'll be off. No messing about at the pool now Kevin,'the warning was given 'and do whatever your sisters tell you. Just see you behave.' the boy nodded 'And if you want any drinks or food just sign for it.'

'Lead the way then Simon,' Perce instructed and in so doing the foursome headed out of the hotel while the remaining three headed for the deep end on the sixth floor.

There was an MRT train station not far from the hotel. After a brisk five minute walk and a couple of downward escalator rides they found themselves standing on a northbound platform awaiting the arrival of the train. Minutes later they were sitting on light green plastic seats along the side of a brightly lit carriage heading for futuristic revelations in air-conditioned comfort.

As the train gathered speed Glad turned to her son and asked

'Why are half the people sitting opposite asleep, and the other half talking on mobile phones?'

He laughed before answering 'You are observing two of the four favourite pastimes of Singaporeans. Which, in no particular order, are - talking on the 'phone, sleeping on buses or trains, shopping and eating.'

'Sounds OK to me,' Perce commented 'right up my street in fact that little lot.'

'How do they know when they are at their station though if they're asleep?' Glad now directed the questioning to Siew Moi.

'Built in radar, they just wake up.'

'Amazing,' Glad summed up the situation and thought she'd best sleep on it.

The visitors were surprised when the train came up above ground and wound its way northwards above busy roads and highways. They had thought of it as an underground system, not realising there were actually long stretches above ground. Half an hour later they alighted at Yishun MRT Station and followed Siew Moi's lead in making their way out of the busy station. They crossed the road to one of the Housing Development Board blocks nearby and Siew Moi stopped to check the number.

'Have you been to this lady before?' Glad asked.

'Yes, though a long time ago.'

'And was she any good?'

'I think so, quite accurate I believe, though I can't remember fully. My mother and my aunt come every Chinese New Year for a reading and they seem to think she's OK.' She smiled before adding 'We shall soon see, won't we?'

Siew Moi again consulted her notes as they entered the lift and headed up to the tenth floor. They then took the stairs down one level and turned right past potted plants along a narrow balcony to the apartment in question. Siew Moi asked them to remove their shoes as she knocked on the door which opened within seconds.

A lady in her mid thirties smiled at them as she spoke to Siew Moi in Chinese. She responded to their smiles by standing back and inviting them into the flat. A small temple stood on top of a red cupboard immediately inside the door, a square card table took centre stage, awaiting occupants. The table had a number of chairs at one end, a single seat at the other and two packs of well-worn cards in its centre.

The temple had a numerous statues of deities within its confines plus a lit candle floating in a bowl of thick temple oil in front of the central figure. Flowers, fruit and sweets covered the front. Smouldering joss-sticks with their grey smoke added to the decor.

'This is Da Jie, or to translate the name into English, *Big Sister*.' Siew Moi informed them, introducing the smiling lady.

'G'day darls,' Perce smiled back 'I'm Percival Constantinople Skeer from Aurstrarlia. Call me Perce,' he shook hands regally 'By way of a little bit of background can I mention that I am in business on my own as well as with my brother who is a draftsman, though I prefer Snakes & Ladders myself,' none of which was understood by the Chinese-speaking other party. He smiled, happy to be doing his bit for overseas Aussie relations, and sport overall.

'This here is my wife Gladys,' Glad smiled and shook hands 'and this is our wandering son Simon, about whom we have no idea what he's up to for most of the year. Which is probably a good thing.' Simon did as his mother had.

Da Jie greeted them with a 'Ni hao?'

'She is saying *hello* or *how are you?*' Siew Moi translated.

'Foine darls, weez bloody foine,' Perce answered for the family. 'OK, who wants to go first?'

'Go on mother, you get yer mitts on the table then,' Perce pushed Glad forward.

She sat opposite their hostess on a small plastic stool. Siew Moi sat next to her with Perce and Simon in the second row. Da Jie took hold of Glad's hands, palms up, looked at them and declared things acceptable.

'What's she doing that for?' Glad quietly asked Siew Moi.

'Lookin' to see if you washed them this morning,' Perce quickly answered.

'Not really,' Siew Moi explained 'she just wants to check that your hands are OK to handle the cards.'

All three visitors gave out an impressed 'Ooooooohhhh.'

Da Jie picked up one of the packs, shuffled it, placed it before her and asked that Glad cut the cards. She did as bid. Another shuffle followed and the cutting request repeated itself before Da Jie spread the cards and invited Glad to choose one. *Big Sister* placed the card on top of the pack and shuffled once more. She then dealt out four rows of nine cards, face up, and studied them carefully.

Siew Moi sat close to Glad for translation purposes. She held a pen and notebook to record what was said for later reference and review.

Da Jie started speaking in Mandarin, directing her comments to Siew Moi 'She says you have a strong connection to the number six.'

Glad thought about the claim before answering 'No, not that I know of, I only have four kids.'

'That's what yewz tell us…could be that bloody postman's been delivering his special packages again,' Perce chipped in and received a belt from the front row for his wicked thoughts.

The Chinese ladies spoke again at some length. Da Jie looked at the cards once more before repeating the statement.

Glad's response was the same, an emphatic 'No,'. They sat in silence as everyone pondered the connection, including those in the back stalls. From the second row Perce spoke up.

'Yes you do. Course you do.'

'How do I? I can't see any six in my life.'

'She said six not sex,' Perce clarified for his listeners.

271

'None of that either,' Glad confirmed. Perce ignored her and went on with his rather deep theory.

'Well weez from Aurstrarlia — the land 'down under' — roight?' They nodded.

'And this lady lives in Singapore which is just north of the equator — roight?' more nods 'So when she sees a number six what she really sees for us Aussies is the same number but upside down. Get it?' Detective Perce had fathomed out the answer 'And what number house do we live in on Wombat Way mother?' he asked of his puzzled wife, who still wasn't entirely convinced.

'Nine.'

'Exactly. Which is yer Number 6, upside down…or to yewz…'down under.' And with the kids and us it totals 6 anyway…so she's right in both hemispheres ' He was triumphant, what a brainy fellow he truly was, he felt. 'Quite right, quite right,' he confirmed to the card lady giving her a wink and the thumbs up sign. *Big Sister* smiled back. 'Carry on darls, all correct so far.' The green light came back on as far as Perce was concerned.

'All correct? She's only said one thing,' Glad countered, still in need of certain convincing.

'I know that, but it's right. So move on darls.'

More chat followed between Da Jie and Siew Moi.

'She says you are under the influence of Mars.'

'Actually she prefers Kit Kat.'

Glad thumped him again. Siew Moi continued 'And that your planet will have Jupiter in line with The Plough at the end of the ninth moon, which is in early November.'

'Which means what?' Glad asked.

'That you should clean up the bloody back garden for a change,' She again hit out backwards.

'That this will be a likely time for you to come into a lot of money,' Siew Moi answered the original question. The three Aussies moved forward at the revelation, wide eyed.

'What kind of money?' Glad asked.

'What do you mean *What kind of money?* Perce asked 'Any kind of bloody money will do woman – as long as there's a lot of it. Any currency is foine darls,' he confirmed across the table.

Siew Moi and Da Jie spoke again while the latter moved a few cards about the table before answering.

'She says she sees a lot of horses.'

'November, horses…??? I really don't know,' Glad wasn't very clear.

'It's the bloody Melbourne Cup in November. That's it,' Sherlock Perce again solved the mystery 'Youz obviously gonna back the winner, and maybe the quinella, and the bloody trifecta too darls, and weez gonna be rich.' He nearly fell off his stool with excitement.

'Oooohhh, maybe you're right. Maybe. Fancy that,' Glad whispered, imagining herself in jockey's silks collecting bags of money from the local bookie and going home in her own personalised security van.

Simon spoke for the first time 'Will the lady give us the numbers of the horses she should back?'

Siew Moi put the question and answered 'No, she says your mum already has them within her and that they will all come out correctly on the day,' The family grinned in full anticipation before urging that the reading continue over a few more furlongs.

Da Jie invited Glad to have another shuffle of the cards. All attendees sat back to re-group somewhat, calm down and think about racehorses and winning posts. They agreed to rename their cat Flemington after the Melbourne Cup track – never having been very keen on Rover anyway. Rather basic they felt, and had wanted a dog anyway.

For the next reading Da Jie dealt the cards in a circle before speaking to Siew Moi 'Did you know your element is Iron?'

'No.'

'Da Jie says you should make better use of it.'

'What do you think that means?' Glad asked.

'It means you should iron my bloody shirts more often, that's what,' Perce received another backhander.

'She says your yin and yang are not balanced and you need to take in more Chi, or energy flow.'

'Oh, fancy that. What's my yin and yang, will it itch when it rains?' Glad was rather worried.

'It's your inner being and how the opposite parts balance with each other in the body.'

'So I'm rather unbalanced?'

Siew Moi nodded.

'Runs in their family,' Perce claimed 'lots of nutters amongst her lot.'

Glad struck out again at her tormentor 'So I need what – more Chi?' Siew Moi nodded 'And how do I get a packet? Do they sell it in Woolies here?'

'No, you can't buy it. What you can do is go for deep breathing exercises or take brisk walks,' Glad thought about her options 'Don't worry, we'll discuss it later.'

Da Jie sat back, scooped the cards into the pack and announced that the reading was over. The travelling punters smiled as Glad and Perce changed places.

Big Sister checked his palms and invited him to cut the cards twice. Four lines of nine cards were again dealt out across the table and the lady reader started speaking. From time to time she would glance at the altar above and to the right of her. The eyes would roll back in their sockets before she continued, a movement her Australian watchers observed with certain concern. Da Jie began speaking again.

'In the next month she says you should watch out for Pluto as there could be some problems for you.'

'That's next door's dog and the little bugger is always trying to bite me,' Perce told his listeners 'tell her thanks, and I'll certainly whack the feller where it matters next time he has a go at me.'

The two Singaporeans spoke to each other again..

'There is a lot of movement in the eleventh moon – January – and you will experience asteroid problems if you are not careful.'

'That's OK darls, I have pills and cream for them. She's right though, they can be painful if you don't watch it.'

Siew Moi continued 'Da Jie says you are going on a long journey very soon.'

'Well everyone knows that. Course we are – back to God's Own Country, Perth, Aurstrarlia. Tell the dear lady she should go there for a holiday some time, bloody marvellous, I'm sure she'd love it.'

The two Singaporeans spoke.

'She thanks you for the invitation to visit Perth but she already has two houses there and goes quite regularly actually.' Perce's mouth fell open as he took in *Big Sister's* Aussie property status.

He turned round to Glad and announced 'Better get a couple of packs of these cards before we leave mother as there's obviously a fortune to be made doing this. We'll set you up on our front lawn in Kevin's old tent and you can give readings for twenty five dollars a time – dead easy.'

Siew Moi went on 'She says she sees a big bird in the sky.'

'That'll be my homing pigeon, Gertrude, the pride and joy of my life. I spend all my time talking to her, when she's not away of course, and unlike Glad she doesn't usually talk back.'

His punishment came from behind this time. He beamed 'Very good – five bonus points. Thumbs up again.'

'Da Jie asks if you have trouble with your feet.'

'No,' he answered emphatically.

'I do,' Glad chipped in 'they stink most of the time. Drives me bloody mad.'

Siew Moi went on 'What about your right knee? Da Jie says there is a problem.'

Perce grimaced and clutched said knee 'Correct. It's an old war wound which gives me trouble in cold weather.'

'No it's not, it's from falling off the ladder when trying to clear out the gutter the other Sunday afternoon. Which wouldn't have happened if he hadn't been drinking earlier in the day with his mates down the pub. War wound indeed!'

Big Sister read again before speaking to Siew Moi.

'In the tenth moon you will have some luck as Uranus will be rising.'

Perce looked at Siew Moi 'Is she being funny?'

'No, why?' she was puzzled but moved on 'And she says someone will bring you money that you should invest.'

'On a horse?'

Siew Moi checked and shook her head before continuing 'She asks if you know someone with orange hair.'

'Yes, that lad Harbour Bridge who's doing a bit with the lass from Queensland, why?'

'Da Jie says you will be seeing a lot of them by the tenth moon – around Christmas time.'

Glad chipped in 'It's not the Harbour Bridge feller, it's that bloody barmaid Doris at the Koala Arms Pub near home with her dyed orange hair. Always has had the hots for him that one. Tart.' She glared at him 'So no egging her on at the Christmas Party this year, you hear!'

'Or Father Christmas won't be coming your way with any nice prezzies,' the previously silent Simon warned his father.

Da Jie again moved the cards about and spoke to Siew Moi 'She says you have to be careful as your magnetic field is out of balance and you could have problems.'

'I know it is darls. Before we moved into this house many years ago some drongo buried mouldy batteries down the bottom of the back garden and ever since then I've never been able to grow anything. Amy radishes and carrots simply refuse to come up. So tell her she's right and I promise to dig 'em up before spring.'

The reading ended, the cards were put away and though encouraged by all to have a reading Simon declined. They paid a small amount, shook hands with the good lady of mysterious talents, saying they would keep an eye open for her down Freo Markets, and headed back to the station.

Talk during the ride back to the hotel was unanimous that it had been a quite amazing experience and that they couldn't wait for the first Tuesday in November to come around – Melbourne Cup Day.

After a light lunch Siew Moi went shopping with the twins while Simon joined the remainder of his family by the pool. Having returned with dresses, skirts, blouses and reams of cloth following their expedition to numerous shops Oona and Kate were more than happy with their purchases. Each kept thanking Siew Moi profusely.

'You can call her Da Jie,' Simon told them.

'What does that mean?' Oona asked.

'Big Sister,' Simon, Glad and Perce answered in one voice.

Dinner was taken by the river and an early night was in order, some folks having to work the next day. Others had a flight home to think about.

The family did their own thing on Tuesday morning. Their flight back to Perth was just before nine in the evening so Simon and Siew Moi met them after work and following a farewell drink in the hotel they headed off to the airport around six o'clock.

After check-in Siew Moi presented Glad with a box of orchids as a parting gift and Kevin gave Siew Moi his bushman's hat which was indeed a sacrifice.

'Kevin this is so kind of you. Xie xie,' Siew Moi thanked him in Mandarin before kissing him on both cheeks. The reaction to which was an embarrassed wriggling, squirming and colouring of the cheeks.

Yet again Simon got the same hollow feeling in his stomach as departure time neared and told himself he would never again take part in an airport farewell. Came the moment though and via hugs, kisses and tears the family of five said goodbye to the remaining two. The twins were teary and even strongman Kevin proved to be not so strong in trying to present a cool farewell behind watery eyes.

'Thanks son, it was great, really great,' Perce hugged his number one son. 'Seez yews at Christmas,' he confirmed behind a quivering mouth that was trying hard to find a smile.

'Sure,.' Simon confirmed, himself holding back as best he could.

'And yewz too darls,' Perce reached out and hugged Siew Moi who was dabbing a few drops away. She nodded in silent agreement.

Glad was both smiling and crying 'Marvellous, just marvellous. Thanks to you both…and all your friends. Wonderf….' the word jammed in her throat as she hugged them both.

With cork hats in place – just four of the original five for the return journey – they made their way to the Immigration Desks. Baby dingoes were waved all the way from passport checks deep into the departure area beyond. And then they were gone.

'Phew,' Simon let out a deep breath 'I think I need a drink.'

'Me too,' Siew Moi took his hand and led him out of the terminal to a taxi stand.

They had dinner at the East Coast Seafood Centre in almost total silence, each filed with their own particular memories of the last few days. There was no need for words. Nothing needed to be said as they were both at complete ease in their own silence.

As they were leaving Siew Moi looked at him through still-damp eyes 'It was great you know, really great, every minute of it. You did them proud.'

Simon smiled and held her close, not wanting her to see his own tears.

Chapter 12

Hello – Goodbye

Simon walked up the verandah steps of the house rather wearily. He had been marking midterm test papers all afternoon and needed to relax tight neck and shoulder muscles as soon as possible.

As he reached the front door he found the entrance blocked by a large brown dragon-patterned plantpot. A tall, spiky palm reached out on all sides to repel any attempt to enter.

He looked at the green and brown mass for a moment before pushing the heavy pot to one side with an outstretched leg and squeezing his way in. As he walked into the lounge, puzzled as to exactly what the pot was doing there Cazza greeted him from the lotus position on a small red rattan mat in the middle of the room.

'G'day. Glad to see you managed to get in, though I will have to move it back in a minute,' she announced, a book titled '*Feng Shui & A Harmonious Home*' in hand. He also noticed that the coffee table in the middle of the room now had a large frying pan sitting in its centre.

'What is going on?' he asked, though he had basically worked out the answer.

'Feng Shui,' Cazza announced from behind two long legs and one short skirt 'It's time to make things more harmonious and tranquil around here,' she had obviously taken on the task with the delight of an inspired artist.

'Which means we can't get in the front door any more?'

'Well, sort of. The back door is under used anyway,' logic will always win. 'You see, according to this book, all the Chi – that's the energy – within the house is being lost because it's going right out of the front door instead of circulating around us, the occupants, and doing us good.'

'Could that be because the door is always open?'

'Maybe.'

'And why couldn't the Chi be coming in through the front door, rather than going out, and therefore adding to the energy of the house?'

'I thought of that but the chart I have for this room shows that the front door area is actually an outgoing triple negative. It aligns triangularly to both the kitchen and back door which means that the chi flows down from the trees behind the house, in through the rear, twice round the sink and straight out.'

'Like a good dose of chilli?'

Cazza took a deep breath 'Don't make fun Simon, the Chinese have been doing this for thousands of years.'

'What, blocking off their front doors with giant plant pots and putting empty frying pans on tables?' he brought the discussion round to the cookware.

Cazza looked at the pan before continuing 'According to the book this room is in need of positive indication of the presence of food as it represents the sustenance of life. And, although we eat in here a lot the food comes and goes of course. So, to represent the continued presence of man's basic needs what better than a frying pan?'

'How about a wok?' he countered 'Wouldn't it be more Chinese and rather fitting?'

'Hadn't thought of that, you could be right. Though we don't have one, so No.'

Simon probed the situation a little 'Where did the book come from?'

'From K.C. who else?' she smiled dreamily at the mention of his name.

'His latest hair colour comes out of the Happy Hairdressers Feng Shui Chart does it?'

'I don't know, maybe. But it does work and I'm sure we would all like more harmony and good fortune coming our way, so I decided to do the whole house. Then we can all benefit.'

Simon walked into the kitchen and pulled up short as he saw that the dining table now had a birdcage sitting in its centre 'And who is this?'

'Oh this is Aldo, he's a singing bird. Very lucky.'

'And where did he come from?'

'The tree outside.'

His eyes opened wide 'You mean you caught it?'

'Well I actually hypnotised it first so I wouldn't waste my time climbing the tree only for it to then fly off.' Cazza's hidden talents were coming out in a rush.

'How did you hypnotise it?'

'First of all I sang to it and then I gave it my hypnotic whistle.'

'And where did you learn that?'

'Oh there's also a tape which comes with the book.'

'So having climbed the tree…?' he paused to check with her, she nodded 'you then caught the bird…?' she nodded again 'and brought it in here..?' third nod 'and the cage?'

'Spare one from next door.'

'And how did you bring it out of its trance.'

'I counted to three and clapped my hands.'

'In bird talk?'

'No, in English.'

'Oh I see. This bird can count in English?'

'Seems to be the case, though maybe it was the noise when I clapped. Anyway, he's been singing ever since,' Cazza was indeed happy with her feathery work.

Simon sat down, checking first that the chair he was aiming for was still there 'Other than counting, what else does this bird do?'

'Brings luck, I just told you.'

'And how do you know when he's brought you luck?'

'When you win money of course,' she was beginning to tire of the questioning and was rapidly deciding Simon was a pain in the beginners Feng Shui.

'So now we all just sit back – if we can find enough chairs that is – and wait to become rich?'

'Exactly,' she smiled and headed off towards her bedroom 'Excuse me but I have to move my bed up against the door. It's in a double negative area at the moment and facing the wrong way too.'

'Then how will you get in?'

'Through the window of course.'

By the time all occupants returned home a number of other Feng Shui revelations had come to light. The downstairs toilet now had a huge white orchid plant in full bloom positioned in the bowl. 'And what are we supposed to do when the need arises to use the loo, Miss Feng Sushi?' Sheila Three asked.

'Well you can either lift it out – but don't forget to put it back – or go upstairs or outside and use either of those loos.' Cazza felt the options to be obvious.

'But exactly why is there now an orchid plant down the dunny?'

'Because all the good feng shui would be washed away if the thing were left as it has been. It says so in the book!' the botanical Cazza explained.

'Then why not just keep the lid down until needed?' Sheila Three pleaded.

'Well I suppose you could but it says under Positive Flower Power in Chapter Six that each room should have native plants in them. So by putting an orchid there I felt we'd be achieving success.' It was all perfectly reasonable to her.

'While our needs and desires to use the bloody dunny in peace and comfort go out the window,' Sheila One came in with the killer comment.

Tyrone asked why the carpet that once lay on the dusty upstairs landing was now hanging on the bathroom wall.

'Because natural fibres should be where there is a constant water flow.'

'We already have them, you call them towels,' Tyrone advised Ms. Wind & Water, as the term Feng Shui translates.

'Right, but the towels are not silk as the carpet is and it will bring those coming into contact with it more success in business.'

'Can't really dry yourself with a carpet very easily can you though?' he asked before adding 'And how can we come into contact with it when it's hanging on the bloody wall?'

Cazza was beginning to come under attack from all sides and it was Sheila Two who came to her rescue 'OK folks, let's stop for a while. We all know that the changes have been done with an objective of improving things for all of us,' they nodded.

'And if we feel some of the new placements are rather odd then so be it. For the sake of homely harmony though I suggest that we leave things in place for a week and seven days hence we will sit down – if we still have chairs without goldfish bowls on them that is – and review the overall situation quietly and analytically. OK?'

Everyone agreed and emphasised that they didn't mean any ill towards the Cairns Cookie, it was just that they felt the changes were rather sudden, as well as slightly odd. For her part Cazza asked that each of them promise to look at the book on Feng Shui so they would have a better appreciation of what she was trying to achieve and improve.

The request was accepted by all participants in the Towards Better Feng Shui Harmony Campaign who agreed that there must be something in it – after all five hundred million Chinese couldn't all be wrong – and that one week hence all would be revealed. Or removed.

Bruce had been on edge ever since the barbeque and with each passing day had become increasingly agitated whenever the phone rang. He made a habit of sitting near it, though tried hard to disguise the fact that he was now acting as the in-house telephonist.

When a call came he would rush to answer, at times knocking one or two housemates flying in his attempt to get there first.

At a quarter to eight on the Wednesday morning of the third week after the barbie he was packing his bag for school when the phone rang. He answered. For some reason he had expected her – him – to call in the evening so when a voice asked 'Can I speak Mr. Big Boy please?' he went into immediate shock.

Dropping the bag with a thud, his mouth dried up immediately as his tongue tried to create speech from a drought-stricken area. Choking somewhat and signalling to the waiting Tyrone and Sheila One to go on ahead without him he managed a dry and very squeaky 'Speaking.'

The gush of excitement that came down the line was palpable.

'Oooohhhhh hello Big Boy! Is me – your Tutti Fruiti.'

He tried to remain calm whilst watching for passing housemates. 'Yes, I know.'

'I here in Singapore,' the caller advised as he kept silent 'I come and see you later.'

'No you won't,' he told her – him.

'Why not? You like me, No?'

'No,' he was emphatic.

'Oh yes you do, you joking I know. We have nice time in Batam, now we also have nice time in Singapore.'

'No we didn't and no we won't,' he was trying to be stern though he was still squeaking somewhat and wondered if he was going to faint at any minute.

'OK then, I here for just one night. I come to you tonight – seven o'clock, is OK?'

'No, I'm just off to Australia,' he threw in the googly.

'That's nice, I come with you.'

'No you cannot,' he was going to be sick.

'I sing special song for you,' Tutti promised 'I see you later Mr. Big Boy.' The line went dead.

He missed the next four buses before calming down enough to feel he could walk in a reasonable manner without falling over.

He couldn't really have a drink, though felt the immediate need for a tinnie or two, so tried deep-breathing while wondering about the impending disaster and pondering who would be home in the evening.

During the day he considered how to best handle the situation. There were a number of options available — emigrate: stay out all night: keep the residents away by telling them the place had burnt down: put a double padlock on the front gate and lose the key: borrow two fierce dogs to frighten everyone away. The final thought was to kill himself after the last class of the day.

He ran into Simon along one of the school corridors during the early afternoon. His housemate asked if anything was wrong as he looked pale. A problem shared is a problem halved they say and so Bruce told him.

'She's here,' he whispered.

'Who is?' Simon asked, looking down the corridor to see who he was talking about.

'Tutti,' the whisper was enveloping.

Simon gasped 'Oh no. How do you know?'

'She – he – called this morning which threw me completely as I never expected a morning call. The ship must have docked early today and she — he — called to say she — he — is here for one night…and is coming round to see me this evening.' His voice rose as he gave out the details and had to slap his cheek in an attempt to calm himself down.

'What can I do?' he wailed.

'So we are in for a good old sing-along after all then?'

'No. Please, no. I don't want her – him – coming to the house. The girls will cotton on to what she really is very quickly … and will think I'm like that too!' the wailing started again.

'That's OK, nobody cares these days anyway.'

'I know, but I do as I'm not,' he was rambling.

'What you should have done was arrange to meet her somewhere in town and then you'd have been able to keep her away.'

'I know. I thought of that after I put the phone down and while considering my sixteenth way to commit suicide but by then it was too late. I don't know what ship she's on or where it is so I can't do anything…Oh God, help me!'

Simon felt sorry for his agitated chum but couldn't resist milking the situation somewhat. 'OK, Plan B. We will get you one of Siew Moi's dresses, you can get a wig from that trendy wig shop Shock! and put them on when we get near home. It'll be like looking at Diana Ross in Duplicate with the two of you all dressed up,' he suggested with a straight face.

Bruce went into even deeper dismay and sat shaking his head.

His more tranquil colleague continued 'Listen, you either tell the girls, and Tyrone, the full story so they will know you're not into fishnet stockings, sequined tops and cracking whips. Yet…' he paused to let that one sink in 'Or you say nothing and bluff it out to whoever's there. Your choice.'

'None of the above.'

'Then we go directly to the pub after school – happy hour prices and all that - as I want you paralytic by the time she – he – turns up.' This seemed the better option.

By six o'clock they were half pickled in the bar of the Dancing Tiger Pub just two streets away from school. Another option they hadn't considered was not turning up at all and the more Anchor beers they had the more appealing this idea seemed. Simon's mobile phone rang at quarter to seven. He spoke to the caller with a series of 'Yes' and 'No' responses before cutting the connection.

Turning to Bruce - who refused to carry a mobile phone as he felt them intrusive and was running his own anti-mobile phone

'Stop the bloody ringing' campaign - he told him 'That was Sheila One, Miss Tutti Fruiti is presently sitting on the verandah waving her legs in the air, waiting for you.'

Bruce juggled his beer and gasped 'Well I hope she's got some knickers on. Did she say anything else?'

'No. Just asked if I was with you and when I said yes she just said that Tutti was there, and that she'd given her a drink.'

'Hopefully a knockout potion,' Bruce wailed before continuing 'but then, she – he – gets worse when she drinks. What shall we do?' He wanted to die.

'Let's go. Play it by ear when we arrive. Come on, just go for the laughs and see what happen,' Simon summed it up perfectly, what was the point of panicking anyway? It's amazing how positive one gets when half-sozzled he thought as they left the bar to seek out a taxi.

Their yellow and black conveyance stopped a short distance from the house by request. The duo crept forward and were soon standing outside the gate taking in the scene as the dim verandah lights picked out the wild hair and flashy clothing of the visitor. Tyrone was sitting next to her in animated conversation as well as his usual trusty green and gold shorts and t-shirt.

They quietly opened the gate and on getting closer noticed the lady was pawing at Tyrone's bare knees, both of them giggling with delight 'If you only knew,' Bruce said quietly.

Their crunching footsteps on the gravel were finally heard, causing the verandah duo to look up. When Tutti spotted Bruce she screamed and leapt in the air before rushing down the steps and throwing herself at him.

'Big Boy. I see you again,' she attempted to kiss him. He tried valiantly to dodge the attack, pulling away and falling backwards onto the grass in doing so. Tutti took this as a welcoming sign of encouragement and dived on top of him. They rolled about for a moment or two – reruns of their original Batam bout flashing through his mind – before he managed to break the headlock her legs had him in. Having finally untangled himself he shakily regained his stance and tried to do the formal introductions but Tutti wasn't the least bit interested. She smiled meekly at Simon as she continued to grab at Bruce.

'Stop it!' he shouted.

'We go your room now? I ready Big Boy,' she was hardly discrete.

'No. No. No. You sit here with Simon and Tyrone,' his eyes pleaded for help from his colleagues as he guided her back to her seat 'while I go inside for a minute.' He placed a drink in her hands, ordered 'Stay there!' and went into the house.

'Well hello Big Boy,' Sheila Two grinned a red-edged double-gum exposure at him.

'Well aren't you the dark horse?' Sheila One asked as Sheila Three galloped in fast with her questions.

'Can you tell us how you got the rather impressive title some time please? We're all dying to know.'

'And when can we see proof of the claim?' Sheila One moved on behind knowing eyes. Only Cazza was missing. His worse nightmare was coming true.

'Look, it's not what you think,' he told them, starting to shake.

'And exactly what do you think we think?' Sheila One asked the half-pickled paramour.

'Well that she is my friend. Because that's not true,' he tried to clarify things.

'Then why has she come to see you and apparently jumped ship to stay with you for *ever more* – as she's been telling us?' Sheila Two asked.

Bruce was both speechless and in shock.

In the distance an arriving 'Coooeeee,' could be heard as the last member of the household turned up.

From the verandah a responding 'Cooooeeee,' was provided by Tutti as a welcoming echo. She seemed to be settling into the routine of things rather well and making instant friends everywhere.

Bruce staggered to a chair, fell into it and gasped 'Look this isn't supposed to be happening. I never wanted to see this, this…' he paused before maintaining his approach to the gender of the person outside '…woman again. Once was enough – believe me.'

Sheila Three brought him a much-needed coldie which he grabbed with silent thanks. It barely hit the sides of his throat on the way down. Cazza came into the lounge, wide eyed.

'Just who is that with Simon and Tyrone?'

'It's Bruce's special friend from Batam,' Sheila One informed 'who has just thrown herself overboard from the SS Karaoke Kween to spend the rest of her life with Mr. Big Boy here.'

Cazza was in shock 'Well, what can I say? Good for you and all the best for your life together…' she was trying to say the right thing. The other girls were not trying to hide anything though and were rolling about the place laughing as Bruce felt the barbs coming his way from all sides.

'Stop,' he declared 'Just stop. Enough is enough. I can't take any more.'

Silence reigned. It was time for action, confession, execution and immediate death he told himself.

'Yes but it looks like she – or should I say he – can.' Sheila Three offered her thoughts.

Bruce looked at her in open-eyed surprise 'You know?'

'Well you don't have to be bloody Agatha Christie to work out that there's a bloke out there, not Miss World. Just one look at the chin darls and you'd soon see that she – he – hasn't shaved for a while,' Sheila One presented the evidence.

'So, what weez want to know is, are you 'going that way' now or what?' Sheila Two grinned with certain gusto, red hair aflame.

Bruce shot up to defend himself 'No. Not at all. Look, I met this …er…person…in Batam the other week in a bar. It was dark, she – he – spoke to me and said she was the resident singer there which proved to be true as she kept going on stage and singing.'

'And?' Cazza joined the inquisition.

'Well by the end of the night I'd had quite a few tinnies and I was on a little holiday so when she – later he – suggested coming back to my hotel I agreed.'

'And?' Sheila Two grinned again.

'Well when we got there I still didn't know she was a bloke until well, you know.'

He paused.

'No, we don't know,' Sheila One claimed, ordering the accused to 'Continue.'

He was squirming now but went on 'Well you know....'

They gasped collectively in exasperation.

'OK, OK,' he agreed to tell 'Well you see she got me on the bed, stripped me and said I should lie there with my eyes closed until she told me to open them.'

'And?' Cazza prompted.

'Well when I did things weren't quite as I'd been expecting. Simple as that,' he looked at them, the confession was on the table, even if the frying pan wasn't any more.

'So?' Sheila Two came in again, still grinning from her red background.

'So I told her – now him – I wasn't like that and she – he – could go.'

'And?'

'Well that was the hard part,'

'The only hard part?' Sheila One wndered.

'In his case, yes – not in my case,' he shuddered at the memory of it all. Anyway, he didn't want to go but in the end after a bit of a struggle I got rid of him – her – I mean him. Though he was a she again when he – she – finally left.'

'Then why is she – he – here to see you?' Cazza asked, helping herself to the contents of a bottle of cold dry white wine which had conveniently appeared.

'Don't give up do they?'

'Well, she tells us she's a singer on a cruise ship but has jumped ship to be with you - for ever.' Sheila One mentioned again.

'Well she can't.. It's all so bloody stupid,' Bruce summed it all up 'I have to get her – him – back to the ship as soon as possible. I can't take any more of this, I'm going to have a heart attack.'

'Don't do that, have another beer instead,' Sheila One passed another coldie across.

Tyrone wandered into the lounge, avoided the large porcelain tiger positioned in the 'Fortunate Blessings' zone directly in front of the telly, and announced 'Geez Bruce what a great girl you've got there, a million laughs.'

'You can have her. She's yours,' Bruce came up with an offer too good to refuse, he hoped.

Tyrone collected more drinks for the outside party and asked 'Why? She seems to be great fun if you ask me.'

'She's a drag queen and I don't want her here,' the revealing statement was made.

'Is she? No!' now it was Tyrone's turn to be shocked and seek out a chair.

'Are the fellers all simple around here, or what? Though it is rather dark out there darls,' Sheila Three chipped in 'but if you check out the chin you'll see that she needs a close chat with Mr. Gillette rather badly.'

'And this is … er … your friend? You going AB-CD now or whatever they call it?' Tyrone asked.

'No she is not and no I am not. When I met her – him – I honestly thought he was a she,' Bruce wailed 'How many times will I have to say this?'

'Until weez all satisfied,' Sheila Two informed him from the jury area on the well-worn floorboards.

'OK enough. Operation Instant Divorce is obviously required,'

Cazza declared.

'Before this gets out of hand you have to get her back to the ship before it sails. So why don't you just go and sit with her on the verandah for a while, be nice to her, have a drink and we'll put the plan into action?'

Bruce could have kissed her 'You will?' She nodded, they all nodded.

'The real women in the house will sort it out,' Sheila Three summed up the situation.

Mates he thought, where would we be without them. His heartbeat slowed down to six thousand a minute.

'Big Boy!' Tutti declared as Bruce returned to the verandah and sat down.

'I'll refresh your drink,' Simon told her and disappeared with her glass.

'I miss you, lover boy,'

'What's the name of your ship?'

'Java Dream but finish already. Now I retire as job only part-time anyway. Now I stay with you…full time. Nice ah?'

'Cannot lah,' he told her, slipping in a touch of Singlish.

'Can lah,' she countered positively.

'No,' he took a swig of his beer 'you cannot stay in Singapore, you have to go back to the ship. Think about your fans, what will they do without you? Who will sing if you're not there?' He was appealing to her professional musical side.

Simon returned, passed Tutti a fresh drink and quickly went back inside.

'Never mind, they can play CD. I like it here. I like you,' she was persistent if nothing else.

'No. You are a man, I am a man. It doesn't work like that for me.'

'Can lah, is OK,' she wouldn't give up and reached out to grab him again.

'Stop it!' he pushed her away 'Cannot lah. Do you understand?'

he spoke slowly, emphasising the last three words.

Tutti pouted and knocked back her drink before smiling again, dipping her head into her neck and winking at him excessively.

'I will take you back to your ship soon, where is it?' he was digging gently.

'World Trade Centre,'

He sighed as he now had both the name and location of the maritime jigsaw. Tyrone appeared as Tina Turner music started up from the hi-fi and Tutti got up to dance with him. She was soon belting the song out like a professional, supporting moves coming naturally.

Two of the Sheilas came out and took their places as backup giving out timely *Wah wah ooh's* as they swayed along, memories of their Phuket evening of fame rushing back. The third Sheila appeared with a tray of snacks, beer and more wine, the party was far from over.

Cazza finally joined the group, grinned at Bruce and quietly advised 'Under control. K.C. is coming over with the BMW in about half an hour and will run her to the ship – you'd better go too and make sure she gets on,' he nodded 'In the meantime let's have a laugh and give him – her - a good time.'

Things seemed to be going in a better direction now Bruce thought as he noticed Tyrone taking a close-up look at Tutti's chin as he swayed past her with a few tinnies in hand. Their visitor was loving the spotlight and after a couple of songs with the Sheilas in support did a twenty minute solo session.

Cheers and encouragement helped things along and after her sixth song she threw herself onto Bruce's knee and declared 'I never leave you, this is so great here.' Just then a car honked from outside the gate and Cazza nodded.

Bruce shook her off and announced 'OK, we have to go now. Say goodbye everybody.' And with that the complete household huddled and fussed around their visitor while ushering her slowly towards the gate. Rather bemused, but very happy with the attention, Tutti asked Bruce 'Where we go?'

'Surprise,' he announced, pushing her into the back seat of the BM and quickly sliding in alongside and locking all doors to prevent any escape. Cazza slipped into the front passenger seat and told Tutti as the car moved off 'This is K.C., my boyfriend.'

'Nice. Love your hair, you want to gloss over me some time?' Tutti pouted into the driver's mirror. Cazza was rather shocked at the fast forward approach, even by her standards.

As the car headed for East Coast Parkway the back seat action could be clearly heard if not clearly seen by those in the front. It consisted mostly of Tutti trying to grab Bruce in certain parts, and he trying to rebuff the attacks with certain blocking movements. The cries of 'Yes!' and 'No!' that passed between the two wrestlers were about equal in emphasis as each strove to make their moves a success.

A hard-fought fifteen minutes later and K.C. was driving into the car-park at their destination, slowly scanning the waterfront for the vessel in question.

'Oh look, there my ship. Come my cabin we have party and plenty fun,' Tutti did the identifying for them as she pointed to a small off-white steamer along the dock.

'No, just you and me. Come on then,' Bruce told her 'let's go and have a look.'

Taking her by the hand he slid out of the car, mouthing 'Stay here' to Cazza, and pointed the visitor towards the ship.

Two sailors at the bottom of the gangway grinned at them as they approached and spoke to Tutti in rapid-fire Indonesian. She chatted back animatedly, then turned to Bruce and asked 'You like now come my cabin? I have waterbed for deep dive.'

'No thanks, I have to get back and mark some homework actually,' he told her lamely. It was the best excuse he could think of.

'I come too. I sharpen your pencil,'

'No you will not. No more, thanks,' he repeated 'Finish!' pointing her towards the gangway.

'Serious?' she sought clarification.

He nodded.

'OK I go then,' she smiled 'I miss you Big Boy,' and with a peck on the cheek and more laughing and chatting with the dockside crew she climbed daintily upwards towards the main deck and out of sight.

His body sagged wearily as he walked away from the ship. He slipped into the still-waiting car with a huge sigh of relief. 'Thanks. Thanks to both of you. I owe you a drink, or two, or three – even a keg perhaps.'

'Pleasure,' K.C. announced 'seems a very nice girl.'

'Oh yes, she is,' he lay flat out on the leather 'though just not my type really.'

'What's that large red patch on your cheek?' Cazza asked as she looked sadly at the prone figure on the back seat. Bruce gingerly felt the area in question.

'Whisker rash.'

Chapter 13

Always A Winner

Simon and Siew Moi were having a pleasant 'Drain View' dinner one Friday evening when she passed him a red invitation card with gold Chinese lettering on the front.

'Very nice, what is it?' he asked as he sought out some baby kai-lan vegetables.

'My cousin is getting married and we are invited. You don't have to come if you don't want to, but I thought it would be an experience for you. You know, a real Chinese wedding and all that.'

'I hate weddings.'

'Well, Chinese weddings can take up much of the day, and evening,' she revealed 'but you may find it interesting and even enjoy it. Or some of it. Perhaps.'

'When is it?' he looked at the Chinese writing inside the card.

'Two weeks tomorrow. Though you don't have to commit yourself just yet.' He took another sip of the ice-filled beer and decided

'That's OK, I'll come. I'm sure it will be great.'

'I hope you say that after the event,' she was both relieved and concerned.

Ten days later Siew Moi filled in the details for him. The traditional tea ceremony would take place at 8.30am on the Saturday morning at her auntie's home. This was the major element of the event, the showing of respect by the newly-married couple to the parents of the groom, with whom they would then live.

'OK,' he declared 'in for a penny, in for a pound. If I'm going to see this I may as well catch all parts. We'll be there for the eight thirty kickoff.'

The aunt lived close to Siew Moi's family home so it was agreed that she would meet him off the train at the station at eight o'clock and they would then go straight to the apartment from there. The thought of such an early start on a Saturday morning was not so appealing but on the day in question Simon duly awoke slightly before seven and was on the bus into town by quarter past. Siew Moi had told him to dress 'smart but casual' so he sported a pair of fawn coloured trousers and a long sleeved light blue shirt, no tie.

He came out of the MRT station just before eight and she was waiting for him. A peck on the cheek and a 'Good morning, so you managed to get here,' welcomed him as they then made their way towards a block of flats she had targetted.

'Why does it have to be so early?' he asked as they strolled along the winding paths.

'Well, according to a seer they went to it's an auspicious time for them.'

'Bit of an early start,' he commented, still trying to wake up fully.

'Actually the original time was 4.30am.'

He looked at her wide-eyed.

'So half past eight is second choice.'

'I hope they don't have a lifetime of problems just because of a lack of alarms clocks,' he thought out loud.

When they arrived at the apartment it was packed with family, friends, well-wishers and just about everyone he'd ever seen in Singapore.

'The groom, my cousin, has already gone to the bride's home to collect her from her family as from today they will live here. So now we await their arrival,' Siew Moi informed him as he was passed a waxed packet of chrysanthemum tea.

From the outside balcony someone shouted excitedly in Hokkien causing great commotion inside the flat. It was the signal to move out and most of the group started heading downstairs to welcome the arriving couple. Simon and Siew Moi were swept along with the crowd and soon found themselves standing on the kerb watching the white-ribboned car slowly arrive.

Though early, the day was already hot and as the rear door opened to allow the bride to emerge cheers and clapping broke out. The girl was wearing a long, flowing, white dress and obviously feeling the heat as a drop of perspiration gathered on the end of her nose before falling daintily into the bouquet of yellow orchids she held. Should keep them nice and moist Simon thought to himself as the young lady sought to smooth out the folds of her dress under the beating sun. While doing so a large round tin was thrust before her and after some quick words between her and the holder she dipped a white-gloved hand inside and pulled out a piece of paper. A smiling helper opened it, shouted something, folded it up and dropped it back into the tin which was then shaken. The action was repeated three more times.

'What are they doing?' Simon whispered to Siew Moi 'Is it some ancient Chinese custom calling on the Gods of Happy Marriages via pieces of paper?'

'Not really, she's picking the numbers for tonight's lucky draw.'

'In the middle of a wedding they are working out their bet for tonight's numbers?'

'Of course, why not? This is her lucky day so maybe she can pick some lucky numbers for the people here,' it all made perfect sense to her.

'Quite reasonable,' he agreed with the obvious logic.

The groom appeared from the other side of the car. Dressed in a midnight blue dinner suit with a huge white dickie-bow as the focal point his hair had been recently set into a bunch of curls.

'Very smart,' Simon told Siew Moi 'don't know how they'll feel by the wedding dinner tonight though after getting through the heat of the day in all that gear.'

'Let's wait and see,'

The dozens of people then made their way back upstairs to where the groom's mother and father were sitting on stools in the centre of the lounge awaiting the couple.

The bride and groom made their way forward and knelt before them, an attendant passed them small cups of sweet longnan tea which each in turn then offered to the older couple.

The watery offerings were accepted and sipped after which the parents presented the couple with a gift. Other senior members of the family then took their places on the stools and were also served the sweet tea. Siew Moi mentioned to Simon that older unmarried relatives would not be included in this ceremony.

'What happens next?' he asked from his position at the back of a group of chattering aunties all looking very smart in their best silk cheongsams.

'Nothing. That's it, now they are considered married. We stay here for a while, then I take you across the road to the hawker centre for some breakfast. After which you can go home until you meet me at the hotel for the wedding dinner this evening.'

'Painless,'

'So far, still a long way to go,' Siew Moi was rather apprehensive about events to come.

Simon chatted to both bride and groom, who seemed very pleasant, as well as umpteen other people who came and went over the next half hour or so. After a while Siew Moi tapped him on the shoulder and quietly requested 'Come,'. She led the way to the lift-well and pressed the button, the lift finally clunked its arrival and they joined another half dozen or so people inside. After alighting at the ground floor they made their way to a lively hawker centre and sat on red plastic chairs at a round light-brown table under a wide awning.

'So what do they do now?' Simon asked as she brought him a plate of noodles and mixed vegetables. All would be washed down by the thick black coffee steaming before him in a shiny glass, a spoon sticking out of the top.

'Stay there for a while before returning to her parent's home for lunch. Then they go to have photographs taken this afternoon at a suitably exotic location and then it's the wedding dinner this evening.'

'Long day, they'll be ready for bed by the end of it.'

She looked at him.

'Only joking, said it before really thinking. And so what do we do?'

'Well you go home after this. I have to go back to attend the events as programmed and I will meet you at the hotel around eight. OK?'

'Fine, thanks for sparing me,' he was grateful for the most kind consideration.

He spent the afternoon preparing lessons for the next week, had a pleasant doze under a huge Angsana tree in the back garden and as it got dark slowly made his way to the hotel in his best, and only, suit.

A sign in the hotel entrance read:—

WEDDING DINNER
7.30PM
MR. DESMOND LIM XING GUAN
&
MS. BLOSSOM TAN MEI MEI
BALLROOM, MEZZANINE FLOOR

He made his way up a wide and winding staircase to the level in question then along a corridor to where a table of three girls, presumably bridesmaids, were checking off the arriving guests.

He gave his name to the one on the left who smiled and ticked him off the list in front of her. She spoke to her neighbour in Mandarin and then informed him 'Table Ten. On the left as you enter,' she smiled again as she pointed to the entrance of the ballroom.

The place was about a third full as he entered and he wondered if he was early. Despite the official 7.30pm start Siew Moi had told him to be there by eight and it was exactly that by his watch. Making his way to Table Ten he saw her sitting there talking to a couple of people, all other seats were empty. She smiled when she saw him approaching, stood, kissed him on the cheek and introduced him to the other guests.

'Are we too early?' he asked as he settled down.

'No, it's always like this at a Chinese wedding. It's supposed to start at seven thirty but very few will arrive until at least an hour later and the bride and groom by nine, perhaps.'

He looked at her quite puzzled 'Why?'

'Like dat lah,' the fellow sitting next to Siew Moi answered for her 'tradition.'

'Right.' Simon accepted things and took a sip of the Chinese tea that had been poured out before him.

'Beer?' a waiter asked and he nodded a silent *Yes please* in response. This could be a long night a little voice inside told him.

Siew Moi was right and it was indeed almost an hour later that the event finally got underway. The nine course dinner was long and drawn out and as all the table talk around him was in Hokkien he decided to make the most of things by eating and drinking the night away in his own little corner of the world.

'Are you ok?' she asked a few times and received a smiling nod in response. Their table had been filled up by two other couples plus two children. After the third of the nine courses Simon settled on playing face-pulling with the two girls opposite, who were about eight and ten, which kept the three of them happy for quite a while, despite the mother's disapproval.

'Did we give them a gift?' he asked Siew Moi as the thought suddenly struck him that none had been mentioned. She looked at him questioningly.

'You know, electric blanket, alarm clock, toaster, hot water bottles, convection heater, a one year subscription to Readers Digest, that kind of thing?'

'No. We don't give gifts, we give red packets at weddings here.'

'No matching dressing gowns or microwave ovens then?'

'No,'

'So how much do I owe you?' he whispered, labouring the point rather. His eyes were becoming somewhat red she noticed.

'Nothing,'

'You mean we didn't give anything?'

'Of course we did,' she was getting tetchy with his carrying on.

'Well then, how much do I owe you?' his voice was rising.

'Shhhh,' she told him 'I'll tell you later.'

'Then let me settle the bill.'

'What bill, this is all paid for,' he was confusing her.

'My bill to you, I don't like owing anyone anything,' he declared, knocking back his umpteenth beer.

'You are drinking too much.'

'Nothing else to do, is there?' he asked 'I have no idea what's going on, can't understand a bloody word so I am having a nice little drink and talk with myself.' He grinned at her rather oddly.

'I knew we shouldn't have come,' she told him, regretting the invitation mention.

'No. It's fine, great, I love it. Just pass me a programme translation when you can. Meanwhile I will simply sit here smiling away like a loony at every Tom, Dick and Harriett passing by,' He took another swig of the beer in self-martyrdom. She had never seen him like this and wondered what she could do to keep him under control, rather concerned as to what he might do.

A drawn-out cry of 'Yaaaaaaammmmmm Seng!' rang out from the far side of the room. The bride and groom had started their visits to each table of guests for the traditional toast.

'What's happening now?'

'The bridal party are going from table to table. The guests at each table will toast them by shouting *Yam Seng* - 'Cheers' in your talk. They all knock back their drinks and the idea is to get the groom fairly tipsy by the time they've visited everyone.'

'Sounds like a good idea to me,' he laughed 'better start practicing now.' He knocked back the remains of his current beer in one.

It took a while for the bridal party to reach Table Ten but when they did Simon was waiting. He'd noticed that the idea of the toast was to draw out the first word as loudly and for as long as possible and was indeed fully prepared.

As the group arrived he leapt to his feet, then on to his chair and, with arms waving wildly like a mad orchestra conductor, led the table chorus in a rousing and drawn out 'Yaaammmmmmmmmmm…yammmm….yammmm….yammmm….' that went on for what seemed like five minutes.

Siew Moi wanted to crawl under the table with embarrassment.

At the end of it all - on the finishing 'Seng!'- the whole room applauded his vocal prowess, performance originality as well as overall content and presentation. Simon in turn bowed and waved to all four corners in recognition and appreciation of his audience. He gave suitable recognition to his table support and returning to ground level flopped back into his seat exhausted.

'Great!' he declared, grinning happily.

'Everyone was looking at you,' Siew Moi whispered, not daring to look towards where her mother and father were sitting.

'That's because I was standing up and showing them how it's really done,' he confirmed rather breathlessly.

'And making an exhibition of yourself.'

'Not at all. Just leading the wedding chorus on behalf of Table Ten, which they all loved,' he informed her, knocking back another drink in timing with the 'Seng!' of the chant now taking place at a nearby table. She was not amused.

Just before eleven everyone suddenly stood up and started leaving.

'Come on. It's over, we're going,' Siew Moi stood.

'Just like that. All out?'

She nodded and taking his arm guided him towards the bridal party now standing by the Exit sign smiling farewells to guests as they made their way out. She was praying that he wouldn't fall over or do anything silly to draw attention to himself again. As they started passing down the line of groom, bride, best man, bridesmaids, relatives and others she kept close to her guest.

The exchanges were all in Chinese. Simon kept it simple by shaking hands with everyone in the line, wishing them 'Goodbye, Yam Seng,' and bowing as he made his way towards the heavy ballroom doors, confident in the fact that he was now fluent in 'wedding chat'.

Other than an attempted kiss of the bride which missed her cheek, caught her left ear and resulted in a teardrop pearl earring ending up in his mouth, he managed to stay balanced during the farewells.

Siew Moi was greatly relieved to get him out of the ballroom and once outside told him emphatically 'We will leave quietly and quickly, OK?' as they headed for the staircase. He opened his mouth to reply and the teardrop earring fell out.

Siew Moi caught it before it landed and propping him up against a wall with the instruction 'Don't move!' rushed back into the room to reattach it to the vacant ear of the blushing bride.

Thankfully he was still where she'd left him when she returned, though listing slightly to the left. Moving quickly she soon had him under control and heading down the stairs, one stumble— 'Whoops!' —which nobody noticed. A whispered 'Keep going!' as his knees buckled again and finally they were outside the hotel.

He was in a taxi before he knew it and in a single movement was lying flat out across the back seat. She gave instructions to the driver as to where to take him and having watched the taxi's lights disappear into the distance breathed a sigh of relief that it was all finally over.

'First and last,' she told herself as she walked slowly towards the MRT station and a quiet ride home.

Melbourne Cup Day was a holiday for most Aussie companies and establishments in Singapore. The Antipodean Academy of Learning was no exception though the staff were expected to attend school for the morning, watch the race on telly and attend a celebration barbeque lunch afterwards. The students had the day off.

Everything was under control as a direct telecast of the race was to be shown on television sets around the school. Transmission started at twelve noon local time, the race itself at twelve ten in Singapore which was three hours behind Melbourne. A happy carnival atmosphere set the scene for one of the great days in the Australian calendar. There were twenty-six runners in the event and various in-house Sweepstakes had been organised offering a wide variety of prizes – all of an Australian nature.

Teachers were allowed to wear whatever they wished and encouraged to join in the fun of the event by getting stuck into the mood of the occasion. A 'Fashions In The Field' parade would be held at eleven thirty, prizes going to those selected by a panel of design and fashion experts – led, not surprisingly, by Matilda and Dot Com.

A late arrival had been authorised and Simon arrived with Bruce and Tyrone just after ten. He was wearing his bushman's hat with an Aussie flag sticking out of the band. Tyrone was, on this day especially, in glowing patriotic green and gold. Bruce carried his own didgeridoo, which he threatened to play later.

Simon had worked hard on making things up with Siew Moi following his performance at the wedding banquet a few weeks earlier but was still getting the cold shoulder and was beginning to wonder if she would ever come round.

Other than promising never to drink again, a claim she treated as pure fantasy, and never to again utter the words *Yam Seng* until the end of time, he didn't feel there was much else he could do. He sent flowers to the bookshop and 'Sorry' cards to her home every other day but the lady was not impressed and had refused all his suggestions to meet.

As the first Tuesday in November had drawn closer he reminded himself of the fortune teller's forecast as far as his mother and horses were concerned. He quietly studied the field of runners for the race and passed details of his selections to Perce back in Perth for the placing of a few dollars thereon.

His father confirmed that Glad had been in serious training for some time and that he'd had her galloping round the back garden for the last couple of weeks. She was now declared to be 'in fine fettle and *under starters orders*' and studying the runners night and day, though not rushing into anything just yet. Her final selections were expected on the morning of the race, after a nice cuppa and crumpet in bed.

The school quadrangle was bedecked with bunting as well as posters of horses, Australia and Melbourne. Aussie tunes played over the tannoy and the staff were soon caught up with the merry mood and anticipation of the morning. No one was expected to do any work, simply mingle, join in the fun and the barbeque lunch which would follow the race.

Chauncy cantered into the open arena in fitted jockeys silks, his back obviously fully recovered. His top consisted of a collarless pink and white checked blouse with matching pink peaked cap. White breeches ballooned about his legs above shiny black riding boots, a whip under the left arm completed the ensemble.

'I know, don't say it,' he advised the three Sheilas as he galloped up to them while they checked the odds of the horses on one of the Sweepstake boards 'Jealousy will get you everywhere.' They grinned at him with certain admiration 'Not even a bloody Aussie and look at you,' Sheila Two gave him a cup-winning smile.

'Been down the old pizza palace and snaffled one of their best tablecloths, have you?' Sheila One wondered, checking out the pattern on his shirt.

He grinned in delight, did a twirl and asked 'Don't you love it? You're right, the pink used to be red but I had it especially faded for the occasion.' He turned around to reveal a notice on his back that read ---

'10/1 The Field : 20/1 The Meadow : 100/1 The Back Garden'

They screamed in delight and Sheila Three commented 'Not much hope of any success in the back garden by the look of it, eh?'

'It's all those snails, make everything slippery. Can't get a decent grip,' he told her with a wink before heading off towards the weighing-in area, which was actually the canteen and where coffee warmly beckoned.

The three girls all wore cool pastel summer dresses and wide-brimmed straw hats, one white, one red and one blue. Collectively they made up the colours in the Australian flag and very smart they looked too.

Cazza arrived in khaki jodhpurs, black PVC boots that ended just above the knees, white blouse, white leggings, a black peaked hat and riding crop in hand.

'Where'd you put the horse?' Tyrone asked her as she checked the starting prices at a Runners Board.

'She's outside, will be here in a minute.'

And just as Tyrone laughed at what he thought was a joke an echoing 'Clip Clop' announced the arrival of a real horse.

Everyone in the quadrangle stopped what they were doing as a beautiful light brown mare, with a flowing white mane,made her way into the arena. She was led by K.C. who had dyed his hair white to match that of the galloper for the occassion.

Her four-legged friend was slowly led to where Cazza awaited. She moved to the left of the animal, placed her left foot in the stirrup, flicked her right leg backwards and was assisted upwards and into the saddle by K.C. her travelling head groomsman. The trio slowly set off on a circuit of the inner field to the applause, cheers and waves of those along the route. The horse wore a Number 5 saddlecloth which was noticed by those seeking signs and omens of possible winners. As they returned to the unsaddling enclosure by the entrance the three Sheilas awaited them.

'Good God Cazz, where'd you get this beauty?' Sheila One asked.

'Haven't you met K.C. before?'

'She means the bloody horse,' Sheila Three clarified.

'I know that. This is Sayang, which means *Love* in Malay. She is from the Polo Club where K.C.'s brother O.B. is on the committee. So we just borrowed her for a little ride this morning, that's all. Felt it might add to the atmosphere of the event, you know.'

'O.B.?' Sheila One asked 'Let me guess - Outside Broadcast?'

'No, Outback' Cazza corrected the close try.

'Went to school in Alice Springs did he?' Sheila Two grinned.

'No, Sydney, but he likes the outdoors.'

'Shouldn't he be O.D. then rather than O.B?' Three queried.

'Perhaps, but who knows how he worked it out,' Cazza grinned at them. The choice of letters was rather confusing but as Sayang then decided to make her own Melbourne Cup statement on the grass the point was left unexplained.

Matilda and Dot Com appeared and made their way to the owners enclosure.

'Well, she really is a beauty, isn't she?' Matilda declared, stroking the mane of the tall horse and mentioning 'I'll have that lot for my garden, if you don't mind,' to K.C. who nodded and went off to look for a bucket.

'Absolutely beautiful,' Dot Com agreed 'exquisite,' as she too joined in the fuss of the animal who seemed to be relishing the attention.

'OK, ready to dismount,' Cazza announced as K.C. returned with the bucket. He held the reins tight as she dismounted and fussed the horse. 'Thanks so much K.C. that was really nice of your brother to let us borrow her,' she gave him a big smackeroo on the cheek followed by one for the horse in the same spot. The short visit was over though its effect would be long lasting.

K.C. smiled, bid farewell to the audience and slowly led the animal out of the schoolyard to the float outside. He left the now-filled bucket by the entrance and signalled to Matilda where it was. She smiled and gave him a thumbs-up sign. 'Nice touch Carol. Backed a winner there, for sure.'

Matilda smiled happily as she and Dot drifted away thinking about upcoming races and upcoming prize-winning plants.

By eleven all the sweepstakes had been drawn and the names of those who had a horse were shown on numerous blackboards against their runners.

'Get anything?' Bruce asked Cazza as they checked out the 'Aussie Wine Mine' Draw in which prizes were bottles of fine Australian wines.

'Yes, look at that, I got *Stiff Upper Lip*, is it any good?'

'Dunno darls, let's see,' he checked the likely odds on a paper he carried 'Twenty to one. It's from New Zealand.'

'Hope it's not tired after riding all that way,' she looked concerned. He looked at her and wondered if she was serious or just being simple.

The board for another draw some twenty yards along the path was offering Top Quality Australian Food as prizes in 'The Pucker Tucker Sweepstakes'. The three Sheilas were checking it out as Simon and Tyrone arrived.

'Anything?'

'Yes,' they were a happy trio 'We have *The Drover, High Jump* and *Keyboard* so are confident of a trifecta between us.'

'And you?' Sheila Two queried.

'Well not in this one but I have *Setting Sun* in the 'Goods & Chattels' draw over there and Tyrone has *Smile Please* which might go faster if he stopped grinning at the television cameras. The horse that is, not Tyrone.'

'Isn't that the favourite?' One asked.

'One of them,' the patriotic one agreed 'but it seemingly doesn't like running in the wet and it's pouring down in Melbourne right now so....' He tailed off with a shrug.

'Put its lens hood on and she'll be apples.' Sheila Three felt.

The tannoy crackled into life with a supporting whistle.

'Would the entrants in the Fashions In The Field parade please report to the adjudicators desk next to the canteen. The parade will commence at eleven thirty, which is in ten minutes time. Prizes will be presented to the winners by the School Patron, Mr. Clarence Wong.' The announcer went off the air with another high-pitched whistle and closing 'clunk.'

By the start of the parade a jetty of planks stretched half way across the centre playing field at the end of which sat a table of six judges including Matilda in a bright red dress, light blue belt and wide white hat. Dot Com was wearing a long white dress with a dark blue belt and matching scarf over the left shoulder, held in place by a brooch of yellow wildflowers. The remaining four judges looked suitably 'racetracky' enough to be in their presence.

The compere for the event was Rupert Carrington, Head of the English Department. To the accompaniment of a scratchy *Isn't She Lovely?* by Stevie Wonder he got the show underway.

The actual race was now less than an hour away and some of the teachers had already started personally testing the temperature of the coldies available from the canteen. They lead the cheers as the fashion entrants strutted their stuff up and down the boards. Imagination had certainly had a free rein as most of the exhibits showed remarkable creativity.

A lady from the Mathematics Department appeared inside a

wooden horse in which she 'galloped' up and down the planks to encouraging applause. An assistant from Biology came dressed as a bookmaker, complete with signboard showing names and odds of the runners to one and all along her parade path. Her tic-tac signals added to the presentation, not that anyone knew if they were genuine.

The biggest cheer went to Chauncy who naturally played up to the crowd. Crying out in a continual 'Wheeee' in his rather off-centre imitation of a horse he wheeled and whinnied up and down the runway planks to his hearts content.

The fact that he didn't have an actual horse with him didn't deter him one little bit, at least he had no competition from that quarter. At the top of the runway he cracked his whip at all six judges dramatically before spinning on a horseshoe and galloping off at full speed.

The more sedate entrants in their smart dresses drew applause and whistles with the three Sheilas getting a rousing response. There were some twenty contestants in total and after the parade finished they were asked to line up along the runway.

After much deliberation at the head table Rupert announced that third place had gone to 'The Three Sheilas', second place to 'Cantering Candy' a lab technician from Science who wore an ensemble of horseshoes attached to a dress made of the Australian flag. And to a suitable drum roll the first prize went to…'The Galloping Major' – Chauncy - who with a great flourish took his bows to cheers from the people in the paddock. The Academy Patron, Mr. Wong, did the presentation honours and Chauncy was asked to attend Matilda's rooms after the actual race to collect his special prize.

By five past twelve the excitement was palpable as the many television screens now tuned in to Melbourne showed the runners in the Flemington Racecourse parade ring in their bright colours and finery. Numerous groups gathered around the quadrangle and just after ten minutes past the hour the commentator announced 'They're Off!'

The lead changed hands quite a few times during the long race and as the field turned into the home straight enthusiastic watchers cheered their fancies home. It was a blanket finish involving five horses and the judge called for a photo. Tension remained high around the school while the official result was awaited. Cold beers helped calm edgy nerves.

The result finally came through with *Hobgoblin*, a five-year-old bay gelding from New Zealand, the winner by a nose from *Heaven On A Stick*, a handsome black Irish horse that had travelled half the world to participate.

There was a dead heat for third between *Keyboard* and *Mystery Guest* with *Uncle Neighbour* coming in fifth, a nose further back. The winner was at 25/1, second at 16/1 and the third place dead-heaters came home at 33/1 and 9/1.

Of the house residents only Sheila Three showed a return, her *Keyboard* having produced a box of Queensland Pineapples as the prize for third place in the 'Fruits For My Fruit' draw.

With congratulations and commiserations taking place over the next half hour or so the post-race party got underway as volunteer chefs worked on the barbie to ensure the food would be ready for the one o'clock starting time.

Chauncy trotted into the parade ground and ran into Simon.
'Did you win?'

'No, not a snifter,' Simon told him 'I think my horse is still running.'

'Always the way, same here. I can't even win an argument these days,' Chauncy chuckled into his Dry White Burgundy 'Although I did of course win the best-dressed prize so am now off to see what Madam White Snake has for me. Can't wait!' And with a parting 'Mmmmmmmm.....' he shot upstairs to the Winners Enclosure.

The door to Matilda's room was open. Chauncy popped his head around it, knocked lightly and called 'Hellooooo....'

'Come in Mr. Chauncy,' Matilda beckoned with a smile, coming from around her desk. She signalled for him to sit with her by the coffee table and opened the small fridge behind. A package appeared from within and was placed on the table.

'This is your winning prize, if you'd like to sample the nectar within we can perhaps have a tipple together before joining the barbie?'

Chauncy grinned his acceptance of the suggestion and excitedly opened the wrapping paper. The contents revealed a dozen small cold bottles of Heineken beer. Matilda produced two glasses and Chauncy did the honours by opening a bottle and pouring out the liquid contents.

'Cheers,' he toasted the Head of School happily from beneath his pink cap. 'Delicious,' he announced as he put his glass down on the table. His eyes were drawn to the beer bottles and a small light within his fading memory came on. He paused, looked again at the bottles, looked up at a smiling Matilda and began to feel rather clammy. He coughed before asking 'Do you always drink Heineken m'a'm?'

She nodded, still smiling. He gulped.

'And did you perhaps enter the Desert Island competition a while ago using a Heineken bottle?'

She nodded again.

He was stammering now 'Aaaaaaaaand, you, you, you perhaps….er….won?'

Another nod.

He let out a sigh-cum-gasp 'Wow……' his forehead was dripping with perspiration as he took another drink.

She spoke 'Yes, and you are my prize,' she clarified the winners situation, taking a sip of the frothy beer.

'But, you see, I'm…. well er….emmmm…' he tried to gather

his wits and words together, finally managing 'I'm very flattered but I really don't think I'm….er….. your type…really.'

'Oh I think you are,' she countered 'perhaps I am not your type though. Which is what I think you are trying to say.'

'Exactly,' he confirmed the fact and took a much needed swig of beer, straight from a fresh bottle this time. He tried to bring it all into some form of understanding 'But why didn't you put your name on the entry form?' he was beginning to think once again.

'Could you imagine the reaction if I'd claimed the prize and everyone then knew that the Head of School fancied the Art Master?' she asked, sitting back and being realistic, though enjoying the moment immensely.

'I suppose it could have been rather delicate,' he agreed.

'Though the Art Master doesn't fancy the Head of School,' she summarized the situation and took another sip.

'Well it's not that,' he mumbled, trying to be nice 'it's just that I think you would be wasting such a prize on me. I wouldn't be much use to you… really…'

'Oh that's OK, I know that,' she smiled 'so this will be our little secret. No one will ever know that I was the lucky winner, except you and I.'

'Fine,' he was feeling better.

'The prize will never be claimed on condition that you have to fulfil part of it though.'

He looked worried 'Like what?'

'You and I will have a day out on Sentosa Island in three weeks time where we will build sandcastles all afternoon and eat ice creams until we feel sick.'

'And drink Heineken beer in support of the tasks of the day,' he agreed to the consolation prize details.

She smiled, he smiled, they raised their glasses one more time and toasted each other.

Simon was adding some salad to his plate of steak and well-burnt sausages when his mobile phone rang. The opening hollow silence was followed by a loud 'That you Simon?' It was a rather agitated Perce calling from Perth.

'Yes,'

'Weez won,' his excited father announced 'Your mother has won a bloody fortune on this bloody race,' he yelled in breathless delight.

The excitement spread fast to Simon 'That's great. Well done. How much?'

'Twenty two thousand six hundred and fifty five bloody great dollars,' Perce yelled down the phone.

'Say that again,' Simon requested, just to make sure he had heard correctly.

Perce repeated the figure then told him 'Hold on. Here's yer mother.'

Glad came on the line 'Hello darls, isn't that marvellous, bloody marvellous. That card lady was right you see and weez won such a lot of money.' She was screaming with excitement at their good fortune.

'You got the winner then I take it?'

'And the second and the two that dead-heated for third,' Glad completed the set 'On their own quite a few times, plus a few quinellas and quite a lot of trifectas – the last ones paid a bloody fortune.'

'Amazing. Well done, so how do you plan to spend it?'

'Well, weez havin' a few slurps now. Then weez going down the pub for dinner and a drink or two later on and then we'll think about it in some detail.'

'That's great, just great. I didn't win anything.'

'Never mind darls, I'll buy you an ice cream out of our winnings,' and the line was cut.

Simon immediately called Siew Moi's mobile phone and she

answered. She was rather cool to begin with but as he excitedly told her the racing news from Perth she warmed up considerably.

'We have to make a donation to Da Jie.'

'Sure, any time, any amount,' he told her happily 'and we can perhaps celebrate with a special dinner on Friday night…if you are ready to forgive me…please…pretty please…' he paused, hoping for final release from his exile.

'Oh, OK. But don't ever behave like you did again!'

'I won't, I won't,' he promised as she cut the line to attend to a customer.

Simon joined his housemates at one of the canteen tables and told them about Glad's good fortune. As could have been expected each of them decided they wanted a reading from Da Jie as soon as possible. If she could forecast some winnings for Glad she may be able to come up with some positive news for each of them. He promised to ask the now-reconciled Siew Moi about a group booking with the card lady.

Excitement reigned at the thought as the barbie's well burnt offerings were devoured with relish, as well as chilli sauce. Chauncy was rather late in joining them but when he appeared he plonked nine cold bottles of Heineken on the table and announced 'Drinks on me. The best dressed jockey in town.'

'Heineken,' Bruce read the label 'always popular amongst those who know.'

Chauncy smiled 'Special prize, Bedford,' he announced, winking at him.

'Bruce,'

'Whatever,'

'No sand in the bottles is there?' Bruce had worked it out.

'Certainly not!' Chauncy gave him the evil eye.

'So what yewz doing this afternoon?' Sheila One asked of the Art Master as they were all free after the barbie.

'Well, funnily enough I actually met a jockey in a certain bar

the other evening, which explains where I got this outfit from.'
He smiled at the memory of putting his money on another fast
finisher 'And as I have to return the clothes later I've arranged for
him to come over to my place and promised to do him in oils
At The Gallop, as it were, and as thanks for lending me the gear.'
He smiled at the prospect of a sporting interlude later on.

'Whips and all?' Sheila Two asked.

'And spurs,' he confirmed adding 'Mmmmmmm……' at the
thought of his upcoming racing activity

'Reckon yewz on a winner there,' Tyrone thought out loud.

'A dead cert. I hope.'

The school year was scheduled to end in the middle of the
week before Christmas. For much of the final month of the year
staff chat focused on plans for the three weeks break.

The three Sheilas were returning to New South Wales and taking
a five day Camel Safari Trek out of Alice Springs starting on Boxing
Day. After a few days back home with the folks and they would
return to Singapore together on January 5th.

Cazza announced that she and K.C. were first going to Cairns
so he could meet her family after which they would head for the
Barrier Reef. K.C.'s father was thinking about buying some islands
there and they were to carry out the initial survey of a couple on
the list. Can't be bad, everyone felt.

Tyrone was heading north to Phuket where he would stay a
few days with Pui before they went to Tasmania for ten days. Bruce
was planning to go back to Brisbane and do some sailing with a
few mates in the Whitsundays.

He had stopped looking for Internet friends since his shipboard
romance almost sunk him without trace.

Chauncy announced he would be taking the position of
Onboard Artist on a cruise ship sailing the Gulf of Thailand over

Christmas and New Year.

The vessel had been chartered by a Japanese Nudist Society and his role would be to sketch and paint passengers in nautical settings during the voyage. After the cruise he planned to take some R&R in the Thai resort of Krabi and generally spend the remainder of the break relaxing and 'rinsing out his brushes' as he put it.

'How d'yewz get this painting job then, Chauncy?' Sheila One asked over canteen coffee one afternoon in early December.

'Well it's all rather strange and mysterious actually,' he was soon flowing 'It seems that some lady from Hiroshima was here in town a few months ago and took back one of my nudes which she saw in a shop and took a fancy to,' he smiled knowingly.

'Actually it was the one I call Flying Free which captures a certain body leaping off the balcony of my apartment, sans clothing. And I have to say that he looks BEAUtiful as he heads for a crash landing on the lawn below.'

'Cut the crap, just tell how you got the job,' Sheila Three, like the model, brought matters down to earth.

'Well it seems that the lady is in some Japanese Naturists Club which travels every Christmas-New Year to warmer climes. And she felt it would be rather original to get the artist behind her latest nude painting along for this year's cruise and offer Sailing Moments On Canvas to fellow nudist-cruisers. All created by moi - of course!' he squirmed with delight.

'And?' Cazza queried.

'Well I was then contacted by Hang Loose Holidays of Honshu about the escapade, together with an appealing offer — and of course accepted at once. Everything's included, except clothing.'

'Amazing,' Tyrone thought out loud.

'I know, isn't it? So the outcome is that I will soon be sailing with some 200 or so Japanese of varying genders, ages and sizes and all au natural…which sounds like great fun to me.

Mmmmmm……' his eyes glazed.

'What about all those hooks, hoists and derricks about the place, won't they be rather perilous to the passengers if they run around the deck all day without anything on?' Bruce wondered.

'Well I don't really know. I suppose it depends how many Dereks there are on the passenger list. Not a very common name in Japan though, I wouldn't have thought.'

'Can't be bad,' Sheila Two grinned from her own red rising sun backdrop.

'I know….' Chauncy was already dreaming about his Samurai Spectacular.

Simon had spoken at length to Siew Moi about travelling with him to Perth and after some initial hesitancy, which increased markedly after the wedding incident she had finally agreed to go. The persuasive factor was that she had of course met his family and liked them all immensely.

He kept telling her that Glad was insisting she go with him as she wanted to show her appreciation for taking her to the fortune teller in her own special way. What that meant was that she was preparing a special pavlova complete with Singapore decorations.

When asked what a pavlova was he told her it was a rich lightweight cake made from egg whites and filled with cream, fresh fruit and other secret delights she admitted she couldn't resist the invitation.

He booked seats for them for an evening departure on December 17th after school finished in the afternoon and started planning various adventures and activities for them while they were 'down under'.

The basic plans were shared over a Bun in The Oven coffee close to their departure day.

'We will stay in and around Perth until after Christmas. Then we'll drive up north to see the dolphins at Monkey Mia for a few days and then we'll camp under the stars in the middle of the

Outback for a few nights.'

She looked at him with certain trepidation.

'Well the dolphins part sounds wonderful but I'm not so sure about the camping in a tent for a few nights. What about the snakes, scorpions, dingoes and other frightening creature of evil intent?' she was obviously concerned.

'Don't worry. The only creature coming near you with wicked thoughts will be me.'

'But I may not be able to keep you at bay.'

'Actually that's the idea,' he tried to keep a straight face as she reached over to hit him.

Now being prepared, *Spicy Chinese Takeaway,* featuring
the original characters plus a number of extra-hot
ingredients...and a double dose of laughs!

Order now so you don't miss out...
email: sammylah@pacific.net.sg

A Few Words about the Author

Peter Dorney was born and bred in Manchester, England. Over the years, in seeking warmer climes, he has lived in Africa, Australia and, since the mid-eighties, Singapore.

He has a wide variety of business interests in Southeast Asia with writing providing a growing area of activity for his imaginative and rather fertile mind.

When not observing life through humour-coloured glasses the author lives quietly with his semi-tame ferret, Horatio, and lovingly tends his portable tropical garden.